.The Artful Home®

Edition 2

A Source & Guide for Residential Art

The Artful Home®

Editon 2

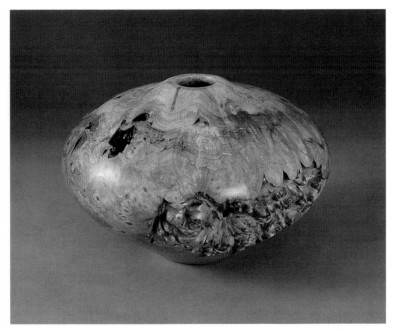

A Source & Guide for Residential Art

GUILD Publishing

Madison, Wisconsin

The ArtfulHome®

A Source & Guide for Residential Art

GUILD Sourcebooks
An imprint of GUILD, LLC
931 E. Main Street
Madison, Wisconsin 53703
TEL 608-227-4135 • TEL 800-930-1856

ADMINISTRATION
Toni Sikes, CEO and Founder
Reed McMillan, Vice President of Sales
Katie Kazan, Director of Guild Publishing
Carla Dillman, Sourcebook Sales Coordinator
Kristina Buie, Administrative Assisstant

DESIGN, PRODUCTION & EDITORIAL
Georgene Pomplun, Art Director
Sue Englund, Project Designer/Production Artist
Rebecca Beckett, Image Specialist
Jill Schaefer, Publishing Coordinator, Writer (Artist Tips)
Susan Troller, Writer (Designer Profiles)
Jessica Levine, Production Intern
Melita Schuessler, Proofreader

ARTIST CONSULTANTS
Nicole Carroll • Amy Lambright
Mike Mitchell • Laura Marth • Paul Murphy

Copyright © 2004 GUILD, LLC
ISBN 1-880140-53-5

Printed in China

Thanks to Louis Sagar, whose contributions to the first edition of *The Artful Home* did so much to set our course.

Page 1: Kurt Piper, cherry cabinets with gray wash. Interior design by Joanna Fritjofson.
Also shown: wood wall hanging by Russell Zuhl. Photograph: John Polak.
Page 2: Joan Weissman, *Wingspread*, hand-tufted wool rug,
architecture/interior design by Robert Strell. Photograph: Matthew Fuller.
Page 3: Bob Hawks, see page 156.
Opposite: Steve Lopes, great room light, copper, steel and mica; steel fireplace doors; copper-clad wall; steel reading lamps. Photograph: Roger Turk/NLP Inc.

■　■　■

GUILD.com is the Internet's leading retailer of original art and fine craft.
Visit www.guild.com.

WELCOME TO THE ARTFUL HOME

The creation of an artful home is a lifelon

It is a journey of discovery and acquisition, as we seek and find the objects and artworks that complement core furnishings. It is an adventure of the spirit, as each of us develops a personal aesthetic along the way, learning to trust our own instincts (knowing, *just knowing,* that a particular piece is something we will want to live with forever). And it is a celebration—of beauty and spirit and personality—as we go about creating a home that is uniquely ours.

Think of this book as *your trusty guide for the journey.* It features suggestions,

Interior design by Stacey Lapuk.
See page 36.

information and practical tips about creating an artful environment. Here you'll find articles about finding and displaying art, suggestions for commissioning one-of-a-kind pieces, and short essays on caring for various kinds of art.

It is also a *wonderful source for finding artists,* the great wellspring of creativity. The book features the work of artists who are available for custom projects, commissioned works of art that fit, hand-to-glove, into the styles, spaces and colors of your home. Phone and e-mail information is also included, and the artists would love to hear from you!

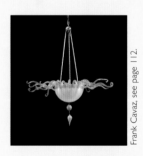

Frank Cavaz, see page 112.

Interior design by Charles Cunniffe.
See page 26.

Finally, *we seek to inspire you.* Our editors have selected outstanding examples of artful homes, accompanied by conversations with the designers who helped create them. The photographs and interviews provide ideas and insights into an intriguing world of possibilities.

Please, let us join you in *your* journey to create a home environment that suits your individual needs, reflects your personality and soothes your soul.

—Toni Sikes
Publisher

ourney, one without beginning or end.

Kathleen Newman, *Distant Call*, pastel.

CONTENTS

1

INTRODUCTION

2

DESIGNER PROFILES

1. Glassic Art, *Ambiance*, carved glass countertop. Photograph: Sampsel Preston Photographers, Las Vegas, NV. 2. Architectural design by Charles Cunniffe.

3

ARTIST GALLERY

4

RESOURCES

3. Lisa Ambler, *Blue Velvet,* oil painting. Photograph: MaxStyles.com. 4. Barbara Barran, *Bars and String-Pieced Columns,* hand-tufted wool rug. Photograph: Michel Friang.

Larry Stephenson, see page 239.

Your Direct Connection to Artists' Studios

The decision to live with art is a decision to live with things of enduring value. The paintings, prints and photographs you place in your home—like the works of art in clay, fiber, metal, glass and wood—enrich your life with a silent and strengthening presence, and with the joy of beauty and imagination.

Because original art can be costly compared to manufactured goods, and because each artwork is unique, shopping for art calls for research and initiative. Hence T*he Artful Home.* This unique volume invites you to browse, buy and commission works of art directly from the studios of exceptional contemporary artists. Works are grouped in two main sections.

- *Furniture, Sculpture & Objects* features furniture, lighting, floor coverings, architectural details and art objects in all media, as well as sculpture for pedestals and gardens.
- *Art for the Wall* features paintings, photographs, prints, art quilts, tapestries and other works for the wall.

Full-color photographs make it easy to find the artists whose style appeals to you most, while complete contact information allows you to get in touch with those artists directly to purchase existing pieces or commission custom-designed works.

You need not be an art collector to purchase works from artists included in *The Artful Home.* In fact, the only qualifications you really need are a sincere appreciation for the artists you call and a genuine interest in owning their work.

PUTTING THE BOOK TO WORK

We welcome you to browse *The Artful Home,* enjoying the artwork, the illustrated designer profiles and the many suggestions for building a home rich in beauty and creative energy. But there's more to this book than that. Every one of our featured artists invites you to call or e-mail to purchase pieces from their studio or to arrange a commission for a custom work of art.

Your call to an *Artful Home* artist can take you in many directions.

- The same artworks shown on these pages may be available for immediate purchase. Some of these works are from an artist's production line or created in limited editions; others are one-of-a-kind pieces.

- The artist may have other available works on hand. If you live near the artist (see the Location Index), consider visiting the studio. If a studio visit isn't feasible, ask to see images; these can often be e-mailed for quick review.
- Alternately, you could hire the artist to create a unique work that reflects your home, your aesthetic and, perhaps, some landmark event in your life or the life of someone you love. For help in commissioning artworks, consider the services of GUILD's Custom Design Center. You can reach the CDC from GUILD's home page (www.guild.com), or call CDC staff at 1-877-344-8453.

When viewing an artist's page, keep in mind that while the projects shown are representative of the artist's work, they don't demonstrate the full extent of the artist's capabilities. If you like a certain style but want something other than the works pictured here, call the artist and talk it over. He or she may be intrigued at the prospect of exploring new forms.

Andrew Muggleton, *Balustrade Chaise*, walnut, makore, aluminum and Ultrasuede®; shown with *Interlocking End Table #1*. Photograph: Kevin Muggleton.

FINDING WHAT YOU NEED
A Roadmap to *The Artful Home*

Want to contact an artist featured in *The Artful Home?* Look for addresses, phone numbers and other contact information at the tops of artists' display pages. Additional information about each artist can be found in the Artist Statements section in the back of the book; listings are in alphabetical order by the heading on each artist's page. This is where you'll find information about the artists' mediums and techniques, their range of products and their notable awards or commissions.

If you know what type of artwork you want to purchase or commission, a search by section will help you find results quickly. You'll find a list of sections in the Table of Contents. Likewise, if you know the name of the artist you want to work with, you can easily search using the Index of Artists and Companies, found in the back of the book. If you would like to work with an artist in your area, check the Location Index.

Curious to know more about an artist's work? Don't hesitate to contact that artist directly; he or she will be delighted to hear from you. And for more information about these and other artists who create works for home environments, visit the GUILD Custom Design Center, a featured service of GUILD.com.

COMMISSIONING A WORK OF ART

Helen Vaughn, see page 223.

There's something exhilarating about engaging an artist to create a unique artwork for your home. Custom-designed (or "commissioned") works of art reflect your personal taste and vision more deeply than "off-the-shelf" art. At the same time, they can significantly enhance the value of your home.

Commissioned works of art may or may not be expensive, depending upon the scope of the project, but they will always require your personal involvement. If you enjoy that involvement, art commissions are the ultimate way to buy original art. Custom-designed artworks—whether movable, as with a painted portrait, or permanently attached to the structure of your home, as with a tile fireplace surround—can become instant family treasures, adding deeply to the heritage of who you are.

CHOOSING AN ARTIST

The most important step you'll take when planning a commission is the choice of artist. What makes a good choice? Someone whose previous art projects appeal to you. Whose previous clients are enthusiastic. Who has undertaken similar projects in the past and delivered completed work within the agreed-upon budget and schedule.

And how do you find this individual?

The Artful Home is a wonderful place to start. Every one of our featured artists accepts commissions for custom-designed artwork, and the contact information included with their individual display pages will put you in touch with them directly. You may also want to talk with friends who have hired artists for commissions similar to yours, or visit artists' studios and art fairs to talk with candidates in person.

Once your A-list is narrowed down to two or three names, it's time to schedule meetings to discuss the project, either face-to-face (for local artists) or by phone. As you talk, try to determine the artist's interest in your project, and pay attention to your own comfort level with the artist. Try to find out whether the chemistry is right—whether you have the basis to build a working relationship—and confirm that the artist has the necessary skills to undertake your project. Be thorough and specific when asking questions. Is the artist excited about the project? What does he or she see as the most important issues or considerations? Will your needs be a major or minor concern? Evaluate the artist's style, approach and personality.

If it feels like you might have trouble working together, take heed. But if all goes well and it feels like a good fit, ask for a list of references. These are important testimonials, so don't neglect to make the calls. Ask about the artist's work habits and communication style, and—of course—about the success of the artwork. You should also ask whether the project was delivered on time and within budget. If you like what you hear, you'll be one important step closer to hiring your artist.

Lynn Basa, *Wild Freedom*, wool rug. Photograph: Russell Johnson.

EXPECT PROFESSIONALISM

Once you've selected the artist, careful planning and communication can help ensure a great outcome. If this is an expensive or complicated project, you may want to request preliminary designs at this time.

Since most artists charge a design fee whether or not they're ultimately hired for the project, start by asking for sketches from your top candidate. If you're unhappy with the designs submitted, go to your second choice. If, on the other hand, the design is what you'd hoped for, it's time to finalize your working agreement with this artist.

As you discuss contract details, be resolved that silence is not golden and ignorance is not bliss! Discuss the budget and timetable, and be sure that these and other important details are spelled out in the contract. Now is the time for possible misunderstandings to be brought up and resolved—not later, when the work is half done and deadlines loom.

THE CONTRACT: PUTTING IT IN WRITING

It's a truism in any business that it's cheaper to get the lawyers involved at the beginning of a process than after something goes wrong. In the case of custom-made works of art, a signed contract or letter of agreement commits the artist to completing his or her work on time and to specifications. It also assures the artist that he or she will get paid the right amount at the right time. That just about eliminates the biggest conflicts that can arise.

Contracts should be specific to the job. If your commission is for a photograph of a beloved country home, a sales slip noting down payment and delivery date should do the trick. If, on the other hand, you've hired a muralist to paint an *Alice in Wonderland* scene in the kids' playroom, a more detailed document will be needed.

Customarily, artists are responsible for design, production, shipping and installation. If someone else is to be responsible for installation, be sure you specify who will coordinate and pay for it. With a large project, it's helpful to identify the tasks that, if delayed for any reason, would set back completion of the project. These should be discussed up front to ensure that all parties agree on requirements and expectations.

PAYMENT SCHEDULE

The more skill you need and the more complex the project, the more you should budget for the artist's work and services. With larger projects, payments are usually tied to specific milestones; these serve as checkpoints and assure that work is progressing in a satisfactory manner, on time and on budget. Payment is customarily made in three stages, although—again—this will depend on the circumstances, scope and complexity of the project.

The first payment for a large-scale commission is usually made when the contract is signed. It covers the artist's time and creativity in developing a detailed design specific to your needs. For larger projects, you can expect to go through several rounds of trial and error in the design process, but at the end of this stage you'll have detailed drawings and, for three-dimensional work, an approved maquette (model). The cost of the maquette and the design time are usually factored into the artist's fee.

The second payment is generally set for a point midway through the project and is for work completed to date. If the materials are expensive, the artist may also ask that you advance money at this stage to cover his or her costs. If the commission is canceled during this period, the artist keeps the money already paid for work performed.

Final payment is usually due when the work is finished or, if so arranged, installed. Sometimes the artwork is finished on time but the building is delayed (as so often happens with new construction); in this case, the artist should be paid upon completion but still has the obligation to oversee installation.

Blaise Gaston, dressing table and chair, see page 54.

WHERE TO FIND HELP

If your project is large and expensive, or if it needs to be carefully coordinated with other aesthetic and functional aspects of your home, consider hiring an art consultant. The consultant can help with complicated contract arrangements and make certain that communication between the artist and professionals such as architects, interior designers and engineers is clear and complete.

Another terrific service is available online through GUILD, the publisher of *The Artful Home*. The GUILD Custom Design Center (accessible through www.guild.com) lets you broadcast project specifications by filling out an online form. Your information is shared with qualified artists over the Internet; GUILD then forwards their proposals to you. This is a great way to find artists when you're celebrat-

ing a family milestone, solving a design problem or looking for ways to make everyday objects artful.

For some people, the process of commissioning a work of art involves a degree of involvement that they just don't want to take on. If that describes you, rest assured—you may still find that treasured work of art! Many artists have a wide selection of completed works on hand in their studios, giving you the option to purchase something ready-made and immediately available. If you find something great among the artist's inventory, don't hesitate to buy it. The piece you choose will still be unique, and it will still reflect your personal aesthetic sense. Your goal should be to develop an individual approach to enjoying art . . . and that includes your comfort level with how you purchase it.

FINDING ART

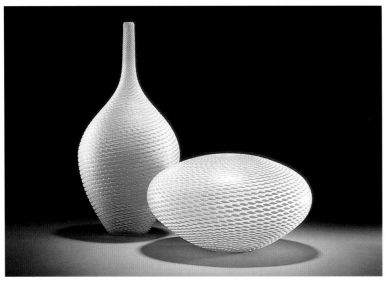

Carrie Gustafson, see page 147.

Arya Azadi, see page 177.

A World of Sources

Your search for a work of art can take many forms. It can be direct and methodical, as when you're looking for a print or painting to brighten the muted colors of a favorite room, or organic and adventurous, as when you're searching for a special something to mark a landmark anniversary. It can be the focus of a month of weekend outings to galleries, art fairs and artist studios, or an evening's pleasant browsing on the Internet. For more substantial purchases, especially those that involve complex installation, you may want to work with a professional art consultant or with the staff at GUILD.com's Custom Design Center.

Each of these methods of finding art has unique advantages. Let's begin with a look at buying art on the Internet, using the GUILD.com website as a handy model.

THE VIRTUAL SEARCH FOR ART
A virtual gallery like GUILD.com offers distinctive benefits, especially if you're pressed for time, prefer to shop at night or want to see a very broad selection of quality artworks. By buying art gifts on the Internet, you also avoid having to ship fragile works yourself; at GUILD.com, for example, packing and shipping are handled by the artist—who knows better than anyone how to do it right.

Internet technology also allows you to search for art items meeting precise specifications. Looking through an extensive collection of online art is similar in many respects to visiting a large museum. Visitors to a museum can meander from room to room, browsing randomly, broadening their understanding of different art forms and kindling new enthusiasms. Alternatively, they can use a map of the museum to select and visit the parts of the collection that interest them the most.

So it is with an online collection, except that instead of a map, the visitor uses search functions to view the collection strategically. At GUILD.com, search criteria include medium, price range, color, theme and size, and they can be used singly or in any combination to fine-tune your search.

GUILD.com uses Internet technology to offer other services that are both useful and fun. E-postcards, for example, allow you to send images of favorite artworks to friends, with your own notes attached. GUILD's Wish List lets you keep a visual record of items you'd like to own someday, while the Gift Registry lets friends browse and shop from among items you've chosen. Another unique resource, the GUILD Custom Design Center, allows shoppers to have artworks customized to their specifications: a perfect way to celebrate a family milestone, fill an unusual space or make everyday objects artful.

When questions arise, or when you want to place custom orders, you can reach GUILD's knowledgeable staff toll-free. Call 1-877-344-8453 to place an order or to find out more about individual artists or works of art.

GALLERIES

Purchasing from a gallery provides the benefit of consultation; you're tapping into the expertise of the gallery staff and the relative assurance that the work meets high aesthetic and professional standards. The artworks will have been selected by the gallery owner or manager, and will reflect his or her personal taste. If your own aesthetic is similar, a gallery can be an excellent resource.

Most galleries specialize in specific types of art and are committed to a stable of artists. Much like interior designers or art consultants, galleries act as professional curators; most select twenty to fifty artists to feature from among hundreds seeking representation.

To varying degrees, galleries act as agents for artists and help create a market for their work. It can be fun and interesting to attend gallery openings in your city or town. If the artwork you see appeals to you, introduce yourself to the gallery owner. Talk about your interest in purchasing art and about the kinds of work you're attracted to. Be sure to mention your budget—and don't feel intimidated if you don't want to spend a great deal of money. Galleries are always looking for new clients, and they'll be happy to spend time getting to know you.

BUYING DIRECTLY FROM THE ARTIST

Every artist whose work is shown in *The Artful Home* will welcome your phone call and your business. Look for artists' contact information at the top of the display pages, as well as basic information about their products and processes in the Artist Statements section at the back of the book.

Many artists keep at least a few completed works in the studio and can provide overnight turnaround for last-minute gifts and the like. This is most often true with artists who make small-scale works, but even artists who produce large-scale paintings or tapestries may keep a few available works on hand.

If you're not in a rush to buy, it can be fun to visit the artist's studio (see page 18). When distance makes that impossible, ask to see photos of available works; photos can often be attached to e-mail if snail mail is too slow. And remember that *Artful Home* artists are available for custom-design projects; see Commissioning a Work of Art, beginning on page 12.

STUDIO VISITS

When visiting an artist's studio, rules of common courtesy apply. Be sure to call ahead; the artist may have limited visiting hours, especially during crunch times. Once there, don't overstay your welcome. Enjoy your visit, but recognize that the artist will need to get back to work.

Some communities offer organized tours of artists' studios on a particular day or weekend each year. These are terrific opportunities to meet artists and learn about the processes they use.

ART FAIRS

Depending upon the crowds and the weather (if the fair is outdoors), art fairs can be a lot of fun. They're also a great way to see the work of many artists at one time. Most art fairs are juried, so you can expect to see high-quality displays and meet artists who work at a professional level.

ART CONSULTANTS

Art consultants work with individuals and corporations, helping them select and place art. This is not a service you'll need for most purchases, but an art consultant can be a tremendous help with complex projects (see sidebar). Although art consultants are familiar with the work of hundreds of artists—and may know many artists personally—they are engaged by, and represent the interests of, the art buyer. Normally, an art consultant is not affiliated with specific galleries or institutions.

Finding an art consultant in rural areas of the country can be a challenge. The Internet can be a great help, of course, and local architects and interior designers may recommend art consultants in your area or with whom they've had successful long-distance relationships. In any case, it's wise to talk with several art consultants to get a feel for the services they can offer and to gauge how comfortable you'll be working with them. Be sure to make reference calls as well, just as you would when hiring any service professional.

Art consultants are normally compensated through a percentage of the art-acquisition budget.

Nancy Nicholson, see page 145.

Jason Watts, see page 244.

WHEN TO USE AN ART CONSULTANT

Art consultants can help with projects of any size and any medium, but their skills and experience are particularly helpful with large or expensive projects, or in the following circumstances.

- When artwork is integral to the structure of the home, as with custom kitchen tile or a wrought iron balcony railing.
- When coordination is needed between the artist and other professionals, such as architects and engineers.

- When installation is complex, as with a heavy atrium sculpture or custom millwork.
- When art from several sources must coordinate, both functionally and aesthetically.

DETERMINING VALUE

FRAGRANCE   BJORN SJOGREN

Bjorn Sjorgen, see page 284.

Let's face it. When we find art that appeals to us, our reaction is immediate. We fall in love with it first—and then think about the pragmatic aspects of buying or owning it.

But before you buy that painting or art quilt, it's important to ask some hard-nosed questions. Do I want to live with this work for years to come? If I buy it, where will I place it? And, equally important: is the piece worth the asking price?

Here at GUILD, we help thousands of customers purchase original art each year. We also interact with hundreds of artists. Based on what we've learned, we can suggest some guidelines for assessing the value of a work of art.

COST AND VALUE

One criterion that all experts and collectors agree upon is this: buy art that you love; all other considerations are secondary. While we agree with the spirit of this suggestion, we also think you'll make better and more confident purchases if you conduct basic research into the artist's background and stature.

PRICING

The cost of a work of art is often related to the experience of the artist. Those who have worked in their fields for many years command higher prices than relative newcomers. The same is true for artists whose work is included in museum collections or publications, or who have mounted one-person shows. These are landmark events; they demonstrate respect for the artist on the part of curators, publishers and gallery managers, and they have a cumulative effect on the artist's prices.

Whether or not a work of art seems expensive, it's good to remember that value and price are different qualities. The value of artwork is perceived and subjective, while the price is set and, usually, firm.

EDUCATION

An artist's academic record sheds more light on his technical background and skills than on his natural talent. Museums and institutions consider an artist's schooling important, particularly when selecting emerging artists to participate in shows. Your choice of an etching or of tile for a fireplace surround, however, should not be based on which institution granted the artist a master's degree—or even whether the artist holds that degree at all. Some of our most esteemed artists developed their skills as apprentices or within an artists' community rather than at an institution.

HISTORY OF EXHIBITIONS

More than schooling, an artist's credibility is reflected in the number and range of shows that have exhibited his work. This is a very important reference point for value. Emerging artists compete to participate in group shows at local and regional galleries. Artists who are more advanced in their careers mount one-person shows.

When reviewing an artist's resume, pay close attention to the dates and locations of exhibitions.

- How long has the artist been exhibiting?
- Has the work been exhibited regionally, nationally or internationally?
- Are the exhibition sites well known?
- Has the artist received awards?

EDITORIAL REVIEWS

Reviews in journals, magazines and newspapers are another benchmark of value. Art critics act as interpreters, and their reviews not only evaluate the quality of artworks, but also place them in the context of history and genre. A strong endorsement by a respected critic can have a significant influence on an artist's career.

COLLECTIONS

It can be interesting to learn which private, public and corporate collections include works by a particular artist. It can also be affirming to learn that others share your passion for a particular artist. With established artists, it becomes substantially more important to know who owns their work. If the work is part of a museum collection, for example, this adds to the value. Likewise, ownership by prestigious collectors and corporations can have a significant influence on price.

CAREER OVERVIEW

Artists go through periods of development influenced by the world around them, producing works that explore particular techniques and themes of influence. When you meet artists or gallery curators, ask them to comment on the artist's body of work. How long has the artist been developing a particular theme or using a specific technique? How refined are the themes and techniques? Is the artist highly prolific? The answers to these questions will provide insight into the artist's depth of experience; in that way, they may influence the value you place on the work.

THE VALUE OF PASSION

Although the factors discussed here relate to marketplace value, they should also be considered as you think about the value you and your family place on a work of art. That said, we couldn't emphasize too strongly that your passion for a work of art should always drive your purchase.

Buying art for your home involves a different set of standards than those faced by a major collector or museum.

The right surroundings and appropriate placement in your home environment are much more important than investment appeal or a history of shows at major museums. Original art has an aesthetic and emotional impact on your home.

This is one area where we urge you to lead with your heart.

THE ANATOMY OF A FRAME

Brian Kershisnik, *Holy Woman*, (available at GUILD.com).

While works on canvas are seldom displayed under glass, other kinds of framed artworks are. These include prints, paintings, drawings, delicate fiber pieces and fragile three-dimensional works in box frames. Typically, four components are used in framing these kinds of works: the frame itself, the glass, the mat and the backing.

FRAMES

Painted aluminum and wood are affordable and versatile choices for frames; finished in antique gold or aged platinum, they're elegant and enduring; painted in bright colors, they're amusing and festive. Natural wood is another excellent choice; it's tasteful, classic and appropriate for most home settings. Vintage frames can be an economical way to add distinct character to an artwork.

As you choose mats and frames, remember that you may want to move the picture at some point in the future. For that reason, it's usually unwise to coordinate frames with specific furnishings.

Frames are usually sold at a certain price per foot based on the measurement around the outer perimeter of the work. When calculating costs, remember that the mat will add to the work's dimensions. Keep in mind, too, that framing is a customized process built around each work of art; costs reflect this individual attention.

Although most of your focus when choosing a frame will be on its appearance, there are some important practical concerns to be considered as well. Obviously, you will need to be sure the frame you choose is strong enough to support the weight of your artwork; if there's any question, select a different style. And be certain that the framing elements are separated from the surface of the artwork, since any rubbing of the frame on the artwork will cause damage. Spacing materials placed between the artwork and the frame will prevent this problem.

GLASS

There are two choices when it comes to glass for framed artwork: standard glass and conservation glass. Standard glass is rarely specified for framing these days, since it provides minimal protection against ultraviolet light—which causes fading—and offers only fractional savings over conservation glass. A third option, plexiglass, is an excellent choice under some circumstances.

Conservation glass, which is coated to shield the framed work against the most harmful rays in the ultraviolet spectrum, is available in various qualities and thicknesses. An optional anti-reflective coating minimizes the visual distractions caused by reflections. Most standard and conservation glass has a slight or noticeable greenish tint, depending on how much iron is contained in the glass. "Water-white" conservation glass eliminates the green tint altogether, making for a very clear glass.

Use a soft, clean brush to dust the glass periodically, along with the other components of the frame. When needed, apply a glass cleaner on a soft, clean cloth rather than by spraying; sprayed cleaner can find its way under the glass and damage the artwork.

PLEXIGLASS

The term "Plexiglas" is trademarked by Rohm and Haas, the largest specialty chemicals company in the United States. However, a number of manufacturers produce the clear plastic sheeting used to frame art, and the terms "plexiglass" and "plexi" are now used universally.

Plexiglass became popular initially for use with lower-priced artworks like posters. However, continued advances have improved the quality of the material so that it's now an attractive alternative to conservation glass. It's also lighter than glass and does not break easily, making it the preferred choice for very large framed artwork and for framed artworks hanging in children's rooms. Plexi is available with optional ultraviolet protection and anti-reflective glazing. Since plexiglass tends to flex and bow, reflecting light from its surface, an anti-reflective coating is a particularly desirable feature.

A few notes regarding plexiglass. The material's slight grayish tint is so pale that it's generally not a concern. Likewise, its resistance to abrasion has improved substantially in recent years, solving one of the traditional concerns regarding older forms of plexiglass: its tendency to scratch. However, it is important that plexiglass not be used for framing artworks made with a loose medium like pastels or charcoal. Plexi creates substantial amounts of static, which can actually pull pastel or charcoal particles off a sheet of paper.

When it comes to cleaning, be sure to use special plexiglass cleaners available from art supply, hardware and home improvement stores. Used as directed, these products clean and protect the plexi without clouding its surface. Do not use glass cleaners on plexi, as they will visibly damage the surface.

MATS

Mats are made of heavy paper stock (called "board") or fabric, and are used to separate the artwork from the frame and glass both physically and visually. Mats come in a variety of finishes, including smooth, textured and linen. Conservators recommend using four-ply, 100 percent rag board or acid-free fabric. Matting materials of lesser quality contain acid and will damage artwork.

Mats have an important functional purpose in that they create a protective space between the glass and the art. They can also dramatically enhance the presentation

of two-dimensional artwork. A wide mat adds presence to any size painting, print or photograph, while double mats lend a refined quality to a framed work. Although mats are available in many colors, most art-works look best against neutral grays, blacks and off-whites; these colors are unobtrusive and they wear well over time. In any case, your eye should never be drawn to the mat; instead, the mat should help to focus attention on the art.

Always be sure there is enough matting around the artwork to enable the work to breathe. Three to four inches is standard, but discuss this with your framer, as his or her experience is invaluable.

A "floating mount" is an interesting alternative to a typical mat—especially when the perimeter of the artwork is asymmetrical. Instead of cutting the mat as a rectangular "window" frame around the artwork, the framer uses cushioning strips to attach the work to the top of a solid mat, so that the art appears to float. This technique is most often used with small pieces. "Close framing," another option, eliminates the mat completely, so that the artwork extends to the frame; this treatment can make an image feel clean and fresh. Professional framers will introduce you to a range of matting techniques to suit a particular piece of work.

CARING FOR FRAMED ART

Direct sun, heat extremes and moist air all pose threats to framed works of art. Avoid hanging framed artwork in direct sunlight or in unventilated bathrooms or other spaces prone to fluctuating heat and humidity.

BACKING

The last structural layer in a framed artwork is the backing, which is usually made of pH-neutral foam core. Tyvek, which is waterproof as well as tear- and puncture-resistant, is also used as a backing material; the extra expense is worth considering for important artwork purchases. A sheet of nonacid paper adhered to the back of the frame seals the framing components against dust.

STORAGE

When not on display, framed artwork should be stored in a cool, dry area. Avoid stacking pieces on top of one another. Instead, stand them on end separated with sheets of acid-free board, available through art supply stores or frame shops. Don't use standard cardboard, which is highly acidic and can ruin artwork.

THE ORIGINAL PRINT

Timothy Duffield, see page 289.

An original fine art print is a work of art, by an artist, in the print medium. What distinguishes it from printed reproductions is the artist's direct participation in the creation of the image. It differs dramatically from a poster, which is a mechanical reproduction of an original work of art. And although there are examples of posters that can be considered works of art because of the artist's involvement in the reproduction process, most posters are executed without the participation of the artist, or even produced posthumously. This will never be the case with original prints. They are new works created by the artist, and for that reason they are considered within the larger body of the artist's work.

Because the various printmaking processes have intrinsic visual characteristics, each technique can be identified by a distinct look. Printmaking techniques can be grouped into four basic categories: relief, intaglio, lithography and screenprint.

- Relief printing is a process whereby areas are cut away from a flat surface, leaving the raised image to be printed. Included in this category are woodcuts, wood engravings and linocuts.
- Intaglio processes, including aquatint, drypoint, engraving, etching, mezzotint and photogra-vure, employ the reverse approach: the images are incised or etched into the surface of metal plates.
- Lithography is a process in which the printed and non-printed areas of the plate lie on the same plane. The image is drawn on a smooth surface and the print is created through direct pressure.
- Screenprint images (also referred to as seri-graphs and silkscreens) are created as parts of a screen are blocked out so that ink prints only on selected areas of the paper.

A fifth category, known as "giclée" or "Iris" prints, has become popular over the last few years. Giclée technology employs high-resolution ink-jet printers to reproduce scanned images; most giclées are made with archival inks and papers. The resulting images, often achieved after many trial runs, have exceptional texture, clarity and tonal gradation.

Original prints made with the four "fine art" printmaking techniques are pulled by hand and should be thought of not as copies, but as original works existing in multiple impressions. Each print within the edition is signed and numbered by the artist.

Adapted from *The Original Print* by Chris Byrne.
Published ©2002 by GUILD Publishing.

FABULOUS AND FAMILIAR

Six Professionals on Designing an Artful Home

Architect Charles Cunniffe's renovation of a New York City penthouse features dazzling spaces for his client's art collection. Artworks in the dining room include a highly sculptural table by Richard Snyder and three paintings by artist Pandora Castelli. The travertine floor features bronze inserts by Michele Oka Doner. Photograph: Philip Ennis.

Every house is, at least, a shelter from the elements, a human nest or den, a more-or-less protective box in which we sleep and eat and carry on the mechanical details of living.

But an artful home is something else entirely.

To the notion of simple shelter we add the emotional content of home—a place where we belong—as well as a creative dimension that reflects who we are and what we value. A truly artful home nourishes our soul and satisfies our psyche. Life-size, it is a kind of sculpture we are delighted to inhabit, providing the perfect stage for the drama of our lives. As such, it is a place of repose and stimulation, comfort and inspiration.

Creating an artful home can be as simple as bringing a perfect little bouquet of wildflowers into the kitchen or displaying a beloved child's drawing in a place of honor. But it can also be as dauntingly complicated as building a house, from vague but passionate ideas to blueprints, and empty site to finished construction.

Usually, we don't need much help to pick a bouquet of flowers. But there are many other times in creating an artful home that we really would like vision and knowl-edge beyond our own as we try to create an environment that looks fabulous and feels familiar.

The very best design professionals at work today—architects, interior designers, builders and the artists with whom they collaborate—bring their artistic sensibilities, skills and experience together as they help create homes that not only surpass their clients' dreams, but also reflect a distinctive sense of unique and individual style.

Please join a handful of top designers in the pages that follow as they both show and tell how they help their clients create *The Artful Home*. You will be inspired by their words, and their work.

—Susan Troller

■　■　■

MARY DOUGLAS DRYSDALE

Washington, DC

Mary Douglas Drysdale is widely hailed as one of the top interior designers at work in North America today. Considered a neo-traditionalist, Drysdale combines contemporary and traditional elements to create interiors that are simultaneously elegant and fresh, serene and distinctive.

Lauded in publications ranging from *Art & Antiques* to *Southern Accents,* and well known through television appearances on the Home & Garden Television network and elsewhere, Drysdale is working at the top of her powers at the pinnacle of her profession.

In 2003, Drysdale's designs were featured in *The Artful Home* as a glorious expression of how beautifully imagined spaces gain verve and personality when they include thoughtfully chosen original contemporary art. This year, the designer shares with us one of her favorite projects: a collaboration with well-known contemporary painter Sam Gilliam.

Together, working with a modest budget, they transformed Gilliam's initially ordinary new house into a dazzling and comfortable family home and a wonderful gallery for the collection of art and beautiful objects that he has acquired in his career as an artist.

Read on to see how Mary Douglas Drysdale and Sam Gilliam inspired each other, and how their experiences can inspire us, as well.

—Susan Troller

As elsewhere in Gilliam's home, Mary Douglas Drysdale improved a rather conventional and crowded living room by opening the space and allowing it to communicate with the adjoining areas. In doing this, she created an atmosphere of light and sophistication that perfectly suits Gilliam's colorful artworks and his simple, elegant Italian furnishings. The glass-topped gilded terra cotta "stump" tables were designed by Drysdale.

"You can literally transform an environment by opening it up, by simplifying the finish vocabulary and then placing the right things in the space," Drysdale says. "Give beautiful things room to breathe! You don't have to force interest by adding more stuff; the trick is in placing the *right* things in the space."

The open geometry and cool colors of this bedroom in Sam Gilliam's home provide a perfect setting for the quilt, paintings and folk art that are part of the artist's collection. With an artful combination of energy and repose, the bedroom projects an atmosphere that is both playful and relaxing.

Like Gilliam, Mary Douglas Drysdale collects quilts, and the designer sees a strong aesthetic connection between paintings and quilts. Here, one of Gilliam's quilts is at home as both functional object and work of art. It is a perfect accessory to other artworks and memorabilia in the room.

"I felt like a curator for Sam's personal art collection," Drysdale says, "helping him place these beautiful pieces to their best advantage. It was my goal that the house reflect his wonderful taste and personality."

Conventional wisdom would probably argue against an interior design project where success hinged on two top artists collaborating closely. Too much individual commitment to personal aesthetics and vision. Too little experience bending to other artistic ideas and expressions. Too much ego.

But conventional wisdom would be wrong.

"Sam Gilliam is a *perfect* client," Drysdale reports, "a client who treats the designer as an artist. As we worked on his home, I was not simply a purveyor of materials. He recognized the artistic process, was familiar with it and respected it."

Gilliam and Drysdale initially talked about the house—a rambling split-level ranch overlooking a park in Washington, DC—and about the kind of outcome Gilliam hoped to achieve. Then, although the budget was limited and the interior spaces problematic, Gilliam gave Drysdale a free hand with the design.

"Initially the house was very, very tight: constricting and controlled. It was filled with small spaces that just didn't work very well—and certainly didn't work very well together," Drysdale says.

Her solution was fundamentally architectural. She advocated moving walls and dramatically opening up the house so that one room communicated with the next, creating a fluidity between adjoining rooms.

Photographs: Andrew Lautman.

"Every space in a house has an impact on the adjoining space. Sam immediately sensed that and could easily make decisions about the shape and volume of the house. When I proposed opening up the house, he was able to visualize the end result. He is a quiet person, but daring and not at all averse to risk. In addition, as an artist, he is very willing to live outside the usual design conventions of a place like Washington."

According to Drysdale, this was a project that depended more on imagination and creativity than on large sums of money. For example, the original unappealing carpet covered a plywood floor. Instead of installing an expensive stone or hardwood floor, Drysdale and Gilliam agreed that a meticulously applied white paint treatment would be just the right expression, providing a dramatic counterpoint to Gilliam's art collection.

"You can accomplish a great deal with a modest budget if there is a sense of creativity, a willingness to experiment and a feeling of trust in the ideas," Drysdale explains.

"In some ways, I would describe a collaboration like this as a kind of dance. The partners need to be listening to the same music and have an appreciation for its beauty. They must share the same sense of rhythm, energy and syncopation.

"For the collaboration to work at its ultimate level, you must believe in your partner's ability; you need to know that he won't let you drop! That kind of trusting environment brings out the best in everyone involved."

Drysdale likes to have her designs reflect her clients and believes that this design, with its elegant-but-unpretentious feel, is well suited to Sam Gilliam.

"I like designs that are artful and intellectual, and I believe a successful design picks up the energy and personality of the client. This space reflects Sam's interests, as well as the essence of his character.

"In the course of my career, I've done two projects with artists. Both have been very special and very satisfying. I would encourage more clients to have the vision and trust of someone like Sam Gilliam. The results are a pleasure for both client and designer."

■　■　■

Mary Douglas Drysdale moved walls and ceilings to open up a previously claustrophobic entryway in the home of artist Sam Gilliam.

The result? A setting that is airy and serene—yet dramatic—for the artist's beloved collection of objects and art. Gilliam collects contemporary works from other artists he knows and admires, as well as African artworks, including masks and sculpture.

The bowling pins shown here—created by Drysdale and painted by Gilliam—are unique and artful accessories within the space. "After working with Sam, I would have to say he is the best colorist I've ever known," Drysdale reports.

In this little vignette, Drysdale arranged objects from Sam Gilliam's collection. Among other things, Gilliam collects glass paperweights, antique toys and African art. Seemingly disparate, the objects work well together because of Gilliam's keen interest in color, shape, content and history and because of his love of playful whimsy.

"The artful home is really constructed from the true tastes and interests of the people who will live there," Drysdale says. "Of course, one pays attention to notions of universal beauty, but any truly good design must have a strong sense of personal meaning and resonance. Otherwise, it will feel hollow."

JANET FRIEDMAN
TRACI SHIELDS

Scottsdale, AZ ■ San Francisco, CA

Interior designers Janet Friedman, ASID, and her partner, Traci Shields, ASID, are known for big, bold, award-winning residential projects alive with unique detailing and one-of-a-kind personality.

Each project, they say, is a true reflection of the client's wishes and desires, enhanced and gently guided by the vision and skills of the design team. This team, they explain, often includes a remarkable cadre of artists and artisans, who enhance every project with their technical virtuosity and aesthetic imagination.

Operating in both the San Francisco Bay area and Scottsdale, Arizona, Friedman and Shields work on high-end, large-scale projects that usually last at least a year and often two or three years. Typically, they become engaged with a project when it is still in the blueprint stage. As a result, they are involved from the very outset, and their work begins by helping clients articulate a dream. They are then charged with helping create the map and overall direction for the project, as well as overseeing every subsequent detail as it evolves.

—Susan Troller

Interior design by Janet Friedman, ASID, and Traci Shields, ASID. Photographs: Dino Tonn.

◄ The foyer of this large Arizona family home has the feel of a warmly welcoming private art gallery, which, in many ways, it is. As the grand entrance to a richly detailed home, the space immediately introduces guests to a place where original art is loved, treasured and appreciated.

Designers Janet Friedman and Traci Shields collaborated with Don Beams of Beams Design to create the unusual, highly sculptural cabinetry that provides a kind of stage for art, including Jan Hurd's ceramic stick figures and Thomas Markesan's copper bowl. Artist Susan Venable's mixed-media piece provides an elegantly textured and tactile statement for the wall. Custom ceiling design, lighting, flooring and handwoven rugs complete an environment that celebrates creativity and excellence in contemporary American craft.

Shields notes that the foyer has a valuable sense of balance and serenity. "Each element—and each piece—complements the next, and nothing is allowed to overwhelm or steal the show."

33

JANET FREIDMAN
TRACI SHIELDS

(continued)

If the divine is in the details, Janet Friedman and Traci Shields want their clients to live in paradise.

"Paying close attention to the details, especially in that last critical ten percent of a job, makes the difference between a job that's merely good and a job that's superlative," Friedman claims.

"Our singular strength is an ability to bring highly creative designs to their fullest expression. We do this especially well, I believe, because of the collaborative way we work with our clients, and with the architects, builders, subcontractors and artists who ultimately make a unique, one-of-a-kind design idea come alive.

"We are consistently in sync as a design team—and that includes the client as a very important member of the team," she explains.

According to Friedman and Shields, the best clients are those who are confident in their vision and willing to say "yes" to an idea that may be only half formed in their own imaginations. Then they let the design team do their part of the job, which is to bring those notions and dreams to life in a plan that will work in the real world, with a real budget and timelines.

"Next, it's our turn to let the artists bring their vision, skills and creativity to the process at hand," Friedman explains.

In their partnership, Friedman and Shields have found that a strong, balanced collaboration enhances their own creativity.

"To have an extra set of eyes, another person's perspective and vision—it's not just twice as good, it's four or five times as good because you bounce ideas off of one another and are stimulated to move in directions you would not have imagined alone. It's more than helpful, it's exciting," Shields explains.

She continues, "We've found true collaboration to be a positive thing in our partnership. And it's also very important in our relationships with a regular group of artists whose work truly helps define and enhance our best and most satisfying design projects. "Trust is key to a great result. In the same way the client trusts the designers, we trust the artists. On the best projects, the results exceed everyone's expectations."

■   ■   ■

Interior designs by Janet Friedman, ASID, and Traci Shields, ASID. Photographs: Dino Tonn.

◄ "It's kind of funny to be known for powder room designs," laughs Janet Friedman, "but in some ways this most private room in the house can have the most personality. I think that's because it really can be a retreat and an expression of individual taste, in contrast to the more conventional expectations of spaces like living rooms and dining rooms. Powder rooms can be very freeing."

These three power rooms designed by Friedman and Shields stretch the notion of what a bathroom, or even a private spa, can be. All three benefit from the extraordinary talents of artists Don Beams and Robert O'Connell, who created magical faux finishes and tile installations, sculptural mirrors, furniture and cabinetry—all combining exquisite craftsmanship with unusual materials and hand-wrought detailing.

STACEY LAPUK

Mill Valley, CA

It is no accident that Stacey Lapuk's elegant interiors have the rich atmosphere of a beautifully composed, three-dimensional painting. The award-winning Mill Valley interior designer has a degree in fine arts with an emphasis on design and photography; she also studied architecture and interior design at the University of California at Berkeley. That aesthetic background is clearly evident in her work as she artfully weaves together elements of color, shape, texture, dimension and light.

The result is a stylish and fresh take on classic design. Lapuk's interiors are known for their sense of balance, harmony and perfect composition. Each interior space she creates reflects not only her solid foundation in art and design, but also her expertise in the ancient Chinese art of feng shui, which directs the flow of energy in an environment to enhance a sense of well-being.

"Good interior design must take the human element into account," Lapuk says emphatically. "It's a kind of fourth dimension that has to do with the way a person responds to and inhabits a space." The bottom line, she believes, is that a beautifully designed environment should provide both stimulation for the senses and nourishment for the soul.

—Susan Troller

Photographs: John Sutton Photography.

In this sophisticated but informal home overlooking San Francisco Bay, the client wanted the feel of an elegant beach house, a place where she could both go barefoot and entertain her well-traveled guests. The walls of the living room have a dimensional and light-reflective quality, the result of a finish that integrates a sea-foam pigment directly into the plaster, which is then sealed with an application of tinted wax. Echoing shades found elsewhere in the room, the strong contemporary painting by artist Aurelio Grisanty pays tribute to the watery expanse beyond the walls and windows and is framed in a joyful, unexpected orange.

Designer Stacey Lapuk describes this lusciously colorful bedroom as feeling like the interior of a candle. Centered over the bed is a sculpture of purple plum tree branches by San Francisco Bay-area artist David Ward. Lapuk explains this unusual choice as follows: "With so much color in the space, a soft counterpiece was required. And in earthquake country, a lightweight artwork is preferable over the bed to a heavily framed painting. This wall sculpture actually creates art with light and shadow; its form seems to be always moving and changing, animating the space."

STACEY LAPUK

(continued)

What are the intangibles that make a room feel good as well as look good? According to award-winning interior designer Stacey Lapuk, a professional member of the American Society of Interior Designers and a California Certified Interior Designer, it takes far more than just lovely furnishings, attractive artwork, pretty fabrics and stunning wall treatments to make a space feel great.

"I believe interior design is about more than simply creating a beautiful space. You should truly love where you live," the designer says. Named one of *Design Times* magazine's "Ten Designers to Watch," Lapuk focuses on the artful manipulation of abstract elements like form, color, line, balance, texture, volume, proportion and energy to create spaces that have both a physical and an emotional impact.

In addition, she believes every space needs to have a distinctive personality that is deeply reflective of the client's interests, lifestyle and passions, while also being responsive to the client's practical needs, uses and budget.

"I see interior design as a three-dimensional sculpture that my clients inhabit. It's an art that brings together energy, balance and scale. Furthermore, every person has a life that develops and evolves over time, and an interior design should have that kind of depth as well. And, because good interior design is an investment, it needs to have a kind of timelessness that justifies the expense."

Lapuk believes that the best interior design work is multi-dimensional, with a focus that is broader than any particular historical era. "I prefer an eclectic style, one that brings together a blend of compatible objects, colors and periods, but this kind of design must be very well planned and purposeful. Ultimately, this has to do with the way your eyes move through the space, the way you experience the space, the way the room makes you feel."

Widely published in design publications and a media presence on the Home & Garden Television network, Lapuk often talks about aesthetically pleasing interiors that combine graciousness with comfort, and that reflect history, diversity and the increasingly sophisticated tastes and imaginations of her clients.

Lapuk routinely utilizes the full vocabulary of design to create an environment that is more than the sum of its individual parts; even her most complex designs are always leavened by a beautiful sense of proportion, color and light. And guided by her own art training, she includes original contemporary art that is bright, engaging and intellectually intriguing.

"As a photographer, I love the sense of composing a room as you would compose and frame an image," Lapuk says. "The fact that you are dealing with multiple dimensions, and that someone will actually inhabit the space you create, just makes it that much more interesting."

◼ ◼ ◼

Photographs: John Sutton Photography.

◂ **Interior designer Stacey Lapuk created** an intimate sitting area within the context of a much larger master bedroom in this Designer Showcase House in Marin County, California.

The two oil paintings by Sandor Bernath, *Rogation Day* and *Love Letters From Tuscany*, are interesting paired together, the designer explains, precisely because they are *not* exactly the same size. Rather, the composition, style and subject matter of the images create the necessary continuity. By placing the paintings over the chairs, Lapuk creates a contained setting, a functional vignette within the larger expanse of the room.

▾ **By integrating antique furnishings** with contemporary art, Lapuk creates a vibrant and balanced focal point for this bedroom. Antique Chippendale night tables, early 20th-century Japanese *koi* lamps with Murano glass, metallic textured wall coverings and an antique Persian rug would all fall into a bland hole were it not for the strong, bright contemporary paintings by Roberto Matta flanking the bed. The subject matter, incorporating images of ancient classical times, lightly crosses the centuries, as do other elements in the design of the room. Their placement forms a boundary or frame for the bed, which is the visual and emotional center of the room.

KENDALL MARCELLE

Aventura, FL

South Florida-based interior designer Kendall Marcelle explains her interest in design quite simply: from as early as she can remember, she had a passion for designing her own space.

"I've always had a strong instinct for nesting," she says with a laugh. "Ever since I was very young, it was something I felt I had to do, wherever I was." So it seemed absolutely natural to Marcelle to major in design and business at Arizona State University, and then to follow that passion halfway across the country to a career in Hollywood, Florida.

Now, as the president of her own four-person interior design firm, Marcelle has found great success in helping other people create homes that feel warm and distinctive, stylish and highly individual. That talent is particularly appreciated by clients who have relocated to the area. Marcelle is able to make a house, apartment or condominium a true home, even when it may be a part-time residence.

Kendall Marcelle, like many other high-end interior designers working today, does not claim a specific signature style, preferring to let the wishes and tastes of her clients help guide the design choices they make together. But there is a recurring element in many of the elegant interiors she creates, and that is the use of original contemporary art and craft.

"Original art can be the most personal thing in a home," she says. "It plays a key role in any design."

—Susan Troller

Photograph: Roy Quesada.

Photograph: Louis Novick.

Kendall Marcelle chose art by Alicia Quaini, a contemporary Florida artist who was born and educated in Argentina, for the light sophistication it loans to this ocean front high-rise luxury apartment.

"We began with a color palette that was bright and natural. The custom built-in furniture features lots of natural maple and pear wood, and the colors are airy and vibrant. We designed a rug and had it made from wool and synthetic blends in three different textures," Marcelle says.

The Quaini artwork picks up the colors of the rest of the apartment, and the subject—an abstract still life of peach slices—is timeless, worldly and playful, perfectly in tune with the rest of the apartment.

There are many reasons why this vibrant Victor Vasarely painting takes a starring role in this dramatic Boca Raton, Florida, residence. Painted by the founder of the Op-Art movement of the 1960s and 1970s, the piece was purchased from the artist at his studio in Paris. Ever since, it has been a treasured centerpiece of an extensive collection owned by a Florida couple with an appreciation for modern geometric art.

Measuring six and one-half feet square, the canvas is large and bright, and full of vivid personality. "We kept most of the furniture and finishes very neutral to highlight and enhance the strong colors of the painting," designer Kendall Marcelle explains. "The multi-colored chairs and a throw pillow on the couch are the only pieces that complement the art. Everything else in the room simply frames the painting to bring out its inherent beauty."

This is the second home Marcelle has designed for this client, and displaying and enhancing original art has been an integral part of each design. The designer says the interiors of both homes were literally designed around the collection.

KENDALL MARCELLE

(continued)

When interior designer Kendall Marcelle goes shopping with a client for home furnishings and accessories, she calls it a "field day." But as she points out, it could also rather accurately be described as a "personality profile," or a "taste tester," or a "style indicator."

"As a designer of primarily residential spaces, I believe it's very important to get to know your client. You need to ask good questions and to listen very carefully, and let those conversations help guide the design process. But it's also important to actually observe what someone gravitates toward, what speaks to him or her," she observes.

She believes that the best interior designs result from a profound confidence between client and designer. "In the most successful collaborations, the designer has the trust of the client. Trust encourages creative freedom. It allows the designer the latitude to create a room or environment that is highly creative, and yet intensely personal and extraordinarily reflective of the client's passions and tastes."

The Florida coastal area Kendall Marcelle Design Associates serves has a large population of people living in apartments, condominiums and upscale golf, recreational and retirement communities. It can be a challenge to create a home with distinctive flair and character from this type of space, which often

Photograph: Shayne Hensley.

begins as a shell with a priceless view but rather rigid architectural parameters. In situations where a client is unable to make large-scale architectural changes in their living space, Marcelle often advocates the use of custom-designed art and furnishings to provide a strong sense of individual personality and taste.

In fact, Marcelle and her group believe custom-designed furniture can often create architectural interest in a space where structural change is not an option.

"We routinely work with a number of fabricators and artisans who can take our idea for a design and make it come to life. It's always a collaboration process, with our ideas and their suggestions and refinements," she explains. The result, she says, is not only beautiful, but often unexpected, with an aesthetic feel that is surprising and distinctive, and most welcome in a space that may be otherwise architecturally unremarkable.

In all Kendall Marcelle designs, there is a marked sensitivity to how original art is displayed, a reverence that informs its placement and presentation, a conviction that its presence in a home is significant and meaningful.

"I've worked with clients who have extensive collections of their own original art, so we design around that collection and let it be the focal point of the home," Marcelle says. "Sometimes I can introduce clients to artists whose work is a complement to their existing art, or who provide an intriguing counterpoint or new direction for the existing collection."

At other times, Marcelle and her team are the catalyst for the client's exploration of original art. "There are so many places to look for inspiration," she says firmly. With her clients, she explores sourcebooks, galleries, books, magazines and even student art exhibitions. "The art does not have to break the budget to impact the setting or have meaning for the client," she notes.

"Original art brings so much energy, excitement and emotion to a room. Whatever the art is, a long-term family treasure or that perfect final punctuation—either found or commissioned—for a newly designed space, what's important is that it expresses the homeowner's personality."

▪ ▪ ▪

◀ A blend of beloved objects and artwork, unusual fabrics and distinctive furnishings come together in this living room designed by Kendall Marcelle for one of her favorite clients.

"This room has a lot of personality, and I think it's a wonderful reflection of the woman who lives here. She is warm, open and curious; very supportive of the arts in general and deeply interested in other cultures and ethnic art. I just love her, and loved working with her to get a room that feels exactly the way she wanted it to feel," Marcelle says. "She says she sometimes likes to sit in here when the room is dark except for the lights that illuminate the painting."

The four-panel painting above the sofa is by Lamar Briggs, a native of Lafayette, Louisiana, whose work is represented in major public, private and corporate collections. His signature abstract paintings, he says, are inspired by nature, music and a positive attitude toward life. The Briggs panels shown here form the centerpiece of the room and beautifully complement the space's other richly distinctive elements: wooden African grave markers, a Tibetan woven rug and a table created from an Asian antique reed bed. The unusual frame chairs and sofa cushions—large and small—feature Donghia fabric chosen by Marcelle.

CHARLES CUNNIFFE

Aspen, CO

Colorado-based architect Charles Cunniffe, AIA, is a contemporary Renaissance artist of the Rocky Mountains.

An award-winning architect with an international practice, Cunniffe is also a private pilot, sculptor, furniture maker and designer of everything from lighting fixtures to dinnerware. His background includes degrees from the Rhode Island School of Design in both fine arts and architecture, and graduate work in real estate, law and alternative energy applications.

As an artist himself, Cunniffe is readily inclined to include original, one-of-a-kind design solutions in his architectural work. He feels there are areas and elements in any project—but especially a home—where elegant, innovative artworks make a natural and significant contribution to the overall design. Typically, these elements include front entries, stair designs, fireplaces, lighting, furniture and various kitchen features, including cabinetry, hood design and tile work. In addition, Cunniffe's projects are designed with spaces and lighting that accommodate and enhance the art collections of his clients.

Interested in the design possibilities of everything from a utensil to a town, Charles Cunniffe believes in the artful home as part of an artful universe.

—Susan Troller

◂ Extraordinary workmanship and a playful eclecticism are combined in this one-of-a-kind kitchen, where virtually every element is a hard-working piece of original contemporary art designed specifically for the setting.

With an ambience that is warm and informal but highly functional, the kitchen features custom cabinetry, custom range hoods in copper and stainless steel, custom lighting and furniture.

The room's centerpiece is a three-disk table/island/workspace; the anchoring middle element features a sink made of granite and steel. Flanked by two attached marble and wood tables for food preparation and informal dining, the effect is clean, sculptural, practical and fun.

The attention to every aesthetic detail, and the homage paid to sculptural form, echoes the rest of the home's interior and exterior spaces.

◂ "Great clients lead to great architecture," says Charles Cunniffe. That is clearly the case with this remarkable New York City penthouse. Cunniffe's open renovation features a dazzling 6,700-square-foot interior space created from a former warren of cramped rooms. The space houses an equally dazzling art collection, commissioned specifically for the project, including a monumental blue glass *Tornado* sculpture/chandelier created in collaboration with legendary glass artist Dale Chihuly.

Cunniffe's client was passionate about art and music, and wanted an environment in which to pursue both interests. The entire penthouse is a kind of gallery, and the living room is designed to accommodate two grand pianos and a wealth of beautiful art created especially for the space.

"Our goal was to bring together a combination of artists and then work with them to create custom pieces that would suit this space. I had known Dale at the Rhode Island School of Design when we were both there, and it was wonderful collaborating with him on this project," Cunniffe says.

This view of the living room shows a fireplace surround, diptych and pink chair, all created by sculptor Forrest Myers. For the diptych and surround, Myers used four sizes of twisted powder-coated aluminum wire. The sculpture against the right wall, suggesting a human figure and titled *Water Boy*, was created by Laura Drake, and is lit from within. Architectural features include a very open floor plan, floor-to-ceiling windows, a state-of-the-art lighting and sound system, and acoustics designed to provide an ideal environment for playing—and listening to—the two pianos.

CHARLES CUNNIFFE

(continued)

The son of a builder, Charles Cunniffe knew he wanted to be an architect by the time he was in eighth grade. He suspects his inclinations toward the profession may have begun even earlier.

"Even as a really little kid I had some pretty strong notions about the way things should look. I could not play with toys that weren't in scale with each other," he laughs.

Born and educated on the East Coast, he has made Colorado his home for the last 24 years, creating a highly esteemed practice with offices in five locations around the state. His firm, Charles Cunniffe Architects, has created award-winning designs for both public and private sectors across the country and abroad. Projects have included residential, resort, office, commercial, hotel, religious and public works settings.

Although his firm is often lauded for its sensitivity to regional contextualism, Cunniffe is particularly proud of his reputation for working well with many clients on extraordinarily varied projects, each ultimately reflecting the client's own passions, priorities and sensibilities.

"I tell my clients, 'We're going on a creative adventure, a journey. Don't be afraid of any idea.' The most rewarding projects and the most rewarding clients are those with that sense of design adventure."

Cunniffe, who has a broad and fluent architectural vocabulary, is delighted to see increasingly bold clients with a curiosity and open attitude towards original design. And although he began building his con-

▸ Charles Cunniffe created this spectacular residence in Park City, Utah, for clients who wanted a place that was more than just beautiful, comfortable and accommodating for their young family. They were seeking a larger-than-life sculpture, a kind of contemporary art on a vast scale that they could also call home.

The house combines a signature cantilevered barrel-vaulted roof over the primary living area. Soaring glass takes advantage of the striking mountain views, and a rugged and graceful exterior combines wood, steel and limestone.

A tribute to the passionate creativity of all members of the design team, the home has won many design and building awards, among them *Mountain Living* magazine's Home of the Year and a Gold Nugget Award from the Pacific Coast Builders Conference and *Builder* magazine.

▸ A bold painting by Oklahoma native and world-renowned artist Joe Andoe is perfectly at home above the large, rugged fireplace in this Colorado mountain home designed by Charles Cunniffe Architects.

According to Cunniffe, virtually every element of this exceptional home was custom designed or hand crafted, from furniture to fireplace screens, and from the stairways to the massive mahogany entry doors.

"We had a great time working on this house; the clients were outstanding, and it shows in the quality of every detail," Cunniffe reports. These were the kind of dream clients, he says, who were committed to a unique vision and enthusiastic about working with artists and artisans capable of creating the one-of-a-kind pieces that become the signature of a true custom design.

siderable reputation as a designer of spaces reflecting a Rocky Mountain heritage and western vernacular, his work reflects a progressively broad range of design ideas.

In a recent interview with a Colorado design publication, Cunniffe reported that, "People seem to be willing to be more creative. They're making their own rules. It's not so much anymore that they do what everybody else does. They want something more original than the typical mountain home."

One of his projects, a Park City, Utah, house that was named *Mountain Living* magazine's 2002 Home of the Year is a perfect example of that spirit of adventure. Designed as an elegant, inhabitable sculpture in wood, steel and limestone, the home reflects a joyful sensitivity to its spectacular site and mountain views. Inside it showcases the owners' significant collection of contemporary art.

But this house is not just a chilly exercise in spectacular design and aesthetics. A family home with a warm and welcoming essence, its grand artistic ideas are blended with a sense of human scale and comfort. The result is a happy mix that ably demonstrates Cunniffe's commitment to making a home livable as well as beautiful.

"An architect has an obligation to consider how space affects the people who live there, or who interact with the space. It is their home, and should provide a retreat. It should nurture their hobbies, their dreams, their sense of themselves. The design is more than just shape or shadow or view. It directly affects all their senses and their well-being. An awareness of all these things is part of the architect's responsibility to his client, and, actually, the world."

■ ■ ■

JUDY GUBNER
COLLEEN JOHNSON

Denver, CO

Interior designers Judy Gubner and Colleen Johnson know they exert an enormous aesthetic influence on all of their projects. Still, they agree that their work is often at its best when it is virtually invisible.

Award-winning partners at In-site Design Group, Johnson and Gubner specialize in high-end home design. Their passion, they explain, is to learn who their clients are and what they want, and then to help them design a home that is an accurate, elegant mirror of their own interests and tastes.

Although the partners deliberately avoid having a signature style, their work is notable for a strong sense of place and personality, and for its distinctive and imaginative use of original art, furnishings and accessories to support the clients' visions of their own dream homes.

Whether it's a New Mexico territorial-style house, a luxurious Rocky Mountain cabin retreat or a California estate with a serene Asian ambience, every In-site Design Group project is, first and foremost, a reflection of the clients' passions. Beyond that, each project is also a tribute to Gubner and Johnson's meticulous attention to every detail that helps create an artful home.

—Susan Troller

Photograph: Estetico, Denver, CO.

▸ Every room in this very large southern California residence seems to whisper in a quietly luxurious style strongly influenced by a Japanese-country aesthetic.

The home's slate floors, exposed timbers, *shoji*-style screens and muted colors all contribute to a sense of restrained elegance.

The serenity of the house and its furnishings provides a perfect background to a genuinely dazzling collection of original contemporary Western and Native American art, including pieces by Georgia O'Keeffe, Fritz Scholder and furniture designer Sam Maloof, as well as both ancient and modern ceramics.

In the family room, pictured here, furnishings, window and floor treatments, colors and lighting are all subtle, allowing the Fritz Scholder painting and Cheyenne headdress to be the focal point of the room.

"We wanted to complement, not compete with, the art," designer Judy Gubner explains.

JUDY GUBNER
COLLEEN JOHNSON

(continued)

Photograph: Estetico, Denver, CO.

"We design other peoples' dreams."

That's how Judy Gubner describes her profession and passion as an interior designer. Since founding In-site Design Group in 1992, Gubner and her partner, Colleen Johnson, have created a body of work characterized by its strong aesthetic appeal and a remarkably diverse range of projects.

And although the scale of Gubner and Johnson's work is often grand, focusing on luxury homes for private clients, the firm itself is small.

"With these rather complex jobs, we prefer to do the actual design work ourselves, as well as the planning and project organization. We're not a firm that assigns the details to someone else," the partners explain. Both Gubner and Johnson are professional members of the American Society of Interior Designers, have decades of experience in all aspects of interior design work and regularly win top honors in ASID competitions.

"When our clients hire the firm, they actually work with the two of us. There's a lot of hand-holding along the way, certainly, but we get great satisfaction from working directly with our clients, along with the architects and contractors." Gubner and Johnson particularly enjoy collaborating with design professionals who share their client-oriented philosophy, and believe that these projects ultimately produce the most exceptional work.

Every project begins with research, drawings and meetings with the client and the design team. Whenever possible, Gubner and Johnson like to be involved in decisions about the interior architectural design and make recommendations about details like interior surfaces and colors. Their involvement ends with the final decorative touches and furnishings.

According to the partners, the most powerful moment often comes at the very end of a project. "We will have worked with the client for months, imagining every detail of their home, choosing furnishings and art, or discussing how and where to use things they already own and love. When it comes time to move in, we prefer to completely arrange the house—down to lighting candles and putting on the music—before the clients arrive. It's quite a magical moment when our clients walk into the home they have been imagining for so long and discover that their dreams have become real."

■ ■ ■

◂ Gorgeous artifact or work of art? What appears to be a heavily beaded leather Indian garment is actually a perfect replica, a sculpture created by artist Janet Nelson using treated craft paper, along with beads and quills cast from a polymer composite.

The sculpture is meticulously painted, decorated and pieced together; in its finished form it is virtually indistinguishable from its historic inspiration. The piece was commissioned specifically for the interior of this Aspen, Colorado, cabin retreat and is beautifully lit to take center stage. An antique French ski poster was also chosen for display, along with a pretty painted panel, a reproduction of a European piece purchased through a design showroom.

According to Gubner and Johnson, an imaginative mix of original art plus other decorative elements creates a warm and lively interior. "Not every piece has to be of the same caliber or expense," Judy Gubner says. "But everything needs to work well together to achieve the overall design."

Sometimes clients ask Judy Gubner and Colleen Johnson to feature a particular piece of treasured art when they create an interior design.

▾ Every design choice and element has an impact on the final atmosphere and feeling of any space.

For example, there is an abiding sense of peace and sanctuary in this New Mexico territorial-style house that extends from the very construction of the walls to the furnishings and art.

Four-coat true plastered walls, finished with beeswax, have a luminous beauty and a rich reflective color. Furthermore, because the plaster treatment has such marvelous sound-absorbing qualities, there is a kind of invisible, but unmistakable, serenity in the room and throughout the home.

In the space pictured here, Judy Gubner and Colleen Johnson chose colors and furnishings to enhance the peaceful atmosphere. The painting, by the late Native American artist Veloy Vigil, is titled *Passing Moment*. Vigil's work is known both for its rich use of color and its abstract, spiritual dimension. The homeowner reports that she loves this room, and finds in its quiet atmosphere a soul-satisfying retreat.

FURNITURE, SCULPTURE & OBJECTS

Joan Weissman, *Forest*, hand-knotted Tibetan rug. Photograph: Jerry Rabinowitz.
Joan Weissman, hand-knotted rugs (detail). Photograph: Dave Nufer.

BLAISE GASTON

BLAISE GASTON, INC. ▨ 686 FAIRHOPE AVENUE ▨ EARLYSVILLE, VA 22936
TEL/FAX 434-973-1801 ▨ E-MAIL MAIL@BLAISEGASTON.COM ▨ WWW.BLAISEGASTON.COM

54

Top: *Helios*, 2003, bubinga with copper paint and glass top, 25"W × 48"L × 16"H.
Bottom: Dressing table and chair, 1996, Japanese ash and cherry with custom brass hardware. Photographs: Philip Beaurline.

ANDREW MUGGLETON

ANDREW MUGGLETON DESIGN LLC ■ TEL 888-886-1805
E-MAIL DESIGNS@ANDREWMUGGLETON.COM ■ WWW.ANDREWMUGGLETON.COM

Top: *Interlocking Console Table*, quilted makore, ebonized oak and glass, 53"L x 18"W x 33"H.
Bottom: *Arch Coffee Table*, figured burbinga, ebonized oak, stainless steel and glass, 45"L x 35"W x 16"H. Photographs: Dean Powell.

CHAJO

JONATHAN EDIE ■ CHANIN COOK ■ 451 MONTECITO BOULEVARD ■ NAPA, CA 94559
TEL 707-257-3676 ■ FAX 707-257-3675 ■ E-MAIL INFO@CHAJO.COM ■ WWW.CHAJO.COM

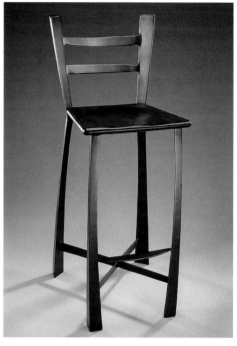

Top left: *Tapered Cocktail Square*, fossilized limestone, jatoba, maple, pau ferro and steel, 36"L × 36"W × 17"H.
Top right: *Bowed Barstool*, steel and maple, 17"L × 16"W × 43"H. Bottom left: *Bowed Entry Table*, ammonite in sunburst walnut with bloodwood trim and steel, 22"L × 22"W × 33.5"H.
Bottom right: *Flared Arc Console*, petrified wood, quilted maple and steel, 46"L ×12"W ×31"H. Photographs: Hap Sakwa.

MARK LEVIN

LEVIN STUDIO ■ PO BOX 109 ■ SAN JOSE, NM 87565-0109 ■ TEL/FAX 505-421-3207
E-MAIL MLEVIN@PLATEAUTEL.NET ■ WWW.MARKLEVIN.COM

Top: *Apple Coffee Tables*, 2003, curly birch with bubinga stem, 16"H × 34"W × 27"D.
Bottom: *Pear Coffee Tables*, 2003, walnut with bocote stem, 16"H × 43"W × 28"D. Photographs: Margot Geist.

THOMAS THROOP

145 GRASSY PLAIN STREET ■ BETHEL, CT 06801 ■ TEL/FAX 203-778-9863
E-MAIL TOM@BLACKCREEKDESIGNS.COM ■ WWW.BLACKCREEKDESIGNS.COM

58

Top: *Trevi Writing Desk*, bubinga, bird's-eye maple and bog oak, 58"W × 30"D × 30"H. Center left: *Essex Console*, cherry and bog oak, 44"W × 13"D × 32"H.
Bottom right: *Durham Cabinet*, cherry and English pippy elm, 32"W × 17"D × 47"H. Bottom left: *Pine Point Table*, bubinga with maple inlay, 22"W × 22"D × 26"H. Photographs: Frank Poole.

SUTTMAN STUDIO

JOHN SUTTMAN ■ 1895 NORTH VENTURA AVENUE ■ VENTURA, CA 93001
TEL/FAX 805-648-1810 ■ E-MAIL JPSUTTMAN@EARTHLINK.NET ■ WWW.JOHNSUTTMAN.COM

59

Left: *Two Tone Gothic*, steel with patina, beveled glass and low-voltage lighting, 72" × 36" × 15". Photograph: Robert Reck.
Right: *Pictoman* series, indoor/outdoor sculpture, left: *Thinman A*, right: *Garden Goddess*, forged and welded steel with patina and fused glass, 67" × 14" × 10". Photograph: Wayne Smith.

JIM GALILEO ■ 176 EAST SEVENTH STREET ■ PATERSON, NJ 07524 ■ TEL/FAX 973-278-5881
E-MAIL RIVERSIDEARTISANS@WORLDNET.ATT.NET

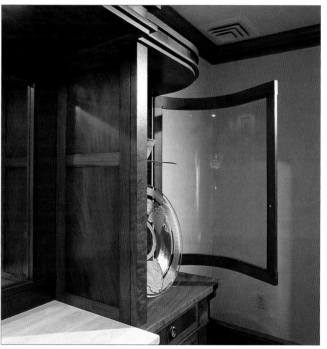

Top: *Fellinger Table*, 1998, mahogany, crotch mahogany and satinwood, 53" × 34" × 25". Bottom left: *Serpentine Cabinets*, 1999,
curly maple and pear wood, 108" × 80" × 25". Bottom right: *Server*, 2001, mahogany, crotch mahogany, travertine and glass, 130" × 78" × 25". Photographs: Bob Skinner.

WILLIAM ROBBINS

WILLIAM ROBBINS FURNITURE MAKER ■ 139 NEWBOLDS CORNER ROAD ■ VINCENTOWN, NJ 08088
TEL 609-859-1790 ■ FAX 609-859-9660 ■ E-MAIL WILLIAMROBBINS@SNIP.NET ■ WWW.HOMEPORTFOLIO.COM/WILLIAM-ROBBINS

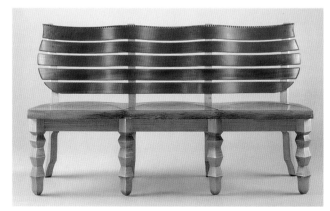

Top: Corner liquor cabinet, bubinga and cherry, 7'H × 54"W. Bottom left: *Journal Settee*, mahogany, maple and stained poplar, 63.6"L × 35.5"H × 20"D.
Bottom right: *Journal Coffee Table*, cherry, hickory and stained poplar, 36"Dia. × 19"H. Photographs: Robert Homan.

KERRY VESPER

3030 NORTH CIVIC CENTER PLAZA #4 ■ SCOTTSDALE, AZ 85251 ■ TEL 480-429-0954 ■ FAX 480-839-5376
E-MAIL KERRY@KERRYVESPER.COM ■ WWW.KERRYVESPER.COM

62

Top left: *Thatza Chair*, 2002, bubinga and Baltic birch, 34"H × 28" × 24".
Top right: *Mesa Ramon*, 2002, Philippine mahogany, base: 20"H × 30" × 30". Bottom left: *Wenge Essence*, 2003, wenge and Baltic birch, 6"H × 14" × 23".
Bottom right: *Seating the Heart*, 2003, sapele and Baltic birch, 34"H × 39" × 24". Photographs: Ron DeRiemacker.

MICHAEL DOERR

DOERR WOODWORKING ■ 4371 COUNTY HIGHWAY M ■ STURGEON BAY, WI 54235
TEL 920-743-5631 ■ E-MAIL MICHAEL@MICHAELDOERR.COM ■ WWW.MICHAELDOERR.COM

Top: Dinette set, curly maple. Photograph: Matt Orthober. Bottom right: Pedestal table, curly maple. Bottom left: *Bobbi's Chair*, curly maple.

ALAN ROSEN

ALAN ROSEN FURNITURE MAKERS LTD. ■ 3740 LEGOE BAY ROAD ■ LUMMI ISLAND, WA 98262
TEL 360-758-7452 ■ FAX 360-758-2498 ■ E-MAIL ALINDYROSEN@EARTHLINK.NET ■ WWW.ALANROSENFURNITURE.COM

64

Top left: Bird's-eye maple and wenge desk and chair set. Photograph: Dana Kershner. Top right: American black cherry and bubinga buffet. Photograph: David Scherrer. Bottom: Bubinga and ebony dining set. Photograph: Dick Wolf.

CITY JOINERY

JONAH ZUCKERMAN ■ 70 WASHINGTON STREET #711 ■ BROOKLYN, NY 11201
TEL 718-596-6502 ■ FAX 718-797-2336 ■ E-MAIL INFO@CITYJOINERY.COM ■ WWW.CITYJOINERY.COM

Top: *Hewn Ding Table and Chairs,* 2001, ash and industrial woven felt, table: 30"H x 44"W x 100"L, chair: 34"H x 22"W x 26"D.
Bottom: *Hovering Console Table,* 2001, black walnut and tiger maple, 32"H x 50"W x 15"D. Photographs: William Boyd.

BRIAN WEIR, WOODWORKER

BRIAN WEIR ■ 797 POTOMSKA ROAD ■ SOUTH DARTMOUTH, MA 02748
TEL/FAX 508-636-1405 ■ E-MAIL BDW@BRIANWEIR.NET ■ WWW.BRIANWEIR.NET

Top: Trestle desk and armchair, walnut and ash, 30" × 72" × 32".
Bottom: Credenza, walnut, 28" × 56" × 21". Photographs: Dean Powell.

KENNETH CARLL

BITS OF LIGHT-ARTS ◼ BRIDGETON, NJ 08302 ◼ TEL 856-451-3204
E-MAIL KEN@BITSOFLIGHTARTS.COM ◼ WWW.BITSOFLIGHTARTS.COM

Top left: *Castle Chess Table*, carved cherry with monolithic granite chessboard, 41" × 32" × 31". Top right: *Cherry Blossom Table*, cherry with cherry blossom carving, 23" × 32" × 23".
Bottom left: Three-tier table, cedar with cedar and slate carvings, 25" × 33" × 24". Bottom right: Six-leaf table set, cedar with cedar and slate carvings, 41" × 26" × 20".

JEANINE A. GUNCHEON

JEANINE A. GUNCHEON STUDIO ■ 7349 WEST MADISON STREET ■ FOREST PARK, IL 60130
TEL 708-366-2360 ■ FAX 708-366-2238 ■ E-MAIL JAGUNCHEON@SBCGLOBAL.NET ■ WWW.JAGUNCHEON.COM

70

Top left: Dye-painted, lacquered table, original, handbuilt design, 35"W × 60"L × 29"H.
Right: Dye-painted, lacquered cupboard, original, handbuilt design, 27"W × 47"H × 14"D.
Bottom left: Dye-painted, lacquered chest, original, handbuilt design, 26"W × 22"H × 17"D. Photographs: Jerry Anthony Photography.

BLUE STAR DESIGN COMPANY

MARGARET ROMERO ■ 55 BALTIMORE STREET ■ CUMBERLAND, MD 21502
TEL/FAX 301-722-7223 ■ E-MAIL MAROMERO@BLUESTARDESIGNCOMPANY.COM ■ WWW.BLUESTARDESIGNCOMPANY.COM

71

Top: *Zoo*, cotton, wood and gold leaf, 24" x 24" x 18"H. Bottom: *Rubicon*, cotton, silk, Ultrasuede®, wood and gold leaf, 43" x 20" x 21"H. Photographs: Vibrant Image.com

HOLMAN STUDIOS

STEVE HOLMAN ■ PO BOX 572 N DORSET, VT 05251 ■ TEL 802-867-0131 ■ FAX 802-867-0255
E-MAIL HSTUDIOS@SOVER.NET ■ WWW.HOLMANSTUDIOS.COM

72

Top left: *Lyre Desk*, 2000, mappa burl veneers with ebony, maple, gold leaf and brass, 28"D × 48"H × 60"L. Top center: *Deep Sea Desk*, 2000, maple, acrylic and bronzing powders, 24"-30"H × 30"W × 60"L. Top right: *Catherine's Hutch*, 2002, Karelian burl veneers, purpleheart, sycamore and rosewood, 24"D × 62"L × 84"H. Bottom: *Checkerboard Desk*, 2001, figured maple, bubinga and cocobolo, 30"H × 30"W × 60"L. Photographs: Cook Nielson.

MILLEA FURNISHINGS

ANNA MILLEA ■ 4229 NORTH HONORE STREET ■ CHICAGO, IL 60613 ■ TEL 773-244-9840 ■ FAX 773-244-9843
E-MAIL ATMILLEA@AOL.COM ■ WWW.MILLEAFURNISHINGS.COM

Top: Coffee table, birch with acrylic surface application, 17"H × 48"W × 24"D. Bottom left: *Tower Cabinet*, birch with acrylic surface application, 72"H × 12"W × 12"D.
Bottom right: *Geo-Tansu Chest*, birch with acrylic surface application, 54"H × 36"W × 18"D. Photographs: Image Studio Ltd.

LEO PECK

PECK TILE, POTTERY AND SCULPTURE ■ 1065 LOS CARNEROS AVENUE ■ NAPA, CA 94559
TEL 707-226-3100 ■ FAX 707-255-6202 ■ E-MAIL LEO@PECKTILE.COM ■ WWW.PECKTILE.COM

74

Top: *Rainforest*, ceramic tile with bamboo style metal legs, 36" × 36" × 21". Bottom: *Jack of Clubs*, one-eyed jack with golf clubs, 43" × 33" × 18".

EILEEN JAGER

LIGHTHUNTER ▨ ONE COTTAGE STREET ▨ EASTHAMPTON, MA 01027
TEL/FAX 413-527-2090 ▨ EILEEN@EILEENJAGER.COM ▨ WWW.EILEENJAGER.COM

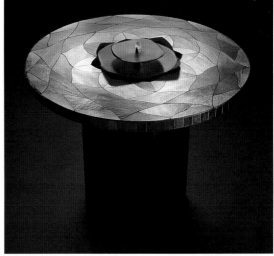

Top left: *Petal Lotus*, 2003, glass mosaic table-fountain, 24" × 24" × 16". Top right: *Star Lotus*, 2003, glass mosaic table-fountain, 30" × 30" × 24".
Bottom: *FloWing IV*, 2003, glass mosaic table-fountain, 54" × 32" × 19". Photographs: Tommy O. Elder.

ZINGARA YULI GLASS STUDIO

39 LINCOLN PLACE ▪ BROOKLYN, NY 11217 ▪ TEL/FAX 718-857-1015
ZINGARA@ZYGLASSTUDIO.COM ▪ WWW.ZYGLASSTUDIO.COM

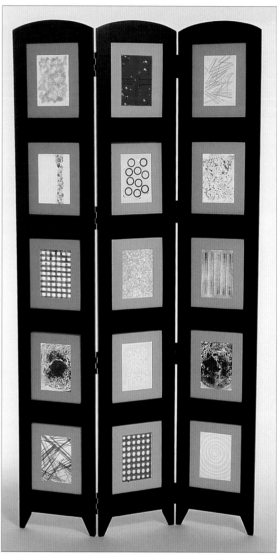

76

Left: Set of three tables with glass samples, 2003, fused glass, 55" × 45" × 23".
Right: Screen door with glass samples, 2003, various glass techniques, 177" × 90". Photographs: D. James. Dee.

MELANIE ROTHSCHILD

MELANIE ROTHSCHILD, INC. ■ TOPANGA, CA 90290
TEL 310-455-1297 ■ FAX 310-455-7587 ■ E-MAIL MELROTHSCHILD@AOL.COM

Top left: *Tivoli Hall Table*, acrylic paint on wood, 47" x 9" x 28". Top right: *Rocco End Table*, acrylic paint on wood, 18" x 18" x 22".
Bottom: *Reddddd: An Archeological Site of Color*, Museum of Art Store, Toledo, OH, mixed media, 47" x 9" x 32".

APRYL MILLER

APRYL MILLER STUDIOS ■ 188 EAST 76TH #29 ■ NEW YORK, NY 10021
TEL 212-639-1836 ■ E-MAIL INFO@APRYLMILLERSTUDIOS.COM ■ WWW.APRYLMILLERSTUDIOS.COM

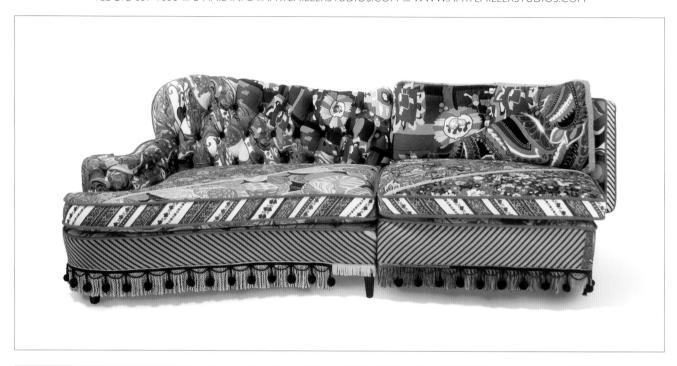

78

Top: *Can he do the rumba, you can do the twist?*, 2001, 33"H × 82"W × 41"D. Bottom left: *The Sun Sprouts with a Back Pocket*, 2001, 51" × 27"W × 27"D.
Bottom right: *Buttons for Hunderwasser*, 2000, 29"H × 33"W × 31"D. Photographs: Scott Petill.

AMY GRASSFIELD

PEAS-ON-EARTH ■ 901 WEST SAN MATEO ■ SANTA FE, NM 87505
TEL 505-982-9411 ■ E-MAIL AGRASSFIELD@YAHOO.COM

Sweet Cano-Pea Bed, copper, steel, barn wood and chicken wire. Photograph: Pat Pollard.

TOM CHENOWETH

ASTRA DESIGN ■ 15 NORTH BELMONT AVENUE ■ RICHMOND, VA 23221 ■ TEL 804-257-5467 ■ FAX 804-257-5928
E-MAIL ASTRADESIGN@MINDSPRING.COM ■ WWW.ASTRADESIGN.COM

80

Top: Day bed, 2002, steel with linen and silk cushion.
Bottom left: Coffee table, 2002, aluminum and stainless steel. Bottom right: Garden bench, 2003, steel. Photographs: Lee Brauer Photography.

JOHN RAIS

JOHN RAIS STUDIOS ■ PO BOX 338 ■ MILFORD, PA 18337 ■ TEL/FAX 570-409-0441
E-MAIL JOHNRAIS@MERCURYLINK.NET ■ WWW.JOHNRAISSTUDIOS.COM

81

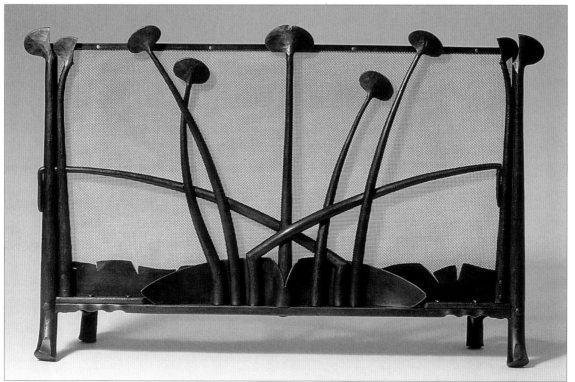

Top left: *Fiery Fire Tools*, forged steel with oxide finish, set: 31"H x 13"W. Top right: *Little Tool Table*, forged steel with patina, 20"H x 10"Dia.
Bottom: *Salt Marsh at Sunrise Fire Screen*, forged steel, bronze and patina, 28"H x 40"W x 13"D. Photographs: D. James Dee.

DAVID CODDAIRE

755 EAST 10TH STREET ▦ OAKLAND, CA 94606 ▦ TEL 510-451-7353 ▦ FAX 510-451-7351
E-MAIL TALLIRONVASES@MINDSPRING.COM ▦ WWW.TALLIRONVASES.COM

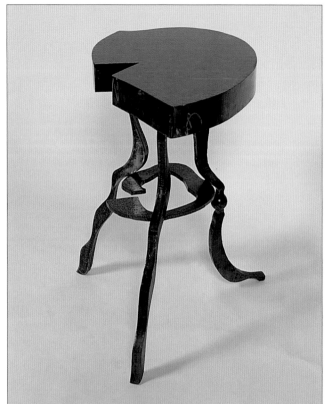 

Top left: *Artist's Table*, 2003, welded and forged steel with an epoxy dye, 20" × 20" × 36". Top right: Metal vase, 2003, welded and forged steel with an epoxy dye, 10" × 10" × 72".
Bottom left: *Spiral Leg Table*, 2003, welded and forged steel with an epoxy dye, 13" × 13" × 42". Bottom left: Steel table, 2003, welded and forged steel with an epoxy dye, 10" × 10" × 30".

82

MITCH LEVIN

HIGH VOLTAGE STUDIO ■ 21180 WEST ELEANOR LANE ■ KILDEER, IL 60047
TEL 847-540-6362 ■ E-MAIL MLEVIN2@MSN.COM ■ WWW.HIGHVOLTAGESTUDIO.COM

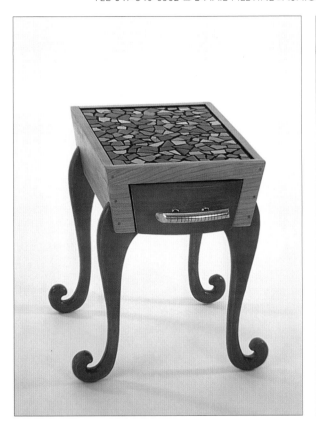

83

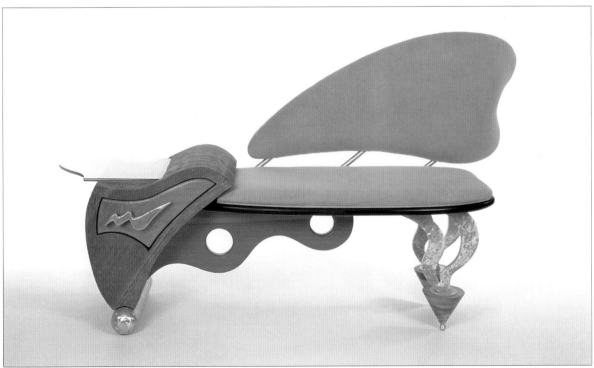

Top left: *Girlie Table*, cherry, dyed poplar, aluminum and mosaic tile, 18"W × 20"H × 20"D.
Top right: *My Heart is Hooked*, recycled metals, purple heart, mahogany, poplar and concrete, 24"W × 56"H × 24"D, glass heart blown by James Wilbat.
Bottom: *Genie Bench*, poplar, aluminum, glass and Ultrasuede®, 72"W × 42"H × 20"D. Photographs: Harold Crane.

MARTIN STURMAN

MARTIN STURMAN SCULPTURES ■ 3201 BAYSHORE DRIVE ■ WESTLAKE VILLAGE, CA 91361
TEL 818-707-8087 ■ FAX 818-707-3079 ■ E-MAIL MLSTURMAN@AOL.COM ■ WWW.STEELSCULPTURES.COM

84

Top left: *Tropical Bedside Table*, 2002, acrylic and steel, 29"H × 19"W × 19"D. Right: *Art Deco Bedside Table*, 2002, acrylic and steel, 29"H × 19"W × 19"D.
Bottom left: *Floral Cocktail Table*, 2002, acrylic and steel, 19"H × 23"W × 21"D. Photographs: Barry Michlin.

BADMAN DESIGN

DAVID BADMAN ■ 18 SOUTH THIRD STREET ■ GRAND FORKS, ND 58201 ■ TEL 701-746-7300
E-MAIL DAVE@BADMAN.COM ■ WWW.BADMAN.COM

85

Left: Untitled cabinet, 2003, terra cotta clay with mixed metals and adjustable glass shelves, 11"W x 22"L x 42"H.
Right: Untitled mirror and cabinet combo, 2003, heated brass and rusty steel, cabinet: 12"W x 31"L x 32"H, mirror: 31" x 31". Photographs: Jason Lindsey.

JOHN T. UNGER

JOHN T. UNGER STUDIO ▨ 3014 SOUTH M-66 ▨ MANCELONA, MI 49659
TEL 231-584-2710 ▨ E-MAIL JOHN@JOHNTUNGER.COM ▨ WWW.JOHNTUNGER.COM

86

Top: *Howie and JoAnn Meet and Fall in Love* (one section of a four-part garden fence), 2003, steel, copper and mosaic, 36"H x 78"W x 11"D.
Bottom: *Acrobat Chairs*, 2003, steel and copper; 34"H x 18"W x 14.4"D; *Swing Side Table,* 2003, steel, copper and glass, 24"H x 20"W x 20"D. Photographs: Richard Hellyer.

STĒL OBJEKT STUDIO

BRANDON WILLIAMS ▪ AMELIA SWEET ▪ 1907 NORTH MENDELL I-REAR ▪ CHICAGO, IL 60622-1205
TEL 317-698-5548 ▪ E-MAIL BRANDART@HOTMAIL.COM ▪ WWW.STELOBJEKT.COM ▪ WWW.STEELOBJECT.COM

87

Top: *Deco Desk/Deco Sit*, 2000, surfaced mild steel, desk: 52" × 36" × 30"; chair: 20" × 16" × 18".
Bottom: *Pod Coffee Table*, 2000, mild steel and neon with resin inserts, 54" × 24" × 18". Photographs: Quarter Moon Photography.

ROBIN EVANS

GLOWING PANELS STUDIO ■ SEDONA, AZ ■ TEL 928-282-6946 ■ FAX 928-204-1750
E-MAIL INFO@GLOWINGPANELS.COM ■ WWW.GLOWINGPANELS.COM

Top: Patinated steel and glass mosaic console table, 60" × 20" × 34"H, design by Robin Evans, steel fabrication by Tom Lever; shown with multi-level glass mosaic mirror, 26" × 38" × 4".
Bottom left: Multi-level glass mosaic mirror (detail). Bottom right: Multi-level glass mosaic mirror (detail). Photographs: Grant Evans.

GUTZWILLER STUDIOS

MICHAEL J. GUTZWILLER ■ 1201 NORTH HIGHWAY 287 ■ FT. COLLINS, CO 80524
TEL/FAX 970-407-8277 ■ WWW.GUTZWILLERSTUDIOS.COM

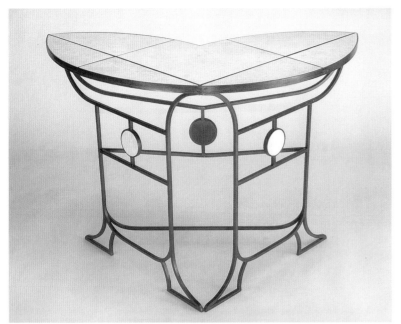

89

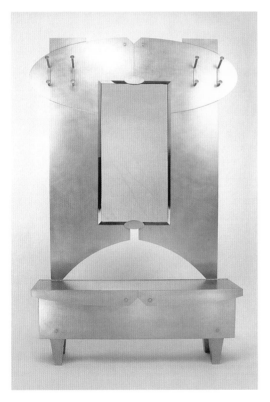

Top left: Table, 2002, steel and travertine, 24" × 35" × 18". Photograph: Jason Reiff. Top right: *Number Nine Rocker*, 2002, steel, 31" × 24" × 35". Photograph: Jason Reiff.
Bottom left: Hall tree, 2001, stainless steel and glass, 80" × 52" × 14". Photograph: Jason Reiff. Bottom right: CD cabinet, 2001, aluminum and ebonized maple, 36" × 54" × 20".

LEPOWORKS, INC.

DAVID LEPO ■ ROBERT LEPO ■ 4640 ALLENTOWN ROAD ■ LIMA, OH 45807
TEL 419-339-5370 ■ E-MAIL DLEPO@WOH.RR.COM ■ WWW.LEPOWORKS.COM

90

Untitled table, 2002, maple, cherry, cerejera, ebonized maple and acrylic, 55"L × 41"H × 20"W.
Untitled mirror, 2002, maple, cherry, cerejera and ebonized maple with convex mirror, 36" × 36" × 6"D. Inset: Untitled table (detail). Photographs: Michael J. Ayers.

91

Leather-back Windsor rocking chair, 2002, wood and leather, patent pending. Photograph: Bryant Photography.

GREG AANES FURNITURE

GREG AANES ■ 319 EAST CHAMPION STREET ■ BELLINGHAM, WA 98225 ■ TEL 360-733-9101 ■ FAX 360-733-2084
E-MAIL GAANES@MSN.COM ■ WWW.GREGAANESFURNITURE.COM

92

Left: *Brendan Rocker*, mango, 22" × 33" × 48". Top right: *Pacific Dining Chairs*, cherry, 20" × 23" × 40" and 24" × 23" × 40".
Center right: *Scooped Seat Stool*, figured maple, 17" × 14" × 17"-30". Bottom right: *Brendan Rocker and Ottoman*, figured maple, 18" × 15" × 12". Photographs: David Scherrer.

DEAN LUDWIG

DEAN LUDWIG, FURNITUREMAKER, LTD. ■ 10034 RAMM ROAD ■ MONCLOVA, OH 43542
TEL 419-877-5185 ■ E-MAIL DLUDWIG@GLASSCITY.NET ■ WWW.DEANLUDWIG.COM

93

Rocking chair (rear view), 2002, No. 1, tiger maple with walnut accents, 44"H x 44"D x 28"W. Inset: Rocking chair (front view). Photographs: Bruce Works, Photoworks.

LH POTTERY

LAURA HERMAN ■ 149 OLD BEAVER RUN ROAD ■ LAFAYETTE, NJ 07848
TEL 973-579-3273 ■ E-MAIL LAURA@LHPOTTERY.COM ■ WWW.LHPOTTERY.COM

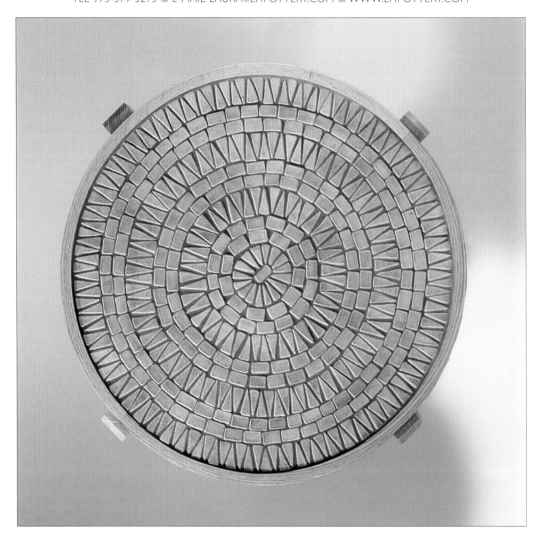

94

Top: *Parker Coffee Table*, stoneware tile, 30"Dia. x 17"H. Bottom: *Remy Coffee Table*, glazed and un-glazed tile, 24" x 48" x 15". Photographs: Digi-Chrome.

CLARKSON McGIBBON

MARK McGIBBON ■ 2316 DELAWARE AVENUE #227 ■ BUFFALO, NY 14216 ■ TEL 888-395-1117 ■ FAX 905-994-7199
E-MAIL INFO@CLARKSONMCGIBBON.COM ■ WWW.CLARKSONMCGIBBON.COM

Top: *Maryanne Table*, pommele sapele and ebonized pear wood, 48" × 27" × 16".
Bottom: *Celeste Dining Table*, English sycamore and walnut, 80" × 44" × 29". Photographs: Pete Patterson.

KURT PIPER

PIPER WOODWORKING, INC. ■ 34 FRONT STREET ■ PO BOX 51502 ■ INDIAN ORCHARD, MA 01151
TEL 413-543-8779 ■ FAX 413-543-5783 ■ E-MAIL KURT@PIPERWOODWORKING.COM ■ WWW.PIPERWOODWORKING.COM

96

Top: *Tanglewood Desk*, black and red oak, 67"W x 34"D x 30"H.
Bottom left: *Melbourne Desk*, black cherry with petrified wood blotter, 75"W x 46"D x 30"H.
Bottom right: *Taos Desk*, carved black cherry with petrified wood blotter, 67"W x 37"D x 30"H. Photographs: John Polak.

ANDY SÁNCHEZ

CUSTOM FURNITURE BY ANDY SÁNCHEZ ■ 4 ARCHIBEQUE DRIVE ■ ALGODONES, NM 87001
TEL 505-385-1189 ■ FAX 505-771-1223 ■ WWW.ANDYSANCHEZ.COM

Top: Cantilever coffee table, juniper, 48" x 26". Bottom: Juniper table with octagon marble base, 7'Dia, chairs by Drexel Heritage Furnishings. Photograph: Sandy Harvey.

YOUR ARTFUL HOME
Tips From the Artist

ARTIST: Brent J. Marshall

PROJECT: *Solomon's Garden*, triptych screen

MEDIUM: Glass, epoxy and mahogany

DIMENSIONS: 63"H x 71"W x 2"D

This decorative glass screen is pictured here in the artist's residence, providing a stunning focal point for the room, as well as a beautiful backdrop for other artworks. Also shown: *Running Rabbit* by Linda Marshall.

An art screen is an interesting entity. Two-dimensional materials such as glass or wood are secured in frames that are folded into a three-dimensional form. As such, screens can serve a variety of purposes, beyond functional room divider. When folded across a corner, an art screen can become the focal point of a room; when expanded, it can capture the light of the day and recede into the background as a warm, glowing presence.

Brent Marshall offers these tips for the care and placement of art screens:

- Glass screens vary in opacity. They can be either freestanding or built into the wall for permanent placement. Think about what you want the screen to do in your room—would you like a functional divider, a decorative piece, or both?

- Despite their dazzling appearance and high quality craftsmanship, glass art screens require no special care. Simply clean the glass with a generic glass cleaner, and polish the wood occasionally with a commercial wood cleaner.

- The wonderful thing about glass is that it captures, holds and refracts light to create its own environment. Glass screens will change appearance with the natural light of the days and seasons. At night, play around with various types of commercial lighting (such as lighting the screen from behind or using a spotlight). Different types of light will enhance the texture and the color of the screen.

AKYROS DESIGN

FRED NULL ■ ZALE GAYLEN ■ CHRIS NULL ■ 2305C ASHLAND STREET SUITE 122 ■ ASHLAND, OR 97520
TEL 800-722-6855 ■ FAX 541-488-6486 ■ E-MAIL INFO@AKYROSDESIGN.COM ■ WWW.AKYROSDESIGN.COM

99

Top: Buckingham, Virginia, slate coffee table with inlay. Bottom: *Raja*, slate coffee table with steel legs. Photographs: Dennis Remick.

WILLIAM POULSON

W. POULSON GLASS STUDIO ▧ PO BOX 705 ▧ 1318 OAK COURT ▧ ARNOLD, CA 95223
TEL/FAX 209-795-5365 ▧ WWW.SILVERHAWK.COM/EX99/POULSON

Top: *Maui No Ka oi*, sculpted koa and art glass screen, 72" × 60" × 12". Photograph: Robert Arnold.
Inset: *Fire Rose*, two-panel art glass screen with cherry frame, 68" × 40" × 12". Photograph: Mike Rothwell.

BRENT J. MARSHALL

32851 TITUS HILL LANE ■ AVON LAKE, OH 44012 ■ TEL 216-431-4408

Left: *The Harvest*, 2001, cast glass, epoxy and mahogany, 68"H × 26"W × 28"D.
Right: *Matrix*, 2002, cast glass, epoxy and mahogany, 69"H × 32"W × 28"D.

ELIZABETH MacDONALD

BOX 186 ■ BRIDGEWATER, CT 06752 ■ TEL 860-354-0594 ■ FAX 860-350-4052
E-MAIL EPMACD@EARTHLINK.NET ■ WWW.ELIZABETHMACDONALD.NET

102

Screen, 63" x 70". Photograph: Bob Rush.

LIGHTING

INNES COPPER LIGHTING

ROBERT INNES ▧ PO BOX 49 ▧ THE SEA RANCH, CA 95497 ▧ TEL 707-785-0061 ▧ FAX 707-785-1987
E-MAIL MRINNES@MCN.ORG ▧ WWW.COPPERLAMPWORKS.COM

104

Top left: Wall sconce. Right: Copper telescoping floor lamp.
Bottom left: Copper telescoping adjustable desk lamp. Photographs: Owen Kahn.

LIGHTSPANN ILLUMINATION DESIGN

CHRISTINA SPANN ■ 2855 MANDELA PARKWAY SUITE 11 ■ OAKLAND, CA 94608
TEL 510-663-9500 ■ FAX 510-663-9550 ■ CSPAN@LIGHTSPANN.COM ■ WWW.LIGHTSPANN.COM

105

Top: Custom chandelier, blown glass and forged iron, 52"H × 48"Dia. Photograph: Paul Hammond. Bottom left: Custom sconce, blown glass and hand-tooled metal, 17"H × 8"W.
Photograph: Paul Hammond. Bottom center: Custom dining pendant, blown, fused and slumped glass, 30"Dia. × 42".
Bottom right: *Amphora Sconce*, blown and painted glass with hand-tooled metal, 16"H × 8"Dia. × 30". Photograph: Paul Hammond.

MARK ROSENBAUM

ROSETREE GLASS STUDIO ▨ 446 VALLETTE STREET ▨ NEW ORLEANS, LA 70114 ▨ TEL/FAX 504-366-3602
E-MAIL INFO@ROSETREEGLASS.COM ▨ WWW.ROSETREEGLASS.COM

106

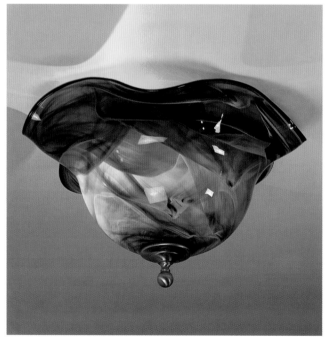

Top left: Ceiling fixture group, 2003, blown glass, amber: 18" × 18" × 12"H; blue-green: 20" × 20" × 10"H; yellow-red: 20" × 20" × 11.5"H.
Top right: *Landscape Sconce,* 2002, blown glass, 14" × 5" × 7.5"H. Bottom left: Amber ceiling fixture, 2003, blown glass, 18" × 18" × 12"H.
Bottom right: Pendant lamp group, 2003, blown glass, cylinder: 7.5" × 4" × 4"; cone: 8" × 4.5" × 4.5"; saucer: 6" × 6" × 6". Photographs: Vicki Stanwyck.

RICK SHERBERT

RICK SHERBERT GLASSWORKS ■ 7300 MACARTHUR BOULEVARD ■ GLEN ECHO, MD 20812
TEL 301-229-4184 ■ E-MAIL RICK@RICKSHERBERTGLASS.COM ■ WWW.RICKSHERBERTGLASS.COM

107

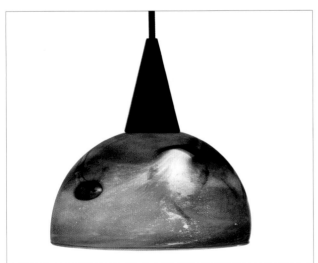

Top: Bar lamps, West residence. Photograph: Lydia Cutter.
Bottom left: *Blue Hemisphere Pendant*, blown glass, 11"Dia. Bottom right: *Gold Vortex Globe Pendant*, blown glass, 9"Dia.

LOTTON ART GLASS

CHARLES LOTTON ■ 24760 COUNTRY LANE ■ CRETE, IL 60417 ■ TEL 708-672-1400/800-661-0950 ■ FAX 708-672-1401
E-MAIL CHARLES.LOTTON@WORLDNET.ATT.NET ■ WWW.LOTTONGLASS.COM

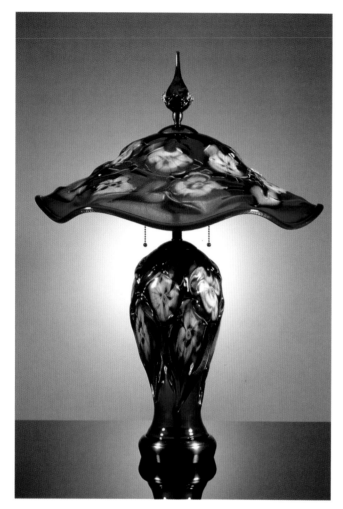

108

Left: *Royal Blue Caged Multi Flora Lamp*, 2003, blown glass.
Right: *Frosted Caged Multi Flora Lamp*, 2003, blown glass; shown with *Frosted Caged Multi Flora Bowl*, 2003, blown glass.

DANIEL LOTTON STUDIOS

DANIEL LOTTON ▩ 24760 COUNTRY LANE ▩ CRETE, IL 60417 ▩ TEL 708-672-1400 ▩ FAX 708-672-1401
CHARLES.LOTTON@WORLDNET.ATT.NET ▩ WWW.LOTTONGLASS.COM

109

Top: *Soft Cranberry Chandelier with Pink Flowers*, 2003, blown glass, sizes vary. Photograph: Steve Ricks. Bottom: *Verre de Soie Chandelier with Pink Flowers*, 2003, blown glass.

YOUR ARTFUL HOME
Tips From the Artist

ARTIST: Daniel Lotton

PROJECT: *Verre de Soie Chandelier*

MEDIUM: Glass and bronze

DIMENSIONS: 32"H x 28"W (without chain)

This chandelier was created for a couple who wanted a piece of original lighting for the dining room in their new home. Also shown are a matching table lamp and vase, both by Daniel Lotton.

Lighting adds that extra touch of warmth and life to a home. Beyond selecting the style and look of your lighting, you should also consider the amount and type of light that will be cast. More than any other element, lighting creates the mood of a room, from cheerful and bright to serene and warm. When not lit, a handcrafted chandelier or lamp is a piece of artwork in its own right. Daniel Lotton's lighting fixtures and lamps are practical and sturdy; once installed, they are virtually maintenance free.

Lotton gives these suggestions for homeowners who are considering commissioned lighting fixtures for their home:

- Lighting can be created in a variety of styles, personalized to your own taste. If you're commissioning a chandelier, consider asking the artist to make a matching wall sconce or table lamp to pull the lighting elements together as an artistic and personalized presence.

- Clean the light when it is at room temperature, not when it's hot. Use a mixture of vinegar and water— or just a basic glass cleaner—to clean and brighten glass surfaces.

- Handcrafted lighting can last a lifetime, so you want to make appropriate choices for your home. Ask the artist to visit your home in person, if possible. He or she may have suggestions for lighting that you had never even considered!

LANSE STOVER

20 BRACKENBURY LANE ■ BEVERLY, MA 01915
TEL 978-922-1391 ■ E-MAIL LIGHT@JILLO.COM ■ WWW.JILLO.COM

111

Top left: *Blue Triple Sconce,* 2003, clay, slip glaze, china paint, mica gilding, ceramic canopy and electrical parts, 13.5" x 10.5" x 4".
Right: Sconce installation *(Salmon Fluted Sconce),* 2003, clay, slip glaze, china paint, mica gilding, ceramic canopy and electrical parts, 12" x 11" x 6.5".
Bottom left: *Orange-Eared Sconce,* 2003, clay, slip glaze, china paint, mica gilding, ceramic canopy and electrical parts, 11.5" x 10.5" x 5.5".

FRANK CAVAZ

BACCHUS GLASS, INC. ■ 21707 EIGHTH STREET EAST #6 ■ SONOMA, CA 95476
TEL 707-939-9416 ■ FAX 707-939-9708 ■ E-MAIL BACCHUSGLASS@EXCITE.COM

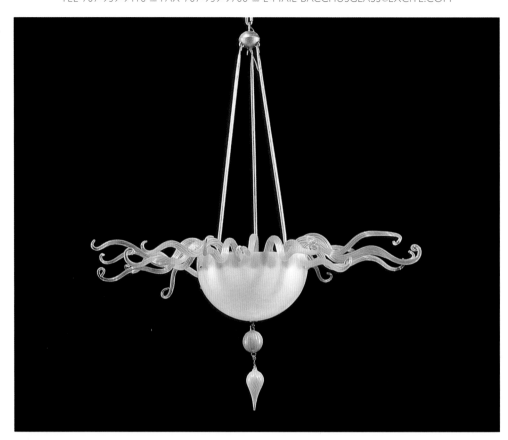

112

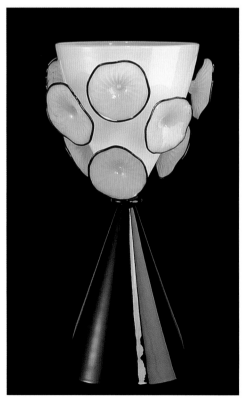

Top: *Turquoise Soleil Chandelier*, 2002, blown glass, steel and gold leaf, 44" × 44" × 60". Bottom left: *Botanical Double Stack*, 2002, blown glass, 24" × 12" × 12".
Bottom right: *Botanical Vase*, 2002, blown glass, 34" × 24" × 24". Photographs: Hap Sakwa.

JOEL D. BLOOMBERG

JOEL BLOOMBERG DESIGNS ■ 600 NORTH COAST HIGHWAY 101 ■ ENCINITAS, CA 92024
TEL 760-942-0298 ■ FAX 760-944-2960 ■ E-MAIL JDBLOOMBERG@HOTMAIL.COM

Top left: *Jellyfish* (white), double dome, iridized, 21" x 14" x 14". Top right: *Jellyfish* (salmon red), double dome, 21" x 14" x 14".
Bottom left: *Jellyfish* (green with light blue), single dome, 20" x 13" x 13". Bottom right: *Jellyfish* (violet), single dome, 20" x 13" x 13".

113

WOODSILKS STUDIO

BARBARA WOODS ■ TOM THOMAS ■ 401A HAMPTON ROAD ■ SANTA FE, NM 87505
TEL 505-466-0834 ■ FAX 505-466-0827 ■ E-MAIL BWOODS@WOODSILKS.COM ■ WWW.WOODSILKS.COM

114

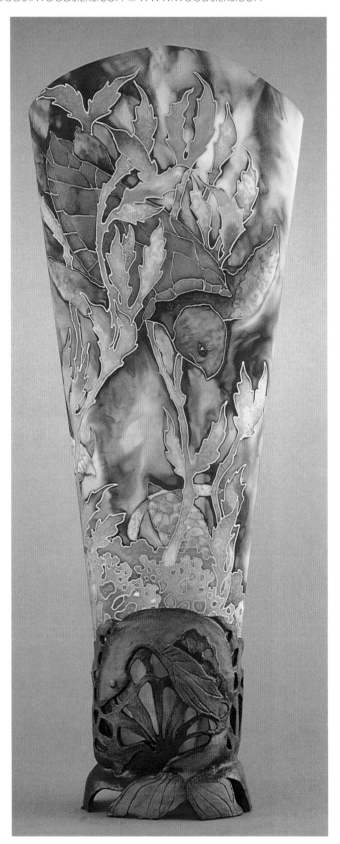

Top left: *Gold Sphinx*, hand-painted silk and carved ceramic, 31" × 28"H.
Right: *Crystal Tower*, segmented hardwood lamp with painted silk shade, 20" × 30"H. Bottom left: *Turtle Garden*, hand-painted silk and carved ceramic, 18" × 10" × 45"H.

HOME ACCESSORIES

BELLOZAR STUDIO

SHARON ZARAMBO ■ 875 EMMETT ROAD ■ ETLAN, VA 22719
TEL/FAX 540-923-5077 ■ E-MAIL BELLOZAR@JUNO.COM

116

Top: *Fantasy Kritters*, hand-painted pillow, 17.5" × 34.5" × 3". Bottom left: *Sunfish*, hand-painted pillow, 17.5" × 17.5" × 3".
Bottom right: *Moon Dog*, hand-painted pillow, 12" × 12" × 3". Photographs: Larry Sanders.

SLAMMING SCREEN DOOR FUNCTIONAL ART CO

BRYAN PUDDER ■ 17120 WESTVIEW TRAIL ■ AUSTIN, TX 78737 ■ TEL/FAX 512-858-5430
E-MAIL SLAMMINGSCREENDOOR@AUSTIN.RR.COM ■ WWW.SLAMMINGSCREENDOOR.COM

Top left: *Looks Like Showers*, acrylic on vinyl, 72" x 72". Top right: *The Shower Scene*, acrylic on vinyl, 72" x 72".
Bottom left: *Eyedrops*, acrylic on vinyl, 72" x 72". Bottom right: *Nude in Shower*, acrylic on vinyl, 72" x 72". Photographs: Scott Metcalfe, Dallas, TX.

MICHAEL GRANT SOLOMON

REFLECTIVE ART ▨ 2 MILTON ST ▨ MAPLEWOOD, NJ 07040 ▨ TEL 973-762-6334 ▨ FAX 973-762-6554
E-MAIL MOSAICS@REFLECTIVEART.COM ▨ WWW.REFLECTIVEART.COM

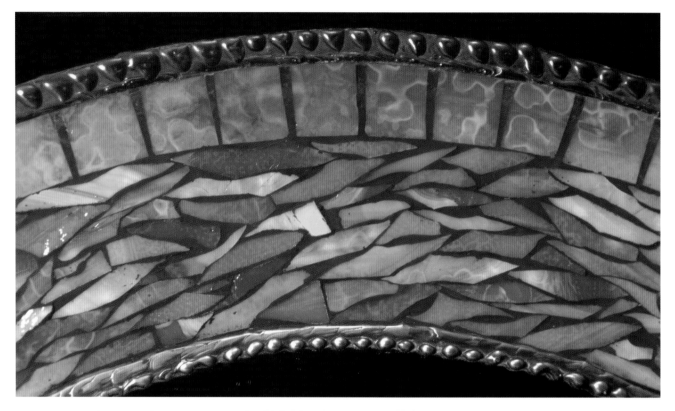

118

Top: *Orange Grove Mosaic Border* (detail), sliver art glass mosaic with decorative soldered border and bronze finish. Bottom left: *Sundial Mosaic Mirror*, private residence, Boca Raton, FL, art glass with decorative soldered border and bronze finish, 48"Dia. Bottom right: *Burgundy Dragon Fly Mosaic Mirror*, private residence, Cleveland, OH, art glass with hammered decorative soldered border and pewter finish, 30" x 40". Photographs: William Tomlin, Maplewood, NJ.

NANCY BENEDICT

5405 OLD ALEXANDRIA TURNPIKE ▨ WARRENTON, VA 20187 ▨ TEL 540-341-0047 ▨ FAX 540-341-0987
E-MAIL NANCY@NANCYBENEDICTDESIGNS.COM ▨ WWW.NANCYBENEDICTDESIGNS.COM

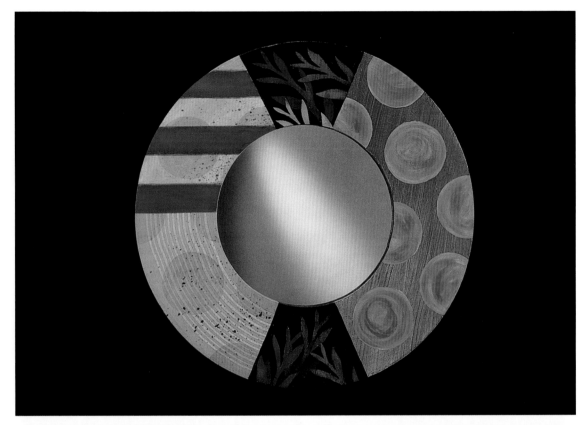

119

Top: *Primary*, 2002, acrylic on wood with mirror glass, 22"Dia. Bottom: *Texture Grid*, 2003, mixed media on wood with mirror glass, 22"Dia. Photographs: Jerry Anthony.

LINDA GAIL RUDELL

RIBBONESQUE INC. ■ 50 LIDO BOULEVARD ■ POINT LOOKOUT, NY 11569-0404
TEL/FAX 516-432-8936 ■ E-MAIL LINDA@RIBBONESQUE.COM ■ WWW.RIBBONESQUE.COM

Top: Pillows, left: *Multi-Ribbon Weaving* on dupioni silk pillow, 20" × 20", right: *Sunburst Weaving* on dupioni silk pillow, 16" × 16".
Bottom left: *For Socks Only™ Ottoman*, black suede cloth with hand-dyed silk, satin weaving and suede.
Bottom right: *For Socks Only™ Ottoman*, hand-painted curved legs, velvet and hand-dyed silk ribbon. Photographs: Jim Strong.

FLOOR COVERINGS

CLAUDIA MILLS

5 BREWER STREET ■ JAMAICA PLAIN, MA 02130 ■ TEL 617-524-5326 ■ FAX 617-524-7164
E-MAIL CMILLS325@AOL.COM ■ WWW.CLAUDIAMILLS.COM

122

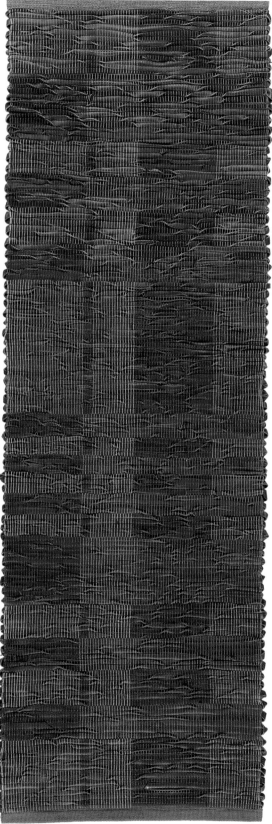

Top left: Runner, double block pattern, 100% cotton yarn and fabric, 4' × 12'. Photograph: Jim Thomas. Right: Runner, log cabin pattern, 100% cotton yarn and leather, 2' × 6'. Photograph: Susan Byrne. Bottom left: Runner, log-cabin style stairway runner and area rug, 100% cotton yarn and fabric. Photograph: Fred Lee.

LYNN BASA

2248 NORTH CAMPBELL AVENUE ▦ CHICAGO, IL 60647 ▦ TEL 773-289-3616 ▦ FAX 773-289-3825
E-MAIL LYNNBASA@LYNNBASA.COM ▦ WWW.LYNNBASA.COM

123

Top: *Portal*, 2000, Seattle University School of Law, WA, silk and wool, 7' × 12'. Bottom: *Formation*, 2001, private residence, silk and wool, 8' × 10'. Photographs: Russell Johnson.

YOUR ARTFUL HOME
Tips From the Artist

ARTIST: Barbara Barran

PROJECT: *Bars and String-Pieced Columns*, rug

MEDIUM: Hand-tufted New Zealand wool

DIMENSIONS: 76" x 95"

This rug was commissioned for a Manhattan residence and is based on a quilt from the *Gee's Bend* quilt collection, a series of over 600 quilts created by African-American women living in Gee's Bend, AL. Artist Barbara Barran has the exclusive rights to make these quilts into rugs. Also shown: *In Favor of Admissions*, wall hanging by Arman. Interior design by Barbara T. Avellino. Photograph by Michel Friang.

When designing a room, homeowners often leave floor coverings for last, according to artist Barbara Barran. Books of upholstery fabrics are pored over, swatches for curtains are carefully considered. What covers the floor is often an after-thought in planning, and this can be dangerous. Rugs are too large and too expensive to be considered an accessory. A custom floor covering means you don't have to settle for something you find at the last minute. For what you might pay for a commercial rug that may or may not match your couch, you can create a custom floor covering to unify your entire room.

The following tips from artist Barbara Barran will ensure a happy floor covering commission:

- Just because your floor covering is a work of art does not mean that it's not functional. In fact, the craftsmanship of a handmade piece should last a lifetime, so feel free to walk on your artwork!

- For wool rugs, you can spot clean new stains with a commercial carpet cleaner such as Resolve®. For ground-in stains, use a powder version of this commercial cleaner. Take your rug to be cleaned professionally, as needed. To reduce the harmful, fading effects from the sun, you may want to consider a protective coating on your windows.

- Floor coverings can also make wonderful wall décor, especially if you have a large space or high ceilings.

JOAN WEISSMAN

3710 SILVER SE ▓ ALBUQUERQUE, NM 87108 ▓ TEL 505-265-0144 ▓ FAX 505-268-9665
E-MAIL WEISSMANJ@ATT.NET ▓ WWW.JOANWEISSMAN.COM

125

Left: *Plum Blossom*, © 2002, hand-tufted wool rug. Top right: *Parasol* (detail), © 2002, hand-knotted Tibetan wool & silk rug.
Bottom right: *Pen and Ink* (detail), © 2002, hand-knotted Tibetan wool rug.

LAKESIDE FIBERS

SUSAN VANDEWALLE ▨ 402 WEST LAKESIDE STREET ▨ MADISON, WI 53715 ▨ TEL 608-257-2999 ▨ FAX 608-257-2996
E-MAIL INFO@LAKESIDEFIBERS.COM ▨ WWW.LAKESIDEFIBERS.COM

126

Fiber rug weaving, 45" x 96". Inset: Contemporary rug weaving, 45" x 96".

OBJECTS

GAIL McCARTHY STUDIO

GAIL McCARTHY ■ 231 NORWOOD AVENUE ■ BUFFALO, NY 14222 ■ TEL 716-884-2195
E-MAIL CERAMICS@GAILMCCARTHY.COM ■ WWW.GAILMCCARTHY.COM

128

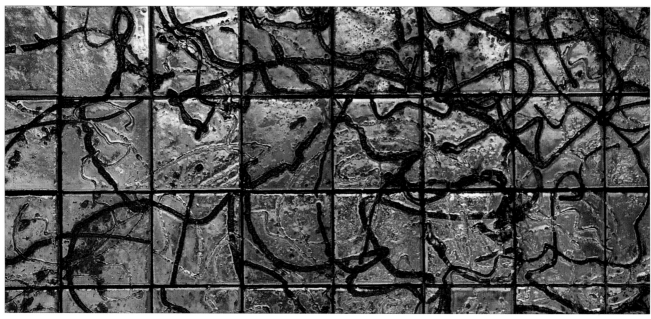

Top left: *Lustered Vessel #106,* 2002, wheel-thrown and altered ceramic lusterware, 16" x 9" x 7". Top right: *Lustered Vessel #116,* 2003, wheel-thrown and altered ceramic lusterware, 14" x 8" x 7". Bottom: *Luster Painting* (detail), luster, slips and engobes on ceramic tile. Photographs: Photographics Two.

BEATRICE WOOD

BEATRICE WOOD STUDIO ▨ 8560 OJAI-SANTA PAULA ROAD ▨ OJAI, CA 93023 ▨ TEL 805-646-3381 ▨ FAX 805-646-0560
E-MAIL INFO@BEATRICEWOOD.COM ▨ WWW.BEATRICEWOOD.COM

Top: Luster chalices, c. 1980s, earthenware, 5.5"H. Bottom: Gold luster tea service, c. 1980s, earthenware, varying sizes. Photographs: Tony Cunha.

BOB POOL

BOB POOL POTTERY ■ 2547 EIGHTH STREET #33 ■ BERKELEY, CA 94710 ■ TEL/FAX 510-841-8135
E-MAIL BPOOLPOTTERY@COMCAST.NET ■ WWW.BOBPOOLPOTTERY.COM

Top: *Full-Bloom Platter,* 2003, stoneware, 22"Dia. x 3"H. Bottom: Platter, 2003, stoneware, 17"Dia. x 2"H. Photographs: George Post.

BRENDA McMAHON

BLUE MOON CLAY STUDIO ■ 2242 COUNTY ROUTE 113 ■ GREENWICH, NY 12834
TEL/FAX 518-692-7742 ■ E-MAIL BMCMAHONSTUDIO@AOL.COM ■ WWW.BLUEMOONCLAY.COM

Top: Saggar-fired porcelain, 2002, 6" × 6" and 14" × 14". Bottom: Saggar-fired porcelain vessel, 2003, 9" × 11". Photographs: Tommy Olof Elder.

SUN & EARTH POTTERY STUDIO

JODI BESSINGER ■ 4636 NORTH RAVENSWOOD ■ CHICAGO, IL 60640 ■ TEL 773-383-7213 ■ FAX 773-973-5093
E-MAIL SUNANDEARTHPOTTERY@HOTMAIL.COM ■ WWW.SUNANDEARTHPOTTERY.COM

132

Top: Tea bowls, 2003, high-fired stoneware, 5" x 4.5". Bottom: Dinnerware plates, 2003, high-fired stoneware, 10.5"Dia. Photographs: Scott Price.

133

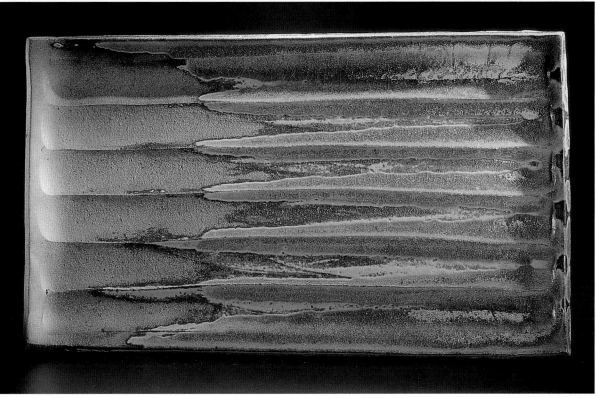

Top: Incense burner, stoneware with feldspar chips, 6" x 9". Bottom: Platter, carved stoneware with ash glaze, 15" x 9". Photographs: Vito Aluia.

LAURA ZINDEL

LAURA ZINDEL CERAMICS ■ 390 CRESCENT AVENUE ■ SAN FRANCISCO, CA 94110
TEL 415-821-2063 ■ E-MAIL ZINDEL@PRODIGY.NET ■ WWW.ZINDELCERAMICS.COM

134

Top: *Snake Platter*, 2003, earthenware, 20" x 17".
Bottom left: *Beetle Platter*, 2002, earthenware, 15" x 11". Bottom right: *Bug Vases*, 2002, earthenware, 8"-11"H. Photographs: Hap Sakwa.

VAJRA GLASSWORKS

WILLIAM L. HENRY ▨ 2155 LAUREL RANCH ROAD ▨ BOZEMAN, MT 59715
TEL 406-994-0902 ▨ E-MAIL WHENREE@AOL.COM

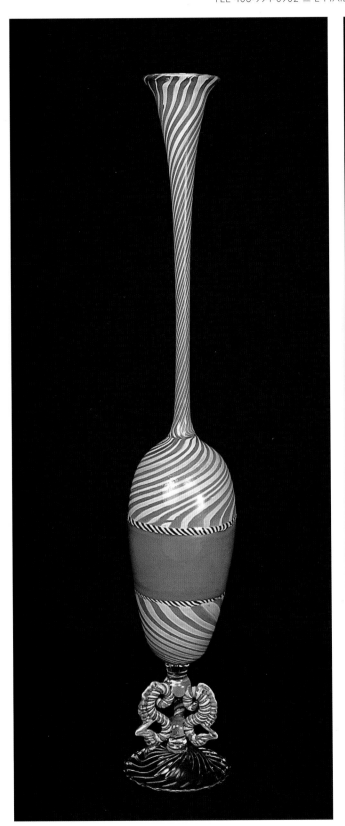 

Left: Incalmo vase, Venetian cane work, 28"H. Photograph: Rikshots Photography.
Right: *Barkeria Spectablilis Exotica*, from the *Orchid 3* series, Venetian-style mantel, goblet and glass chains, 23.75"H.

GARTNER/BLADE

DANIELLE BLADE ▧ STEPHEN GARTNER ▧ PO BOX 185 ▧ 940 ASHLEY FALLS ROAD ▧ ASHLEY FALLS, MA 01222
TEL/FAX 413-229-0058 ▧ E-MAIL BLADE@VGERNET.NET ▧ WWW.GARTNERBLADE.COM

Strata Series: Tangerine Group. Photograph: Jonathan Wallen.

DALE HEFFERNAN

DALE HEFFERNAN GLASS DESIGNS ■ 250 MERRYDALE ROAD #2 ■ SAN RAFAEL, CA 94903
TEL/FAX 415-507-9151 ■ E-MAIL PUNTYBOY@JUNO.COM ■ WWW.DALEHEFFERNAN.COM

137

Top: Coffee table and *Pineapple Pin Vases*, table: 48" × 29" × 18"; vases 20"-22".
Bottom left: *Pineapple Bowls*, blown glass, 15" × 15" × 9". Bottom right: Bowls and vases group, blown glass. Photographs: Hap Sakwa.

KATHLEEN ASH

STUDIO K ■ 2311 K THORNTON ■ AUSTIN, TX 78704 ■ TEL 512-443-1611 ■ FAX 512-851-0662
E-MAIL STUDIOK@ATT.NET ■ WWW.STUDIOKGLASS.COM

138

Top: *U R Here*, collection of fused glass vessels, 14"-24"Dia. Photograph: John Toole.
Bottom: Functional fused glass pieces in the *Breakfast, Lunch and Dinner* palettes.

MARY ELLEN BUXTON AND KEVIN KUTCH

PIER GLASS ▧ 499 VAN BRUNT STREET UNIT #2A ▧ BROOKLYN, NY 11231 ▧ TEL/FAX 718-237-2073

Top left: *Silver Lining Atmosphere,* 2002, blown and faceted glass, 12" × 5" × 5". Top right: *Double Bubble* with stopper, 2003, blown and faceted glass, 13" × 5" × 3.5".
Bottom: *Woven Windows,* 2001, kiln-formed glass, sand carved, woven copper wire and screen inclusion, 12"Dia. Photographs: George Erml.

JUDITH SHAPIRO

ZERO GRAVITY GLASS ■ PO BOX 3394 ■ ALEXANDRIA, VA 22302
TEL/FAX 703-998-9626 ■ E-MAIL MAIL@ZGGLASS.COM ■ WWW.ZGGLASS.COM

140

Top left: *Minuet*, kiln-formed glass, slumped and etched, 12" x 18" x 22". Top right: *Blaze of Noon*, kiln-formed glass, slumped and etched, 12" x 18" x 22".
Bottom: *Carousel*, kiln-formed glass, slumped and etched, 19"Dia., includes metal Artfixtures stand for upright display. Photographs: Tommy Olaf Elder.

GALAZZO GLASS

BARBARA GALAZZO ▨ 16 FISHKILL AVENUE ▨ COLD SPRING, NY 10516
TEL 914-924-0909 ▨ FAX 845-265-7690 ▨ E-MAIL INFO@GALAZZOGLASS.COM ▨ WWW.GALAZZOGLASS.COM

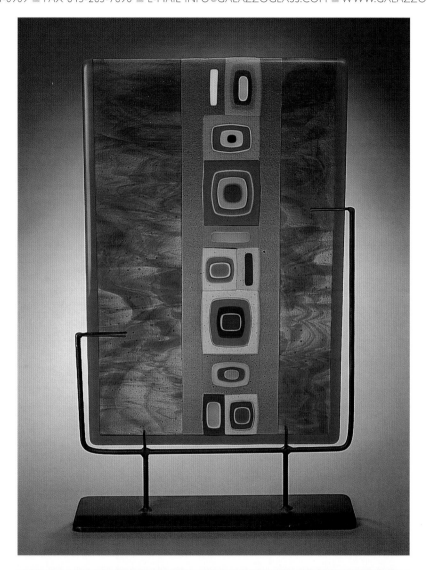

141

Top: *Ribbon Sculpture*, from the *Collage* series, 2003, fused glass, 22"H x 14"W x 4"D, limited edition.
Bottom: *Boat*, from the *Collage* series, 2002, fused, sawed, kiln carved and slumped glass, 24"L x 16"W, one of a kind. Photographs: Allen Bryan.

MARK J. SUDDUTH

3879 MAYFIELD ROAD ■ CLEVELAND HEIGHTS, OH 44121 ■ TEL 216-382-0462 ■ FAX 216-381-5987
E-MAIL MSUDDUTH@EN.COM ■ WWW.SUDDUTHGLASS.COM

142

Top left: Canted form, 2002, blown glass with diamond and stone wheel engravings, 14" × 10".
Top right: Canted form, 2002, blown glass with diamond and stone wheel engravings, 12" × 10".
Bottom: *Line Series*, 2002, blown glass with layered linear drawings, 6" × 13", 17" × 6" and 10" × 8". Photographs: Bill Lemke.

JEFF BURNETTE

JOE BLOW GLASSWORKS ▩ 1191 PARKER STREET ▩ VANCOUVER, BC ▩ CANADA
TEL/FAX 604-215-2569 ▩ E-MAIL JEFF@JOEBLOWGLASSWORKS.COM ▩ WWW.JOEBLOWGLASSWORKS.COM

143

Top: *Ray Gunz.* Bottom: *Ray Gunz.* Photographs: Steve Pinter.

GLOCKE'S GLASS

JULIE AND MARK GLOCKE ■ PO BOX 347 ■ TURTLE LAKE, WI 54889 ■ TEL 715-986-4030 ■ FAX 715-986-4031
E-MAIL CASHLESS@CHIBARDUN.NET ■ WWW.GLOCKESGLASS.COM

144

Left: *Cube Sculpture #3*, 2003, cold fusion glass, 3.5" × 3.5" × 14"H. Photograph: Jerry Anthony. Top right: *Vase #3*, 2003, cold fusion glass, 7.5" × 7.5" × 13.25"H.
Center right: *Vase #7*, 2003, cold fusion glass, 12" × 12" × 15"H. Bottom right: *Vase #10*, 2002, cold fusion glass, 14" × 14" × 30"H.

NANCY NICHOLSON

STAINED GLASS DESIGN AND FABRICATION ■ 232 THIRD STREET SUITE A208 ■ BROOKLYN, NY 11215
TEL 917-696-7882 ■ E-MAIL NANCY@NODISC.COM ■ WWW.NANCY-NICHOLSON.COM

145

Top left: *17th and Broadway*, 2002, free-hanging stained glass panel, 19" × 15".
Right: *South Street (Boston)*, 1996, free-hanging stained glass panel, 25.5" × 55.5". Bottom left: *A Corner in Manhattan*, 2003, free-hanging stained glass panel, 13" × 18".

PETER SECREST

6497 POWELL HILL ROAD ■ NAPLES, NY 14512
TEL/FAX 585-374-5270 ■ WWW.PETERSECREST.COM

146

Top left: Blown murrini/incalmo vase, 2003, 10"Dia. × 8.75"H. Right: Blown murrini/incalmo vases, 2003, 8.75"-17"H.
Center left: Blown murrini/incalmo vase, 2003, 8.5"Dia. × 10"H. Bottom left: Blown murrini/incalmo vase, 2003, 12.5"Dia. × 8.75"H. Photographs: Walter Colley.

CARRIE GUSTAFSON

147 SHERMAN STREET ■ CAMBRIDGE, MA 02140 ■ TEL 781-367-4024
E-MAIL CARRIEJGUSTAFSON@HOTMAIL.COM

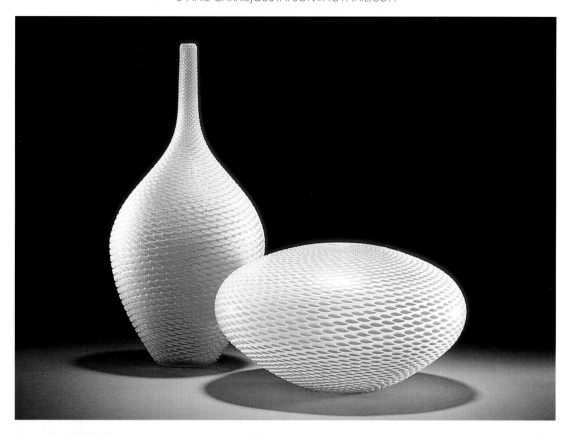

Top: *Sisal*, 2002, 13" × 7.5"; and *Onion Skin*, 2002, 5" × 13". Bottom: *Woven Bamboo*, 2002, sandblasted blown glass, 8" × 10". Photographs: Bill Truslow.

REBECCA HUNGERFORD

THE PEWTER SHOP ■ 3643 CHARLOTTE STREET ■ KANSAS CITY, MO 64109 ■ TEL 816-753-5255 / 877-873-9837
FAX 816-531-2551 ■ E-MAIL PEWTERSHOP@KC.RR.COM ■ WWW.PEWTERSHOP.COM

148

Top: Tea set , pewter and aventurine, teapot: 9.75"W x 4" x 7"H. Photograph: Hartzell Gray.
Bottom left: Vase, pewter, coral, sterling wire, acid-etched leaves, colored pencil and acrylic coat, 12"H x 4"W. Photograph: Kenny Johnson.
Bottom right: Salad set, pewter, 17"H x 4.25"W. Photograph: Hartzell Gray.

ROBERT L. CRECELIUS

ST. FRANCOIS FORGE ■ 5226 HIGHWAY DD ■ FARMINGTON, MO 63640
TEL 573-760-9695 ■ FAX 573-760-9150 ■ E-MAIL RCRECELIUS@SOCKET.NET

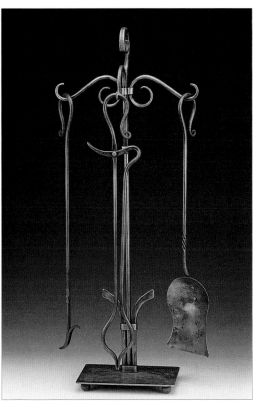

Top left: *Tornado Table* with vessel, forged and fabricated steel, 42"H × 16"Dia. Top right: *Ritual Vessel,* forged and fabricated steel, 20"W × 18"H × 6"D.
Bottom left: Fire set, forged steel, 42"H on 8" × 12" base. Bottom right: Accent table with steel bowl, forged steel, 28"Dia. × 25"H. Photographs: Jerry Anthony.

ROBERT E. ALLEN

ALLEN STUDIOS ■ 328 EAST ORANGE STREET ■ LANCASTER, PA 17602
TEL/FAX 717-394-5857 ■ E-MAIL ALLENSTUDIOS@AOL.COM ■ WWW.ALLEN-STUDIOS.COM

150

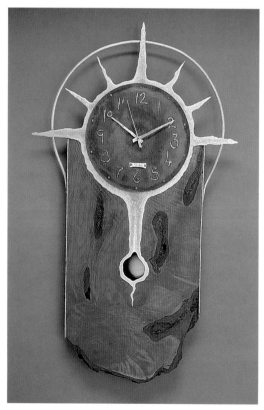

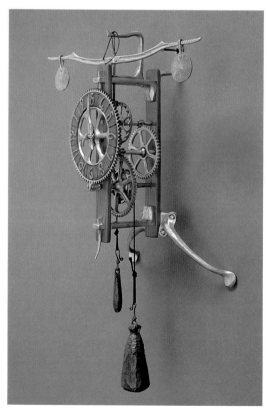

Top left: *Floor Foliot Clock*, cast, fabricated and machined aluminum with cherry wood, 5.5'H x 20"W x 10"D. Top right: *Floor Foliot Clock* (detail).
Bottom left: *Daybreak Wall Clock*, welded steel face with aluminum, brass and cherry wood, 48"H x 24"W x 4"D.
Bottom right: *Wall Crawler Clock*, available in aluminum, brass or bronze, 12"H x 10"W x 6"D. Photographs: Lin Wagner.

CAROL GREEN

CAROL GREEN STUDIO ■ ELBURN, IL ■ TEL 630-365-1238 ■ FAX 630-365-1337
E-MAIL CAROL@CAROLGREEN.COM ■ WWW.CAROLGREEN.COM

151

Top left: Vertical candleholder, cast bronze and bronze with patina, 9"H × 14"W × 7"D. Top right: Horizontal candleholder, cast bronze and bronze, 2.5"H × 17"W × 8"L.
Bottom: Epergne, 2003, cast bronze and bronze with patina, 22"H × 21"W × 17"D. Photographs: Jim Reem.

ETCETERA, COUTURE FOR THE HOME BY SOLOMONIC, INC.

LARISA BELENITSKY ■ 166 PEMBROKE STREET ■ BROOKLYN, NY 11235
TEL 646-644-5399 ■ E-MAIL INFO@SOLOMONIC.US ■ WWW.SOLOMONIC.US

152

Top left: *Caesar*, Norwegian moss on ceramic vase. Top right: *Tree of Wisdom*, Norwegian moss on wooden box.
Bottom left: *Family*, Norwegian moss. Bottom right: *Nature in the Sky*, Norwegian moss, wood branches and ceramic. Photographs: Rais Muharamov.

STACIE ANTHONY

STACIE ANTHONY STUDIOS ■ 19836 EAST MILL ROAD ■ PO BOX 353 ■ GALESVILLE, WI 54630
TEL 608-769-5032 ■ FAX 608-582-4347 ■ E-MAIL SASTUDIO@AOL.COM

153

Left: *Branching Out*, 2002, copper wire and soapstone, 17"H. Right: *Connections*, 2002, silver and brass wires with petrified wood, 13"H.

STEVE SINNER

ROUND WOODS BY STEVE SINNER ■ 5150 CRESTVIEW HEIGHTS COURT ■ BETTENDORF, IA 52722
TEL/FAX 563-332-5611 ■ E-MAIL SSINNER@QCONLINE.COM

154

Ant Farm II, 2002, maple with silver and gold leaf, patina, acrylic and pen and ink, 16.5"H x 7.75"W x 7.75"D. Photograph: Bob Barrett.
Inset: *Ant Farm II* (detail). Photograph: Steve Sullivan.

DAVID WOODRUFF

WOODRUFF WOODS ■ 192 SONATA DRIVE ■ LEWISVILLE, NC 27023 ■ TEL/FAX 336-945-3896
E-MAIL PDWOODS@TRIAD.RR.COM ■ WWW.PDWOODS.COM

Top: Hollow form bowl, white oak burl and ebony, 7"H x 18"W. Bottom: Hollow form bowl, black ash burl and ebony, 12"H x 10"W.

BOB HAWKS

BOB HAWKS TURNED WOOD ▪ 5120 EAST 35 STREET ▪ TULSA, OK 74135
TEL 918-743-4901 ▪ E-MAIL BOBHAWKS@SBCGLOBAL.NET

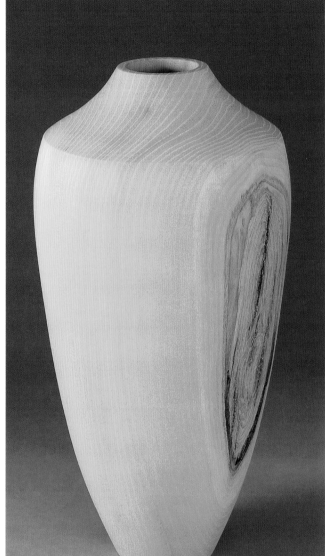

156

Top left: *Longitudinal VII*, 2002, red heart, yellowwood and ebony, 7"H × 10"Dia.
Right: Untitled, 2003, bois d'arc, 15"H × 7"Dia. Bottom left: Untitled, 2003, buckeye burl, 7"H × 10"Dia.

BINH PHO

WONDERS OF WOOD ■ 48W175 PINE TREE DRIVE ■ MAPLE PARK, IL 60151
TEL 630-365-5462 ■ FAX 630-365-5837 ■ E-MAIL TORIALE@MSN.COM ■ WWW.WONDERSOFWOOD.NET

157

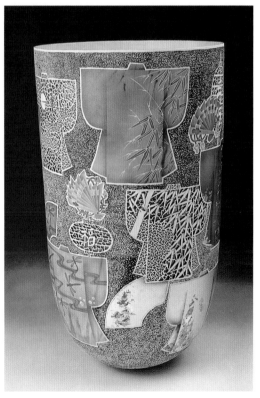

Left: *Otomine and Urashima*, 2002, willow burl, carob and maple, 42"H × 21"W × 4"D. Top right: *Otomine and Urashima* (detail).
Bottom right: *Festival II*, 2002, box elder, acrylic, dye and 22K gold leaf, 18"H × 9"Dia.

STEPHEN ZEH

STEPHEN ZEH, BASKETMAKER ■ PO BOX 381 ■ TEMPLE, MAINE 04984
TEL 207-778-2351 ■ E-MAIL ZEHBASKT@SOMTEL.COM

158

Top: Nesting set of three swing-handle baskets, brown ash, 6", 4.5" and 3"Dia.
Bottom left: *Quadrifoil*, brown ash, 12"Dia. Bottom right: Covered swing-handle basket, brown ash, 10"Dia.

WINDOWS, DOORS & RAILINGS

STEVE LOPES

STEVE LOPES, BLACKSMITH INC. ■ 181 CRAIG ROAD ■ SEQUIM, WA 98382 ■ TEL 360-385-5448 ■ FAX 360-385-4602
E-MAIL SLOPES1@OLYPEN.COM ■ WWW.STEVELOPESBLACKSMITH.COM

160

Stair railing and light fixture, 1999, railing: steel and cherry, 28'L; light fixture: steel, copper and mica, 3'Dia.
Photograph: Roger Turk/NLP Inc.

LARRY ZGODA

LARRY ZGODA STUDIO ■ 2117 WEST IRVING PARK ROAD ■ CHICAGO, IL 60618 ■ TEL 773-463-3970
E-MAIL LZ@LARRYZGODASTUDIO.COM ■ WWW.LARRYZGODASTUDIO.COM

161

Untitled, 2003, private residence, Evanston, IL, fixed sash. Photograph: Susan Andrews.

KAREN ELISE SEPANSKI

CUSTOM ARCHITECTURAL GLASS ■ 2827 JOHN R ■ DETROIT, MI 48201
TEL 313-832-4941 ■ E-MAIL KELISE313@AOL.COM

162

Entry door, sidelights and transom, 2001, private residence, Franklin, MI, glass and mahogany with marine finish, 96"H × 68"W × 3"D. Photograph: Donna Terek.

RICHARD M. PARRISH

FUSIO, FUSED ART GLASS ■ 627 EAST PEACH STREET ■ BOZEMAN, MT 59715
TEL 406-522-9892 ■ FAX 406-556-5802 N E-MAIL RPARRISH@FUSIOSTUDIO.COM ■ WWW.FUSIOSTUDIO.COM

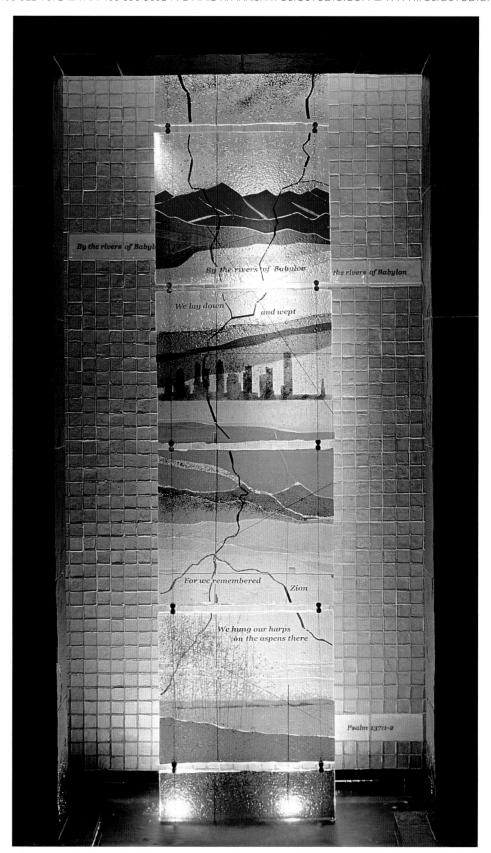

163

By the Rivers of Babylon, 2002, private residence installation, glass panels with water element in wall niche, 24" x 108". Photograph: Karl Neumann.

ERNEST PORCELLI/ART GLASS

ERNEST PORCELLI ■ 543 UNION STREET ■ BROOKLYN, NY 11215 ■ TEL/FAX 718-596-4353
E-MAIL EPORCELLIART@CS.COM ■ WWW.ERNESTARTGLASS.COM

164

Top: *Leaves in the Wind,* leaded glass, each: 24" × 60".
Bottom: *Sprezzatura,* 2003, leaded glass and fused glass, 98"W × 78"H. Photograph: Eva Heyd.

ARTHUR STERN STUDIOS ■ 1075 JACKSON STREET ■ BENICIA, CA 94510
TEL/FAX 707-745-8480 ■ E-MAIL ARTHUR@ARTHURSTERN.COM ■ WWW.ARTHURSTERN.COM

165

Frozen Music, entrance window for private residence, Lafayette, CA, leaded glass with beveled glass prisms, 5.8' × 5.2'.

YOUR ARTFUL HOME
Tips From the Artist

ARTIST: Hugh Culley

PROJECT: Bed frame

MEDIUM: Forged steel

DIMENSIONS: 6'H x 6.5'W

This commissioned bed frame was completed for a couple who wanted a metal bed frame with a scroll design. The clients worked with artist Hugh Culley through their interior designer to get just the right piece for their bedroom.

Whether you're building a new home or renovating an older one, forged metal—in the form of furniture or architectural details—can add a substantial presence. Elements such as railings, hardware for doors and cabinets, and fireplace screens and tools can be created in steel, stainless steel, copper or bronze. Artist Hugh Culley also creates custom furniture upon request, sometimes combining metal with other materials, such as wood or stone.

Culley makes the following recommendations when considering a commission in metal for the home:

- If you're considering a handcrafted architectural detail for your home, it's a good idea to have the artist view the space. Culley prefers to see the setting, then provide sketches to the homeowner based on his visit.
- Polish your metal furniture or architectural element with an oil-based polish. Then buff with a dry rag.
- Culley's architectural elements and furniture pieces are functional, yet unobtrusive and artistic; his pieces of artwork are made to be used and enjoyed on a daily basis. Whether a standalone piece or one that is built into the fabric of a home, handcrafted metal is a solid investment and a unique way to reflect a homeowner's personal style.

ROBERT ODDY

ROBERT ODDY, STAINED GLASS ARTIST ■ 223 SCOTTHOLM TERRACE ■ SYRACUSE, NY 13224
TEL 315-446-0279 ■ E-MAIL ARTIST@ROBERTODDY.COM ■ WWW.ROBERTODDY.COM

167

Left: *Lord of Hurdles*, 2000, residential setting, stained glass, 38" × 9". Top right: *Magnolia #2*, 2000, wall-mounted sculpture in bronze and stained glass, 40" × 28" × 9".
Bottom right: *Rebecca*, 2001, residential setting, stained glass, 19" × 25". Photographs: Albert Fanning.

SANDY AND BILL FIFIELD

FIFIELD'S, THE STUDIO ■ PO BOX 366 ■ CONIFER, CO 80433 ■ TEL 303-838-5072
E-MAIL MACFIFIELD@ATT.NET ■ WWW.MACFIFIELD.COM

168

Phoenix, window panel with stained and hand-blasted *dalles de verre* glass, 28" x 54".

DANIEL MAHER STAINED GLASS

DANIEL MAHER ▧ 500 MEDFORD STREET ▧ SOMERVILLE, MA 02145 ▧ TEL 617-623-8600 ▧ FAX 617-623-8602
E-MAIL DMSG@WORLD.STD.COM ▧ WWW.DMSTAINEDGLASS.COM

169

Top left: *Fish #6*, 2003, leaded found glass objects with hand-faceted glass jewels and stained glass, 26" × 27".
Top right: *Prismatic Rounds* series, 2003, leaded found glass object with hand-faceted glass jewels, 25" × 26". Bottom: *Very Red Snapper*, 2000, found glass objects, 27" × 19".

SPHERICAL MAGIC REVERSE GLASS

JOY DAY ■ B.E. JOHNSON ■ 35010 SKY RANCH ROAD ■ CARMEL VALLEY, CA 93924
TEL 877-437-4225 (TOLL FREE) ■ FAX 831-659-2470 ■ GUILD@SPHERICALMAGIC.COM ■ WWW.SPHERICALMAGIC.COM

170

Left: *Falls*, reverse painting on glass, 8" × 54". Center: *First Kiss*, reverse painting on glass with iridescence, 12" × 24".
Right: *Deep Space*, double-panel installation, reverse painting on glass, 10" × 60".

INGE PAPE TRAMPLER

INGE PAPE STUDIO ■ 23 DEL REY DRIVE ■ MOUNT VERNON, NY 10552-1305 ■ TEL 914-699-8616
E-MAIL INGEPAPETRAMPLER@HOTMAIL.COM

Top: *Angel,* one of four leaded and painted windows created for St. Andrews Presbyterian Church, Groton, CT.
Bottom: *Environmental Destruction,* one of two kiln-fired autonomous glass panels on antique glass.

STEVE TEETERS

ST. ELIGIUS STUDIO ■ 719 BUDDY HOLLY AVENUE ■ LUBBOCK, TX 79401 ■ TEL 806-741-1590 ■ FAX 806-744-8507
E-MAIL STUDIO719@NTS-ONLINE.NET ■ WWW.STELIGIUS-STUDIO.COM

172

McClain Forged Vine Stair Railing. Photographs: Hershel Womack.

CAROLINE RACKLEY

IMAGENM.COM ■ HC68-23A ■ SAPELLO, NM 87745 ■ TEL/FAX 505-425-6092
E-MAIL CAROLINE@IMAGENM.COM ■ WWW.IMAGENM.COM

Far Mountains Tapestry Door, C de Baca Mansion, Las Vegas, NM. Photograph: Kingsbury Studio.

HUGH C. CULLEY ART DESIGN

HUGH C. CULLEY ■ 1425 SOUTH INDUSTRIAL ROAD #13
SALT LAKE CITY, UT 84104 ■ TEL/FAX 801-975-9314

174

Aspen Gate, Deer Valley, UT, aluminum over stainless steel frame, 15.5'W x 9'H x 1'D. Photograph: Dennis Mecham.

SCULPTURE

MARCIA CHRISTENSEN

M. CHRISTENSEN SCULPTURE STUDIO, LLC ▨ 740 CIRCLE K RANCH ROAD ▨ EVERGREEN, CO 80439
TEL/FAX 303-670-1823 ▨ E-MAIL MCEVERGREEN@ATT.NET ▨ WWW.MARCIACHRISTENSEN.COM

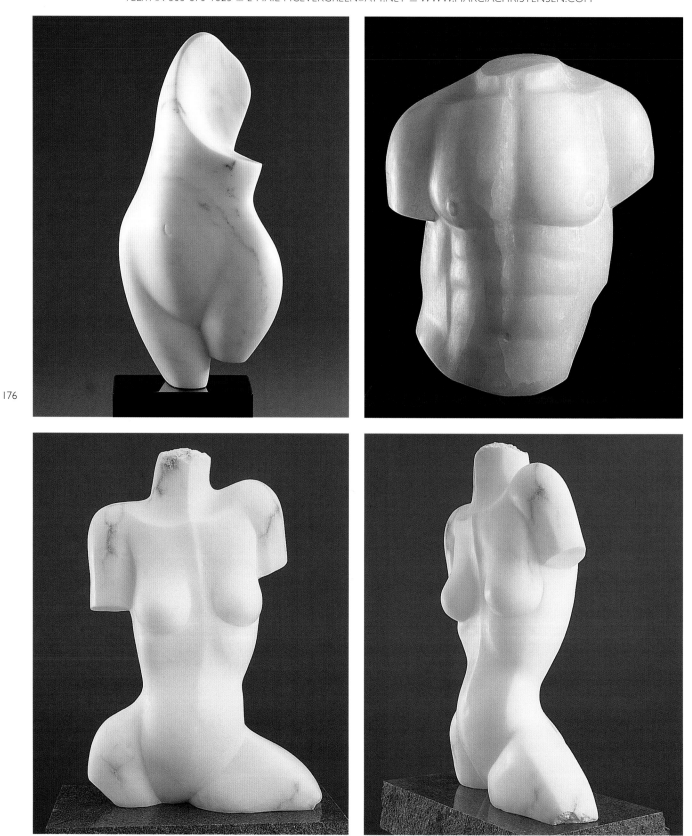

176

Top left: *The Beginning*, marble, 19"H x 6"W x 5"D. Top right: *Male Torso*, Italian alabaster, 22"H x 14"W x 7"D.
Bottom left: *A Mind of Her Own*, Italian alabaster, 32"H x 24"W x 12"D. Bottom right: *A Mind of Her Own* (alternate view). Photographs: Jonathan Eady.

ARYA AZADI

ARYA UNLIMITED ■ PO BOX 189 ■ PAHOA, HI 96778 ■ TEL 808-965-7776
E-MAIL ARYA@MARBLESCULPTRESS.COM ■ WWW.MARBLESCULPTRESS.COM

177

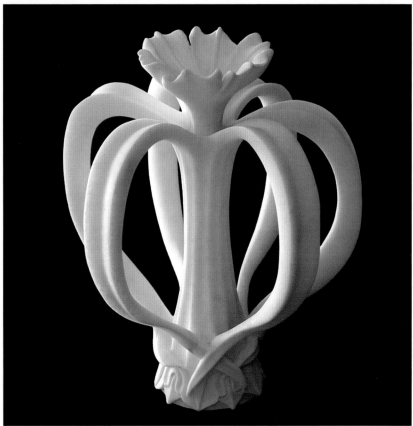

Top: *Orange Flower*, sculpture/water fountain, Rajnagar marble with pink Makrana marble base, 30" × 27" × 24".
Bottom: *Star Ginger I*, sculpture/water fountain, Ambaji marble, 16" × 14" × 14".

GERALD SICILIANO

STUDIO DESIGN ASSOCIATES ■ 9 GARFIELD PLACE ■ BROOKLYN, NY 11215 ■ TEL/FAX 718-636-4561
E-MAIL GERALD.SICILIANO@VERIZON.NET ■ WWW.GERALDSICILIANOSTUDIO.COM

178

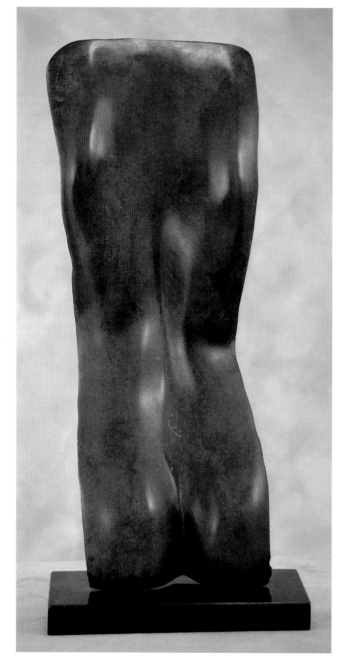

Left: *Dietro,* 2001, bronze, 23" × 10" × 3.5", edition of seven. Right: *Pugilista,* 2000, stainless steel, 28" × 12" × 14", edition of seven.

CHAD AWALT

AWALT WOODCARVING AND DESIGN ■ 4731 STERLING ACRES COURT ■ TUCKER, GA 30084
TEL 770-493-1750 ■ FAX 770-493-1975 ■ E-MAIL AWALT@MINDSPRING.COM ■ WWW.CHADAWALT.COM

179

Vetumnus, hand-carved linden wood, 34" x 20" x 14". Photograph: Neil Dent.

CINTHIA JOYCE

CINTHIA JOYCE FINE ARTS ▪ 800 NORTH DIANTHUS STREET ▪ MANHATTAN BEACH, CA 90266
TEL/FAX 310-376-2427 ▪ CINTHIAJOYCE@ADELPHIA.NET ▪ WWW.CINTHIAJOYCE.COM

180

Serenity, bronze, 22"H x 4"W x 4"D, including base; life-size version also available, 65"H without base. Photograph: Mike Neveux.

CINTHIA JOYCE

CINTHIA JOYCE FINE ARTS ▪ 800 NORTH DIANTHUS STREET ▪ MANHATTAN BEACH, CA 90266
TEL/FAX 310-376-2427 ▪ CINTHIAJOYCE@ADELPHIA.NET ▪ WWW.CINTHIAJOYCE.COM

181

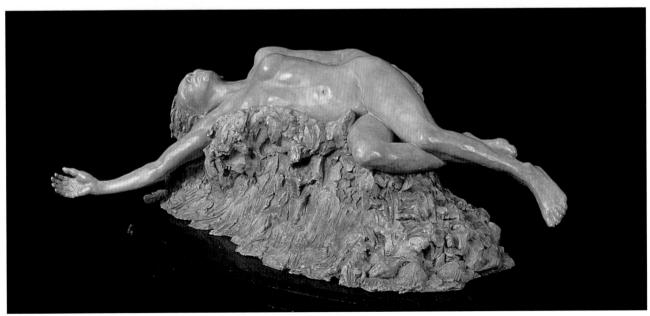

Top left: *Dove*, bronze, 29"H × 13"W × 8"D. Photograph: Paul Moshay.
Top right: *Torso of Aphrodite*, bronze, 22"H × 6"D × 8"W. Photograph: Paul Moshay. Bottom: *Birth of Venus*, bronze, 10"H × 28"W × 15"D. Photograph: Jorge Nuñez.

BORSHEIM ARTS STUDIO

KELLY BORSHEIM ■ PO BOX 340 ■ CEDAR CREEK, TX 78612 ■ TEL/FAX 512-303-3929
E-MAIL SCULPTOR@BORSHEIMARTS.COM ■ WWW.BORSHEIMARTS.COM

182

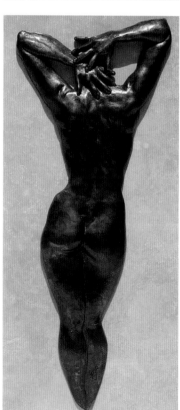

Top left: *Gregg*, bronze, 19.5"H × 5"W × 4.5"D.
Right: *Together and Alone*, bronze on marble base, 26"H × 9" × 8", a 4'H version is available. Bottom left: *Ten*, bronze on travertine, 12"H × 5.5"W × 1"D, 4'H version is available.

JEFF TRITEL

TRITEL STUDIOS ■ 19432 RICHMAR LANE ■ GRASS VALLEY, CA 95949
TEL 800-882-8098 ■ FAX 888-796-3776 ■ E-MAIL TRITEL@TRITELSTUDIOS.COM ■ WWW.TRITELSTUDIOS.COM

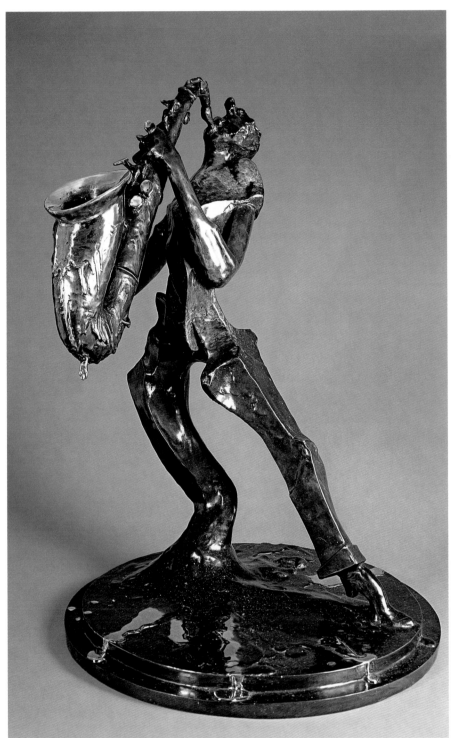

183

Left: *Hot Jazz*, bronze, 25"H, also available 50"H. Top right: *Violinist I*, bronze, 24"H.
Center: *Violinist II*, bronze, 25"H, also available 42"H. Bottom right: *Beethoven*, bronze, 12.5"H.

DUANE MICKELSON

PO BOX 634 ■ HAWLEY, MN 56549
TEL 218-937-5709 ■ E-MAIL DKSKOGEN@RRT.NET

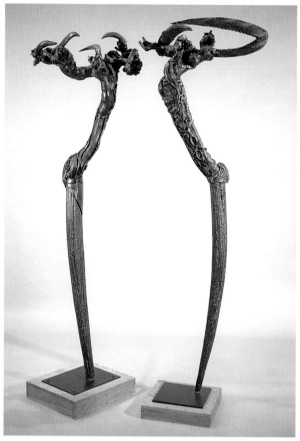

Top left: *Ancestral Visages: The Patriarch,* 2001, bronze, 44" × 14" × 9".
Top right: *Night Dancers I and II,* 2002, welded steel, grapevine and leather; left: 88" × 27" × 20"; right: 91" × 30" × 12".
Bottom: *The Skeptic,* 1996, Rourke Art Museum, Moorhead, MN, welded steel and found wood, 80" × 26" × 57".

LaCASSE STUDIOS

JAMES LaCASSE ▨ 1442 HUDSON STREET ▨ DENVER, CO 80220 ▨ TEL 303-329-8608 ▨ FAX 303-329-0229
E-MAIL LACASSESTUDIOS@AOL.COM ▨ WWW.LACASSESTUDIOS.COM

185

Top: *The Cosmic Play*, 2001, 24" × 16" × 12". Bottom left: *Abundance*, 2002, 27" × 20" × 9". Bottom right: *Fool's Folly*, 1996, 66" × 24" × 24". Photographs: Mel Schockner.

L. BALOMBINI

LAURA BALOMBINI ■ PO BOX 733 ■ BLUE HILL, ME 04614
TEL/FAX 207-374-5142 ■ E-MAIL LAURA@LBALOMBINI.COM ■ WWW.LBALOMBINI.COM

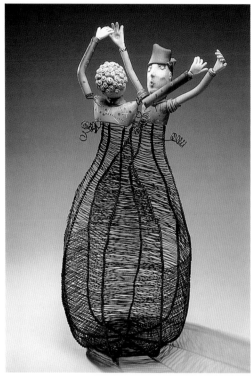

186

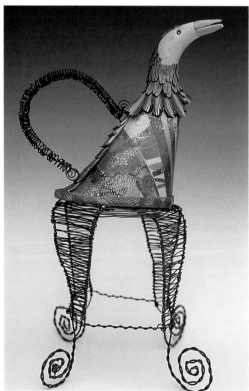

Top left: *House Bought Happy Dance*, 2002, steel wire and polymer; 28"H × 12" × 12". Photograph: Robert Diamante.
Right: *My Last Innocent Year*, 2003, steel wire and polymer, 30"H × 10" × 10". Bottom left: *The Smallest Bird Sings the Sweetest Songs*, 2003, steel wire and polymer, 20"H × 10" × 10".

ROBIN ANTAR

ANTAR STUDIOS INC. ■ 1485 EAST FIFTH STREET ■ BROOKLYN, NY 11230 ■ TEL/FAX 718-375-5156
E-MAIL ANTARSTUDIOS@MSN.COM ■ WWW.ROBINANTAR.COM

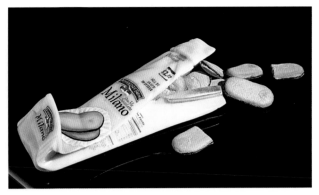

187

Left: *DIESEL Jeans*, ©2002, limestone and oil stains, 29" × 12" × 6". Photograph: Edward Peterson. Top right: *Milano Cookies*, ©2002, bag: marble and acrylic, cookies: resin and acrylic, 3.5" × 15" × 8". Photograph: Edward Peterson. Center right: *Milk and Cookies*, ©2001, glass: alabaster and acrylic, platter: limestone and oil stains, cookies: resin and acrylic, 6.5" × 12" × 12". Bottom right: *Boot in Motion*,© 2000, limestone and oil stains, 12" × 8" × 4".

GLENN DONOVAN

15981 MOLDREM ROAD ■ FERRYVILLE, WI 54628 ■ TEL 608-734-3223
E-MAIL GLENN@WELDERBOY-ART.COM ■ WWW.WELDERBOY-ART.COM

188

Top left: *Courting Crane*, 2003, spring motion creates the illusion of flight, 46"H × 40"W × 30"D. Top right: *Metamorphosis*, 2003, kinetic transformation in balance for indoors or outdoors, 32"H × 20"W × 20"D. Bottom: *Out of Control*, 2003, kinetic spring biker, 36"H × 40"W × 18"D. Photograph: Bill Lemke.

JIM MILLAR STUDIO

JIM MILLAR ■ 375 MILLAR ROAD ■ HOT SPRINGS, NC 28743
TEL 828-622-7367 ■ FAX 828-622-3216 ■ E-MAIL JMILLAR@MADISON.MAIN.NC.US ■ WWW.JIMMILLAR.COM

189

Top left: *Hibiscus*, hand-wrought bronze fountain, 4'H. Right: *Haywood Park*, hand-wrought bronze fountain, 6'H.
Bottom left: *Serenity*, hand-wrought bronze fountain, 5'H. Photographs: Ken Pitts, Asheville, NC.

RICHARD WARRINGTON

WARRINGTON STUDIOS ■ WEST 3907 WASHINGTON ROAD ■ CHENEY, WA 99004
TEL/FAX 509-448-8713 ■ E-MAIL RWARRI3907@AOL.COM ■ WWW.RWARRINGTON.COM

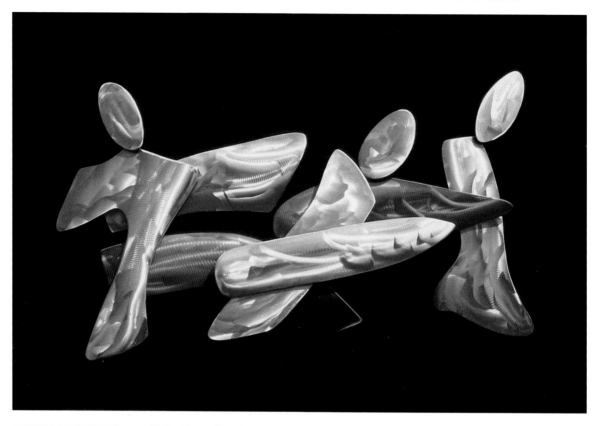

190

Top: *Action People,* 2003, transparent powder-coated aluminum, 40"H x 73"W x 6"D.
Bottom left: *We Stick Together,* 2003, stainless steel, 49"H x 22"W x 11"D. Bottom right: *5 o'clock People,* 2003, powder-coated aluminum, 89"H x 52"W x 24"D.

MK SHANNON

MK SHANNON SCULPTURE ■ 248 JOHN ST SUITE A ■ OAKLAND, CA 94611
TEL/FAX 510-234-6765 ■ E-MAIL MKS@MKSHANNON.COM ■ WWW.MKSHANNON.COM

191

Top: *Laureate*, 1995, bronze, 9" × 12". Bottom left: *Madalyn*, 1982, bronze, 16" × 8".
Bottom right: *Alta*, 1982, bronze, 16" × 20". Photograph: Ted Mahieu.

TERRY WOODALL

PACIFIC CARVINGS ■ 95865 KENTUCK LANE ■ NORTH BEND, OR 97459 ■ TEL 541-756-0752
E-MAIL WOODALL@HARBORSIDE.COM ■ WWW.HARBORSIDE.COM/~WOODALL/

Top: *Bay Fighter*, myrtlewood, 26"H x 24"W. Bottom: *Upstream Duo*, myrtlewood, 18"H x 22"W. Photographs: Robert Jaffe.

TURNER SCULPTURE

DAVID H. TURNER ▪ WILLIAM H. TURNER ▪ 27316 LANKFORD HWY ▪ PO BOX 128 ▪ ONLEY, VA 23418
TEL 757-787-2818 ▪ FAX 757-787-7064 ▪ E-MAIL TURNER@ESVA.NET ▪ WWW.TURNERSCULPTURE.COM

193

Top left: *Fishing Heron*, 2002, 14"L × 10"W × 43"H, created by William H. Turner.
Top right: *Osprey and Silver Trout*, 2002, 22"L × 28"W × 39"H, created by David H. Turner. Bottom: *Stalking Fox*, 2003, 46"L × 12"W × 21"H, created by David H. Turner.

DAN FREEMAN

15417 204TH AVE SE ■ RENTON, WA 98059 ■ TEL 425-652-1739 ■ FAX 425-228-2503
E-MAIL DAN@ELEMENTALCORP.COM ■ WWW.ELEMENTALARTWORK.COM

194

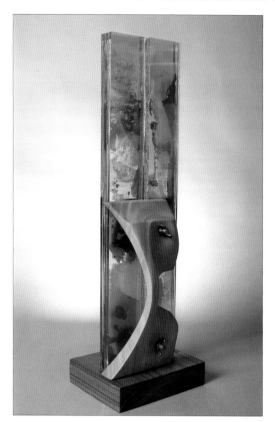

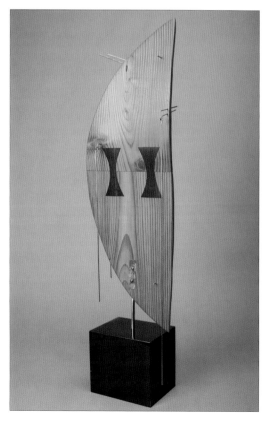

Top left: *Stele*, wood, metal, glass and wax, 23"H x 8" x 8". Top right: *Held*, steel, stone and wood, 21"H x 6" x 3".
Bottom left: *Butterfly Repair*, wood and metal, 39"H x 11" x 6". Bottom right: *Red Rocks Under Glass*, wood, glass and stone, 15"H x 9" x 7".

KEVIN B. ROBB

KEVIN ROBB STUDIOS ■ 7001 WEST 35TH AVENUE ■ WHEAT RIDGE, CO 80033
TEL 303-431-4758 ■ FAX 303-425-8802 ■ E-MAIL 3D@KEVINROBB.COM ■ WWW.KEVINROBB.COM

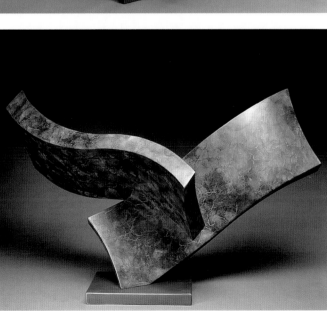

195

Top left: *Blowing Paper*, fabricated bronze, 35" x 34" x 28". Right: *Flight of Triangles*, 2003, fabricated bronze, 54" x 26" x 27" on 5" base.
Bottom left: *Two Waves*, 2003, fabricated bronze, 19" x 31" x 20". Photographs: John Bonath.

AEOLIPILES

JOAN BRIGHAM ▨ 45 MOUNT PLEASANT STREET ▨ CAMBRIDGE, MA 02140
TEL/FAX 617-354-4730 ▨ E-MAIL JOANBRIGHAM@YAHOO.COM

196

Tiara, 2002, glass, water, denatured alcohol and wicks, glass blown by Eric Starosielski. Photographs: Walter Dent.

TALIAFERRO JONES

TALIAFERRO JONES STUDIO ◼ 442 DUFFERIN STREET UNIT N ◼ TORONTO, ON MK6 2A3 ◼ CANADA
TEL 416-538-3304 ◼ FAX 416-538-8272 ◼ E-MAIL TALIAFERRO@TALIAFERROJONES.COM ◼ WWW.TALIAFERROJONES.COM

197

Top: *Cadence*, kiln-cast crystal, 8.5'L × 5.5"H × 7"D. Center: *CordeValle B*, kiln-cast crystal, 60"L × 18"H × 5"D. Bottom: *Sunrise*, kiln-cast crystal, 29"L × 7"H × 6"D.

SUSAN BLOCH

1100 CLEMENS CENTER PARKWAY #126 ■ ELMIRA, NY 14901 ■ TEL/FAX 866-358-5295
E-MAIL SBW@BLOCHSTUDIO.COM ■ WWW.BLOCHSTUDIO.COM

198

Good Will Reflector, 2003, Elmira-Corning Regional Airport (one-year installation), kiln-formed glass, 8.8'H × 6'W × 6'D. Inset: *Good Will Reflector,* (detail).

KELLY BURKE MAKUCH

KELLY BURKE MAKUCH ART GLASS STUDIO ■ 222 BRUSHY HILL ROAD ■ NEWTOWN, CT 06470-2535
TEL 203-426-0509 ■ FAX 203-364-1637 ■ E-MAIL KBMGLASS@EARTHLINK.NET

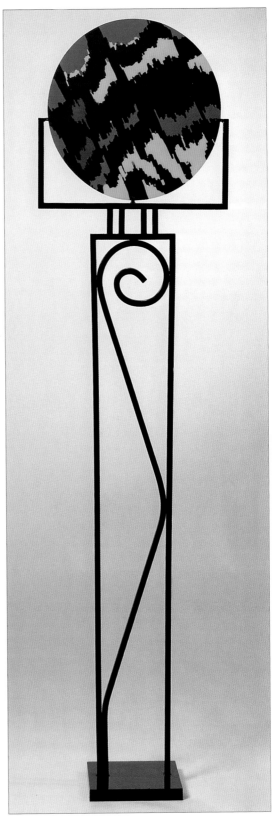

199

Top left: *Fragment Unidentified #5*, 2002, fused glass with iron and steel base, 26.5"H x 16"W x 6"D. Photograph: Linda Napier.
Right: *Lichtenfly Giant Swallowtail Fragment*, from the *Fragment* series, 2003, fused glass with iron and steel, 62"H x 17"W x 9"D. Photograph: Tracy Studio.
Bottom left: *Leaves on the Pond*, 2002, fused glass end table with steel base, 22"H x 14.25" x 14.25". Photograph: Tracy Studio.

WIKTOR SZOSTALO

4398 CHOUTEAU AVENUE ■ ST. LOUIS, MO 63110 ■ TEL 314-652-9720
E-MAIL WSZOSTALO@EARTHLINK.NET ■ WWW.WSART.COM ■ WWW.SZOSTALOSCULPTURE.COM

200

Top: *After Breughel*, 2001, cast glass, 15" × 15" × 2". Bottom: *Temptation in the Desert*, cast glass, 24" × 17" × 2".

MICHAEL J. SCHUNKE

NINE IRON STUDIOS INC. ▨ 203 PROSPECT AVENUE ▨ WEST GROVE, PA 19390 ▨ TEL/FAX 610-869-5926
E-MAIL MICHAEL@NINEIRONSTUDIOS.COM ▨ WWW.NINEIRONSTUDIOS.COM

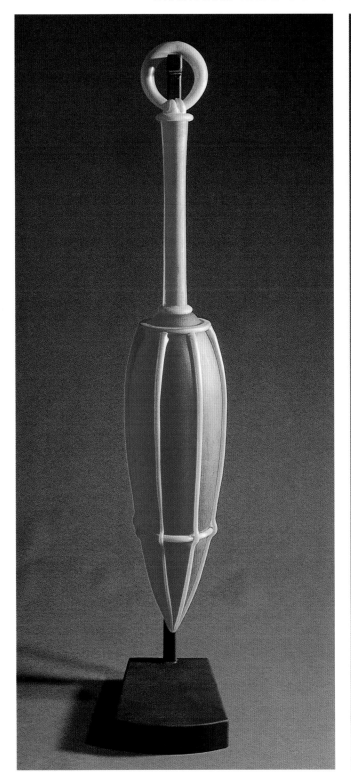 

Left: *Red,* from the *Weight, Float and Hope* series, acid-polished blown glass, hung on steel base, from the collection of Tom and Denise Stern, 47"H x 10"D x 10"W.
Right: *Black,* from the *Weight, Float and Hope* series, acid-polished blown glass, hung on steel base, from the collection of Tom and Denise Stern, 48"H x 9"D x 10"W.

JEREMY R. CLINE

INCLINE GLASS ▨ 768 DELANO AVENUE ▨ SAN FRANCISCO, CA 94112 ▨ TEL 415-469-8312 ▨ FAX 415-469-8463
E-MAIL JC@JEREMYCLINE.COM ▨ WWW.JEREMYCLINE.COM

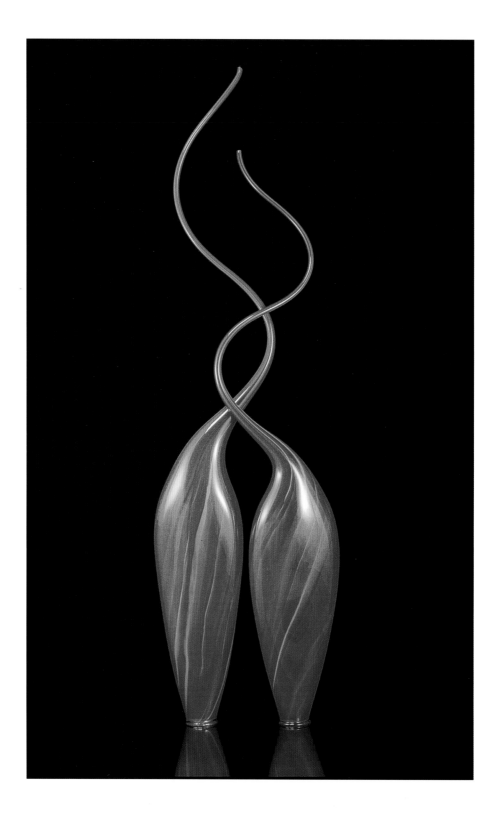

Birds of Paradise, 2003, blown glass, left: 81.5" x 11.5" x 6", right: 71.5" x 11.5" x 6". Photograph: Latchezar Boyadjiev.

GARDEN SCULPTURE

HERB GOLDMAN

GOLDMAN CONSULTING, INC. ■ 1736 NORTH WILD HYACINTH ■ TUSCON, AZ 85715
TEL 520-298-6828 ■ E-MAIL GOLDMANART@COX.NET ■ WWW.HERBGOLDMAN.COM

Left: *Polar Bear,* 1989, Gallery Horizon, Santa Fe, NM, stainless steel, 8'H, available in stainless steel and bronze in various sizes.
Right: *Father and Child,* 1991, Gallery Horizon, Santa Fe, NM, stainless steel, 9'H, available in stainless steel and bronze in various sizes. Photographs: Mary Fredenburgh.

BRUCE ANTHONY & COMPANY

RICHARD DANIELS ■ PO BOX 105 ■ TOUTLE, WA 98649 ■ TEL 800-397-4873 ■ FAX 360-274-2278
E-MAIL OLSONDANIELS@CPORT.COM ■ WWW.BIRDBATHSANDFOUNTAINS.COM

205

Top left: *Short Plant Stand Birdbath,* handspun, patinaed copper bowl on hand-crafted steel stand with powder finish, 23"H x 27"Dia.

Right: *Tall Pyramid Fountain with Spheres and Granite,* handspun, patinaed copper bowl with river rock on hand-crafted steel stand with bronze finish, 23"H x 43"Dia.

Bottom left: *Mission Birdbath,* patinaed copper bowl on hand-crafted stand with powder finish, 39"H x 23"W.

ANDREW CARSON

1531 NE 89TH STREET ▓ SEATTLE, WA 98115 ▓ TEL 206-524-9782 ▓ FAX 425-952-8170
E-MAIL MAIL@WINDSCULPTURE.COM ▓ WWW.WINDSCULPTURE.COM

206

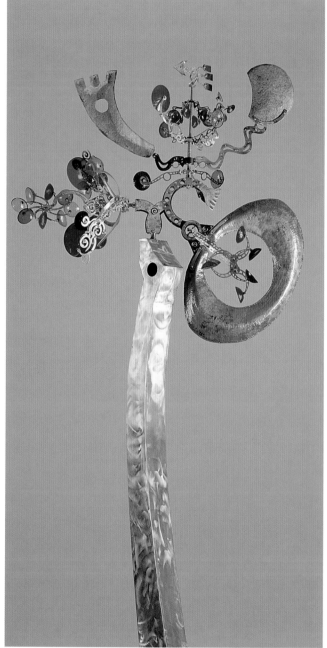

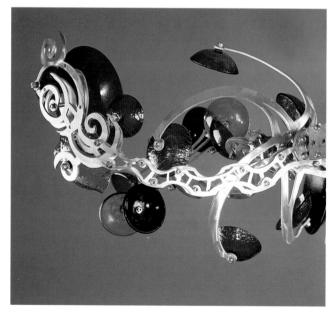

Top left: *Galaxy on Stainless Steel Pillar* (detail). Right: *Galaxy on Stainless Steel Pillar*, mixed metal and glass, 8' × 4' × 4'.
Bottom left: *Galaxy on Stainless Steel Pillar* (detail). Photographs: Bruce Carroll.

GINA MICHAELS

90 EAST CHURCH LANE ▨ PHILADELPHIA, PA 19144 ▨ TEL 215-713-0505 ▨ FAX 215-844-9073
E-MAIL GINA@GINAMICHAELS.COM ▨ WWW.GINAMICHAELS.COM

Top left: *Hand Plant #7*, 2002, bronze, 108" × 60" × 48".

Top right: *Hand Plant #11*, 2003, El Paseo, Palm Desert, CA, bronze, 98" × 42" × 33". Bottom: *Hand Plant # 1*, 1998, bronze, 16" × 26" × 23".

L.T. CHEROKEE

STUDIO 40 PROSPECT AVENUE ■ NORTHPORT, NY 11768
TEL 631-261-3342 ■ E-MAIL LTSCULPT@MSN.COM

208

Left: *Eye of the Storm*, 2001, private residence, South Hampton, NY, granite, copper and stainless steel with water element, 7'H x 5'L x 3'D, weight: 1 ton.
Right: *Beyond the Gate*, 2002, John T. Mather Memorial Hospital, steel resin and bonded concrete with water mist and fog elements, 13'H x 12'L x 4'W. Photographs: Michael O'Neill.

AKYROS DESIGN

FRED NULL ■ ZALE GAYLEN ■ CHRIS NULL ■ 2305C ASHLAND STREET SUITE 122 ■ ASHLAND, OR 97520
TEL 800-722-6855 ■ FAX 541-488-6486 ■ E-MAIL INFO@AKYROSDESIGN.COM ■ WWW.AKYROSDESIGN.COM

209

Montana slate monolith. Photograph: Dennis Remick.

ROBERT PULLEY SCULPTURE

ROBERT PULLEY ▨ 8670 WEST 450 SOUTH ▨ COLUMBUS, IN 47201 ▨ TEL 812-342-6475
E-MAIL BPULLEY@HSONLINE.NET ▨ WWW.ABSOLUTEARTS.COM/PORTFOLIOS/B/BPULLEY/

210

Top: *Blue Heart* and *Tall Fragment*, stoneware, 45"H × 60"W × 28"D. Bottom: *Low Fragment*, stoneware, 23"H × 26"W × 18"D.

KAREN HEYL

1310 PENDLETON STREET ▪ CINCINNATI, OH 45202 ▪ TEL 760-489-7106/513-421-9791
E-MAIL HEYLSTONE2@AOL.COM ▪ WWW.KARENHEYL.COM

211

Top: *The Dreamer*, limestone, 28"L × 24"H × 2". Bottom: *The Great Krohn God*, limestone, 30"L × 24"H × 2". Photographs: Charles Behlow.

ERIC DAVID LAXMAN

ANAHATA ARTS ▪ 478 MOUNTAINVIEW AVENUE ▪ VALLEY COTTAGE, NY 10989
TEL 845-353-8521 ▪ FAX 845-348-3687 ▪ E-MAIL ERIC@ANAHATA.COM ▪ WWW.ANAHATA.COM

212

Anahata Fountain, 2000, private collection, New Canaan, CT, welded silicon bronze, 96"H x 36" x 36". Photograph: Stuart Sachs.

ERIC DAVID LAXMAN

ANAHATA ARTS ■ 478 MOUNTAINVIEW AVENUE ■ VALLEY COTTAGE, NY 10989
TEL 845-353-8521 ■ FAX 845-348-3687 ■ E-MAIL ERIC@ANAHATA.COM ■ WWW.ANAHATA.COM

213

Top left: *Transformation Figure*, 2000, collection of the artist, Vermont marble and steel, 70"H × 20" × 16". Photograph: Sal Cordaro.
Top right: *Dancing Flame*, 2003, collection of the artist, steel and stainless steel, 72"H × 28" × 16". Photograph: Sal Cordaro.
Bottom: *Serpiente Grande*, 2002, site-specific commision for private collection in Madison, CT, welded stainless steel, 50' × 27"H × 15".

YOUR ARTFUL HOME
Tips From the Artist

ARTIST: Eric David Laxman

PROJECT: *Balancing at High Speed,* garden sculpture

MEDIUM: Steel and stone on found wheel

DIMENSIONS: 65" x 24" x 20"

This innovative garden sculpture appears in the collection of the artist. The piece is a metaphor for the life of an artist, who must hold competing demands in precarious balance and be ready for any turns in the road.

A garden sculpture on your patio or lawn is one way to bring your artistic taste outdoors. Depending upon the materials used, a garden sculpture or fountain can blend in with the natural elements that surround it, or animate a space with materials not otherwise found in nature. Like the seasons themselves, garden sculptures tend to weather and change over time; many of these changes are meant to be enjoyed as your sculpture ages.

To ensure the beauty of your outdoor artwork for many years, Eric Laxman shares these tips for caring for garden sculpture:

- Changes to the sculpture surface will vary depending on the materials used and the natural elements in your geographic area. Speak to the artist about what types of changes you can expect so you won't be surprised later on.
- Pollution and dirt can lead to deterioration of some surfaces. General upkeep once or twice a year will keep your sculpture looking its best. Inexpensive products such as wax (to keep moisture out of metal) or clear sealants (for stonework) will protect your artwork without damage or discoloration. Again, the artist can guide you to the best protective strategy.
- Place your garden sculpture so that it may be viewed from all sides, in a courtyard or along a path, for example. Depending on the size of the piece, you may want to place it on a base or stand, to distinguish it from its surroundings. If you've commissioned a fountain, make sure you have a pool large enough to contain the flowing or spraying water.

TUSKA INC.

SETH TUSKA ■ 147 OLD PARK AVENUE ■ LEXINGTON, KY 40502
TEL 859-255-1379 ■ FAX 859-253-3199 ■ E-MAIL TUSKART@AOL.COM ■ WWW.TUSKASTUDIO.COM

215

Illuminates garden screen, welded steel with powder coat finish, 77" x 34". Photograph: Lee Thomas

DAN RIDER SCULPTURE

DAN RIDER ■ 133 BRIDGE STREET #D ■ ARROYO GRANDE, CA 93420
TEL 805-474-5959 ■ FAX 805-474-5955 ■ WWW.DANRIDERSCULPTURE.COM

216

Top left: *Spirit Marker #8*, copper and concrete, 7' × 3' × 3". Right: *Spirit Marker #9*, copper, concrete and slate, 8' × 42" × 12".
Bottom left: *Spirit Marker #6*, copper and concrete, 8.5' × 40" × 18".

SCHULTE STUDIOS

KAI SCHULTE ▨ 41W020 SEAVEY ROAD ▨ SUGAR GROVE, IL 60554-9573 ▨ TEL 630-406-0404 ▨ FAX 630-406-0505
E-MAIL KAI@SCHULTESTUDIOS.COM ▨ WWW.SCHULTESTUDIOS.COM

217

Left: *Obelisk*, 2003, stainless steel, 9'H, base: 24" × 24". Right: *Crane*, 2002, stainless steel, 5.5'H. Photographs: Steve Jorstad.

ART FOR THE WALL

Interior design by Kendall Marcelle, see page 40. Alicia Quaini, *Peach Slices* (detail). Photograph: Roy Quesada.

CLAUDIA McKINSTRY

CMC STUDIOS ■ 15186 SUNRISE DRIVE NE ■ BAINBRIDGE ISLAND, WA 98110
TEL 206-842-6962 ■ FAX 206-780-6873 ■ WWW.CLAUDIAMCKINSTRY.COM

220

Winter Market, 2003, Pike Place Market, Seattle, WA, watercolor, 24" x 38". Photograph: Art and Soul Photography.

CLAUDIA McKINSTRY

CMC STUDIOS ■ 15186 SUNRISE DRIVE NE ■ BAINBRIDGE ISLAND, WA 98110
TEL 206-842-6962 ■ FAX 206-780-6873 ■ WWW.CLAUDIAMCKINSTRY.COM

221

Top: *Jirisha*, 1999, watercolor, 37.75" × 14.75". Bottom: *Alive*, 2000, oil, 90" × 60". Photographs: Bill Wickett.

DONNA JILL WITTY

DONNA JILL WITTY, ARTIST ■ 444 NORTH HILL STREET ■ WOODSTOCK, IL 60098
TEL 815-338-0849 ■ E-MAIL JILWITTY@OWC.NET ■ WWW.DONNAJILLWITTY.COM

222

Top: *Le Barche da Pesca*, 2002, watercolor, 24" x 40". Bottom: *Summer's Bounty*, 2000, watercolor, 24" x 40".

HELEN VAUGHN

HELEN VAUGHN STUDIO ▨ 313 FRANKLIN STREET ▨ HUNTSVILLE, AL 35801 ▨ TEL 256-534-4202 ▨ FAX 256-534-0956
E-MAIL VAUGHNART@ATTGLOBAL.NET ▨ WWW.HELENVAUGHN.COM

223

Top: *Woman in a Dark Slip,* 2002, oil and gold leaf on panel, 16" x 24". Bottom: *Pond Garden in Augusta,* 2003, oil on canvas, 30" x 40".

MARJORIE A. ATWOOD

3627 SOUTH YORKTOWN PLACE ■ TULSA, OK 74105 ■ TEL 918-747-7337
E-MAIL MARJORIEATWOOD@COX.NET ■ WWW.ATWOODART.COM

224

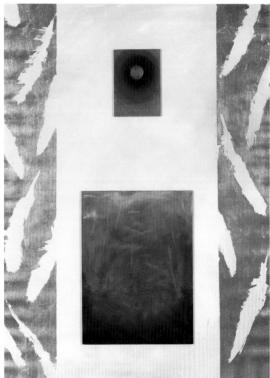

Top: *Blue Joy*, 2003, mixed media, 24" × 72", 48" × 72" and 24" × 72". Bottom left: *Icarus Remembered*, 2001, mixed media, 40" × 30".
Bottom right: *Calla Lillies*, 2001, mixed-media painting, 14" × 18". Photographs: Scott Miller, Miller Photography.

AMOS MILLER

TEL 305-573-2125 ▨ E-MAIL STUDIOAM@BELLSOUTH.NET

225

Top: Untitled, 2003, acrylic on canvas, 38" x 56". Bottom: Untitled, 2003, acrylic on canvas, 38" x 56". Photographs: Daniel Portnoy.

KATHRYN JACOBI

654 COPELAND COURT ■ SANTA MONICA, CA 90405 ■ TEL 310-399-8423 ■ FAX 310-399-5350
E-MAIL KATHRYNJACOBI@ADELPHIA.NET ■ WWW.KATHRYNJACOBI.COM

226

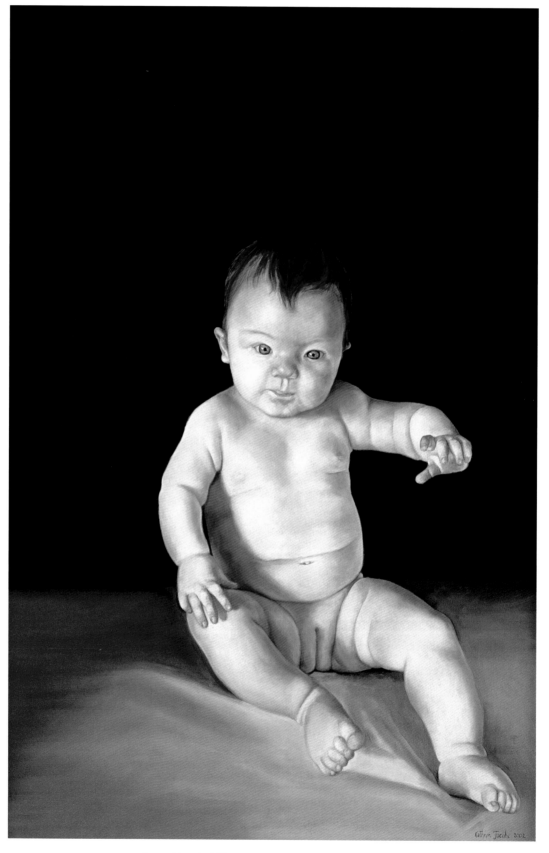

Portrait of Anna #1, 2002, oil on panel, 36" x 24". Photograph: H. van Pelt.

MARY HATCH

6917 WILLSON DRIVE ■ KALAMAZOO, MI 49009 ■ TEL 269-375-0376 ■ FAX 269-375-1069
E-MAIL MARHATCH@NET-LINK.NET ■ WWW.MARYHATCH.COM

227

Top: *The Bridesmaid,* 2002, oil on canvas, 28" x 36". Bottom: *Inside Umbrellas,* 1997, oil on canvas, 40" x 36". Photographs: Karen Rose.

YOUR ARTFUL HOME
Tips From the Artist

ARTIST: Simone DeSousa

PROJECT: *Aqui*, painting

MEDIUM: Acrylic on board

DIMENSIONS: 32" x 48"

This painting was purchased by Simone DeSousa's clients for their contemporary dining environment. The metal frame was custom made by artist Coley McLean to match both the artwork and the residence. Photograph by Dan O'Neill.

Abstract paintings are always open for interpretation. In her experience, artist Simone DeSousa finds that clients come into her studio looking for a painting to match their décor, but then make a connection with a very unexpected piece of work that "they must have." Clients can never explain what it is about a particular piece that appeals to them, but DeSousa believes an abstract painting invites the viewer to find personal interpretations in the work and make new discoveries about its meaning over time.

Below are DeSousa's tips for the placement and care of abstract acrylic paintings:

- Frame the work without glass. Choose a frame that will complement your painting and your residence. Even if a frame is beautiful, it can overwhelm the artwork, so make your selection carefully.
- Keep the painting out of direct sunlight. Dust the piece lightly with a soft brush as needed to keep it clean.
- When you hang the work, give it room to breathe in an environment appropriate for its scale. Do not allow the painting to simply become part of the pattern of the room. You may want to consider moving furniture and other elements in your room so that your painting can be prominently featured and enjoyed.

LAURIE GODDARD

9 BRIDGE STREET ▪ SHELBURNE FALLS, MA 01370
TEL 413-625-8120 ▪ FAX 413-625-4650 ▪ WWW.LAURIEGODDARD.COM

229

Top left: Gilded diptych with patinas and ink, 36" x 24". Top right: Gilded diptych with patinas, acrylic and dye, 36" x 24".
Bottom: *Lucca*, gilded panel with patinas and acrylics, 36" x 24". Photographs: Paul Turnbull.

LORETTA MOSSMAN

290 COLLINS AVENUE #5A ■ MOUNT VERNON, NY 10552
TEL 914-699-2112 ■ E-MAIL LORETTM@VERIZON.NET

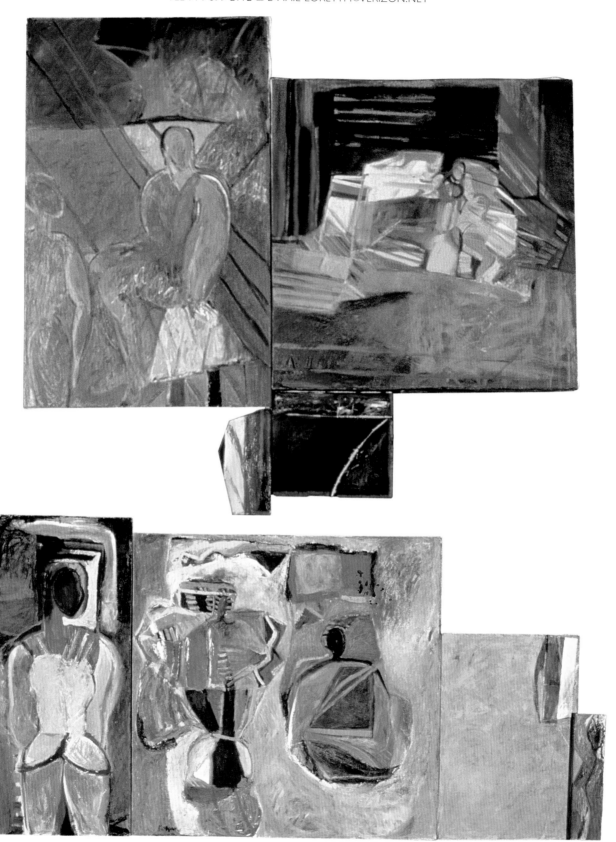

230

Top: *Nocturnal Lightness*, oil on canvas with mixed media, 4' x 3.4'. Bottom: *Symbiosis*, oil on canvas with mixed media, 6.6' x 4.2'.

JAMES NOCITO

JMAN ART STUDIO ▧ 2868 ELM STREET ▧ SAN DIEGO, CA 92102
TEL/FAX 619-795-9544 ▧ E-MAIL JMAN15@COX.NET

231

Top left: *Blue Bathers*, 2003, mixed media on paper, 20" × 26". Top right: *Green Bathers*, 2003, mixed media on paper, 20" × 26".
Bottom left: *White Roses*, 2003, mixed media on paper, 16" × 20". Bottom right: *Red Roses*, 2003, mixed media on paper, 16" × 20". Photographs: Patrik Ryan.

KATHLEEN NEWMAN

12325 90TH AVENUE ■ PALOS PARK, IL 60464 ■ TEL/FAX 708-448-0607
E-MAIL INFO@KATHLEENNEWMAN.COM ■ WWW.KATHLEENNEWMAN.COM

232

Top: *Early Morning Breeze*, pastel on paper, 28" x 34".
Bottom left: *Mario's on Taylor Street*, oil on board, 20" x 15". Bottom right: *Lunch Hour, Lake Point Tower*, pastel on paper, 26" x 19".

LAURIE REGAN CHASE

1255 CALIFORNIA STREET ■ SAN FRANCISCO, CA 94109 ■ TEL 415-203-2676
E-MAIL ARTIST149@AOL.COM ■ WWW.LAURIECHASE.COM

233

Top: *Reservations for Two,* 2002, oil on canvas, 16" × 20", also available in giclée on paper, 16" × 20".
Bottom: *Golden Girls,* 2002, oil on canvas, 49" × 60", also available in giclée on canvas, 30" × 40".

HOLLYE DAVIDSON

STUDIO HD ■ 2655 LEJEUNE ROAD SUITE 814 ■ CORAL GABLES, FL 33134
TEL 786-552-0018 ■ E-MAIL ART@STUDIOHD.US ■ WWW.HOLLYEDAVIDSON.COM

234

Top: *Nana's Pink Chair*, 1999, oil on canvas, 30" x 30".
Bottom: *Fleurs de Pamela*, 2001, oil on canvas, 72" x 96".

MIRANDA MOSS

252 FIRST AVENUE NORTH ■ MINNEAPOLIS, MN 55401 ■ TEL 612-375-0180 ■ FAX 612-342-2424
E-MAIL MMOSS@YAMAMOTO-MOSS.COM ■ WWW.MIRANDAMOSS.COM

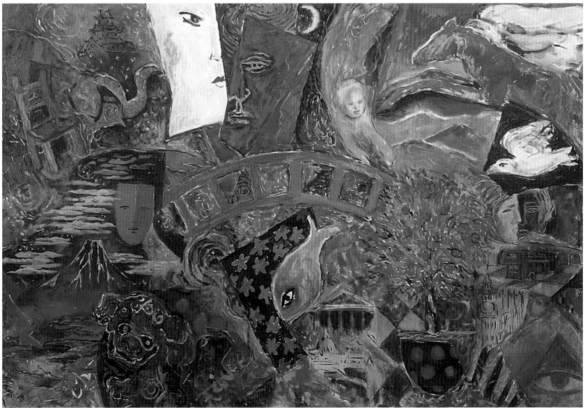

Top: *Signs of Life, Miami Edition,* 2001, oil in canvas, 8.5' × 5.75'. Bottom: *East Meets West,* from the *Koi* series, 1998, oil on canvas, 6' × 4'. Photographs: Paul Najus.

NOMA

26 WALLKILL AVENUE ▨ MONTGOMERY, NY 12549 ▨ TEL 845-457-9821 ▨ FAX 845-457-3951
E-MAIL JBLISS@FRONTIERNET.NET ▨ WWW.NOMAARTIST.COM

236

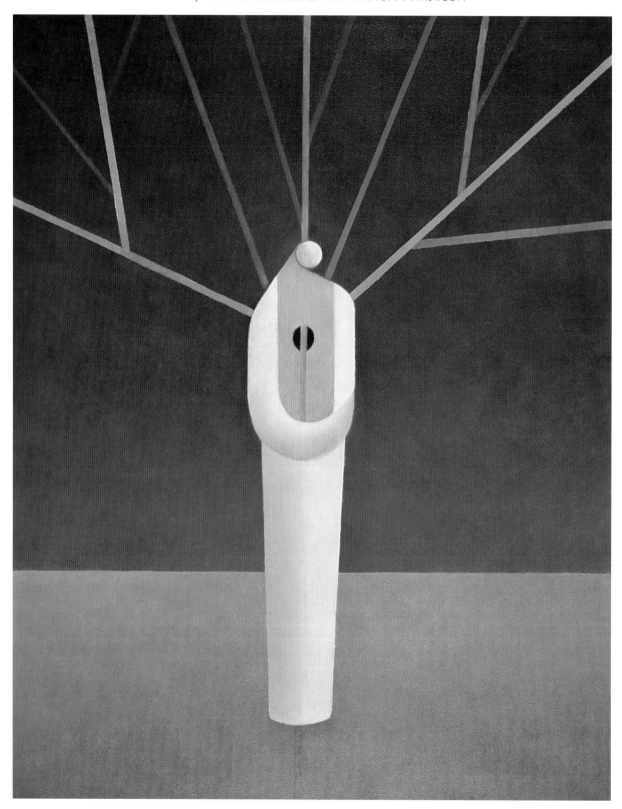

Structurally Sound, 2003, oil, 24" × 28". Photograph: Ron Palmer.

TODD STARKS

9216 SERNS ROAD NORTH ▪ MILTON, WI 53563 ▪ TEL 608-868-3020
E-MAIL TODD@TODDSTARKS.NET ▪ WWW.TODDSTARKS.NET

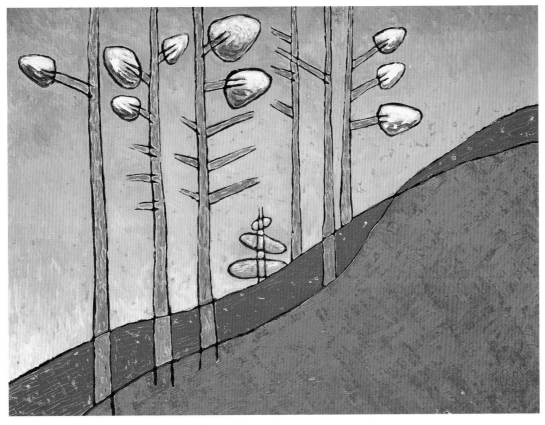

Top: *Underdog.* 2003, oil on canvas, 27" × 32". Bottom: *Belief.* 2003, oil on canvas, 30" × 40". Photographs: Hyperion Studio.

TOBY ATTICUS FRALEY

FRALEY'S ARTSHOP ▨ 309 TAYLOR AVENUE ▨ WASHINGTON, PA 15301 ▨ TEL 724-222-5236
E-MAIL ARTSHOP@PULSENET.COM ▨ WWW.PULSENET.COM/~ARTSHOP

238

Top: *American Southwest #3*, 2001, oil on canvas, 20" x 30".
Bottom: *Restaurant 17 Miles South of Bingham, NM*, 2001, oil on canvas, 42" x 28".

LARRY STEPHENSON

TOYZ ▨ 324 LAKECREST DRIVE ▨ ANDOVER, KS 67002 ▨ TEL 316-733-9654
E-MAIL LSTEPHENSON3@COX.NET ▨ WWW.LSTEPHENSON.COM

Top: *Simple Treasures,* 2003, watercolor and egg tempera on paper, 18" × 60". Giclée print available.
Bottom: *Flight Line,* 2003, watercolor and egg tempera on paper, 29" × 40". Giclée print available. Photographs: Dan Siedhoff, Rock Island Studio.

YOUR ARTFUL HOME
Tips From the Artist

ARTIST: Lisa Ambler

PROJECT: *Grace Foretold*, painting

MEDIUM: Oil on canvas

DIMENSIONS: 34" x 44"

This painting is from Lisa Ambler's series *The Stones Will Cry Out*, a collection of scriptural allegories. The piece hangs in Ambler's garden room, encouraging contemplation in this restful space. Photograph by MaxStyles.com.

A nature or landscape painting offers a wonderful way to bring the natural world indoors. In addition to complementing the color or theme of a particular room, a natural painting can fill a space with rich, beautiful color, no matter what the season outdoors. Organic elements can be a simple reminder of nature's beauty or symbolize a more complex sentiment or allegory. A natural painting may be particularly refreshing for anyone who lives in an urban setting, providing a serene reminder of Earth's basic yet remarkable adornments.

Lisa Ambler recommends the following for the care and placement of natural paintings in oil:

- Oil paintings are very durable. Provided that the artist has properly varnished the dried oil paint, your piece should last a lifetime. Oil paint will even withstand touch, which makes it a nice option for children's rooms.
- Keep your oil painting clean by wiping it with a damp cloth periodically. Because oil is impervious to water, you won't damage your artwork.
- If you're commissioning a natural painting of a particular place, give the artist many photographs to work from. You should also discuss where the piece will hang in your home, whether you'd like it to hang vertically or horizontally, and what features you'd particularly like to see in the painting.

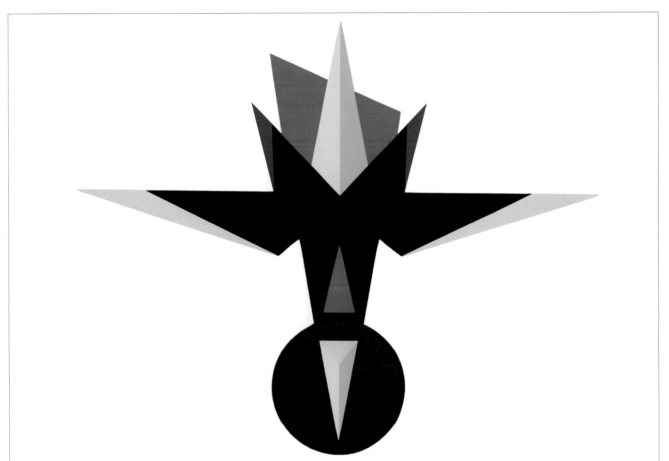

241

Top: *Feng Shui*, acrylic paint on wood, 75" x 92". Bottom left: *Gul Dukat*, acrylic paint on wood, 86" x 63". Bottom right: *Faros Lighthouse*, acrylic paint on wood, 89" x 51".

ANNE LEUCK FELDHAUS

ANNE LEUCK FELDHAUS STUDIO, LTD. ▨ 2156 NORTH OAKLEY ▨ CHICAGO, IL 60647
TEL 773-772-1085 ▨ E-MAIL ANNE@ANNESART.COM ▨ WWW.ANNESART.COM

242

Top: *And Then We Saw The Bird*, 2001, acrylic on canvas, 24" x 36". Photograph: Steve Greiner.
Bottom: *Eleven Tree Road*, 2002, acrylic on canvas, 12" x 24". Photograph: Glenda Kapsalis.

PATT DALBEY

PATT DALBEY STUDIO ▨ 10155 GREENBRIER ROAD #101 ▨ MINNEAPOLIS, MN 55305
TEL 952-525-5960 ▨ E-MAIL PDALBEY@MN.RR.COM ▨ WWW.PATTDALBEY.ARTSPAN.COM

243

Top: *Morning Light on Fields,* 2003, acrylic on canvas, 22"H x 28"W.
Bottom: *Purple Night Falling on the City,* 2003, acrylic on canvas, 20"H x 24"W. Photographs: Mike Habermann.

JASON WATTS

933 DIVISION STREET ■ OAK PARK, IL 60302 ■ TEL 708-386-2436 ■ FAX 630-858-5868
E-MAIL JEILERWATTS@EARTHLINK.NET ■ WWW.WATTSPAINTINGS.COM

244

Top: *The West Side*, 1999, oil on wood panel, 38" x 48". Bottom: *Highway Runs Through*, 2002, oil on canvas, 48" x 60". Photograph: Paul Doughty.

LISA KESLER FINE ART

LISA KESLER ■ 12015 THIRD AVENUE NW ■ SEATTLE, WA 98177
TEL 206-782-3730 ■ FAX 206-784-3304 ■ E-MAIL LISA@LKESLER.COM ■ WWW.LKESLER.COM

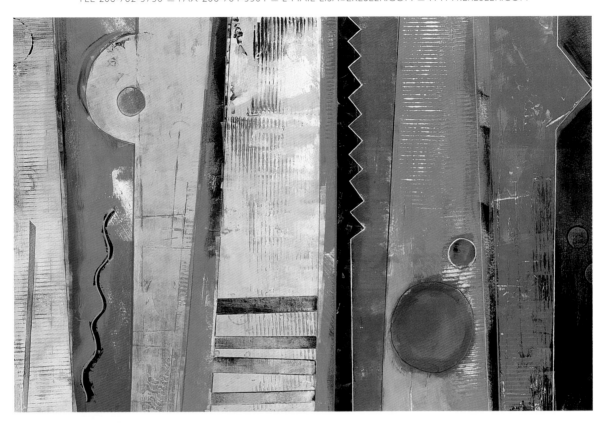

Top: *Structural Rhythm 3*, 2003, mixed media on paper, 24" × 36". Bottom left: *Opening Night*, 2002, hand-painted linoleum block print, 24" × 18".
Bottom right: *Tropical 2*, 2002, hand-painted linoleum block print, 19" × 15". Photographs: Art & Soul Photography.

JULIANN JONES

THE FLAT SPACE ■ 124 NORTH MAIN STREET ■ LIVINGSTON, MT 59047
TEL 406-223-0021 ■ E-MAIL JULIANN@JULIANNJONES.COM ■ WWW.JULIANNJONES.COM

246

Top left: *Houses*, 2003, casein on board, 20" x 20". Top right: *Florals*, 2003, casein on board, 20" x 20".
Bottom left: *Fish*, 2003, casein on board, 20" x 20". Bottom right: *Apples and Oranges*, 2003, casein on board, 20" x 20". Photographs: WMC Photography.

GWEN AVANT

157 JACKSON STREET ▓ MADISON, WI 53704 ▓ TEL 608-772-8192
E-MAIL GWEN_AVANT@TDS.NET ▓ WWW.GWENAVANT.COM

Top: Untitled, 2003, oil stick on paper, 9" x 18".
Bottom left: Untitled, 2003, acrylic and pencil on paper, 41" x 26". Bottom right: Untitled, 2003, acrylic and pencil on paper, 41" x 26". Photographs: Eric Tadsen.

CHRISTINE KUHN

FLOURISH STUDIOS ▓ 138 OLD GEORGETOWN STREET ▓ LEXINGTON, KY 40508
TEL/FAX 859-258-9277 ▓ E-MAIL INFO@FLOURISHSTUDIOS.COM ▓ WWW.FLOURISHSTUDIOS.COM

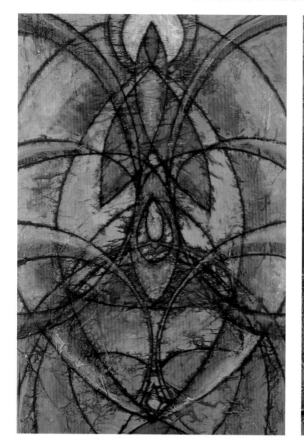

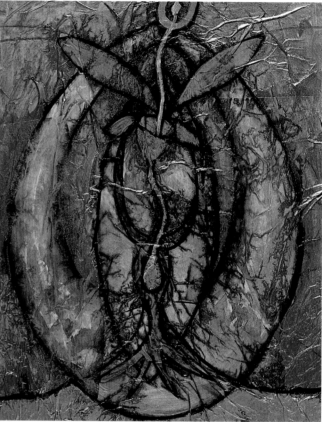

248

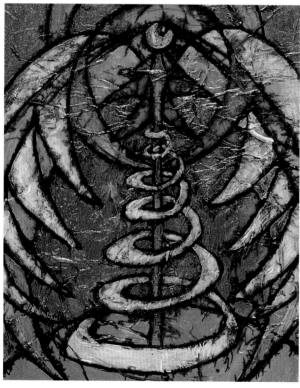

Top left: *Talisman for Career Advancement*, 2003, mixed media, 18" x 24". Top right: *Talisman for Abundance*, 2003, mixed media, 8" x 10".
Bottom left: *Talisman for Spiritual Ascent*, 2003, mixed media, 8" x 10". Bottom right: *Talisman for Remembrance and Forgiveness*, 2002, mixed media, 35" x 42". Photographs: Mary Rezny.

STEPHANIE ANN STANLEY

SANGITA ARTS ■ PO BOX 6571 ■ MALIBU, CA 90264
TEL 310-924-9630 ■ E-MAIL GITA03@AOL.COM ■ WWW.SANGITAART.COM

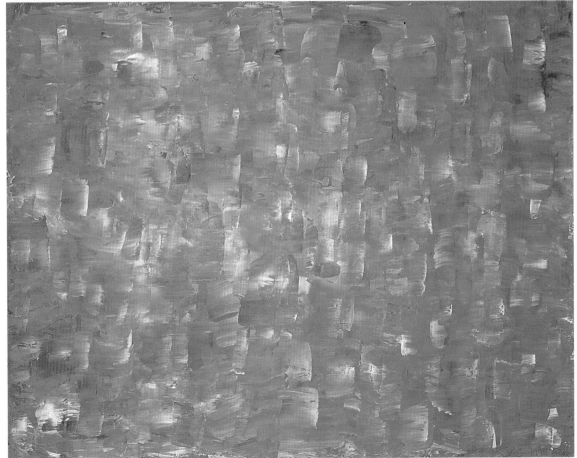

Top: *Desert Horizons*, oil on three canvases, each: 18" x 36" x 1". Bottom: *Nude*, acrylic on canvas, 28" x 22" x .75".

SIMONE DeSOUSA

SALT-MINE STUDIO—PAINTING ■ 1610 CLAY AVENUE ■ DETROIT, MI 48211 ■ TEL 734-417-3633
E-MAIL SIMONE@SALT-MINESTUDIO.COM ■ WWW.SALT-MINESTUDIO.COM

250

 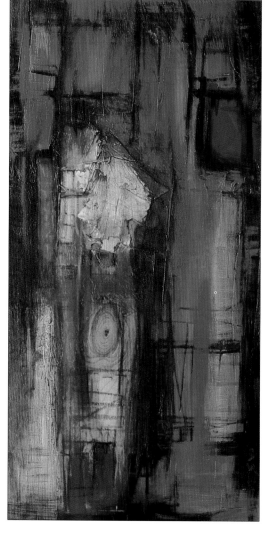

Top: *Construções* 2002, acrylic on board, 26" x 48".
Bottom left: *Revelando,* 2003, acrylic on wood, 48" x 24". Bottom right: *Beyond,* 2003, acrylic on wood, 48" x 24". Photographs: Dan O'Neill.

FRAN BULL

PO BOX 707 ■ 250 HERBERT AVENUE ■ CLOSTER, NJ 07624 ■ TEL 201-767-3726 ■ FAX 201-767-7733
E-MAIL FRANBULL@FRANBULL.COM ■ WWW.FRANBULL.COM

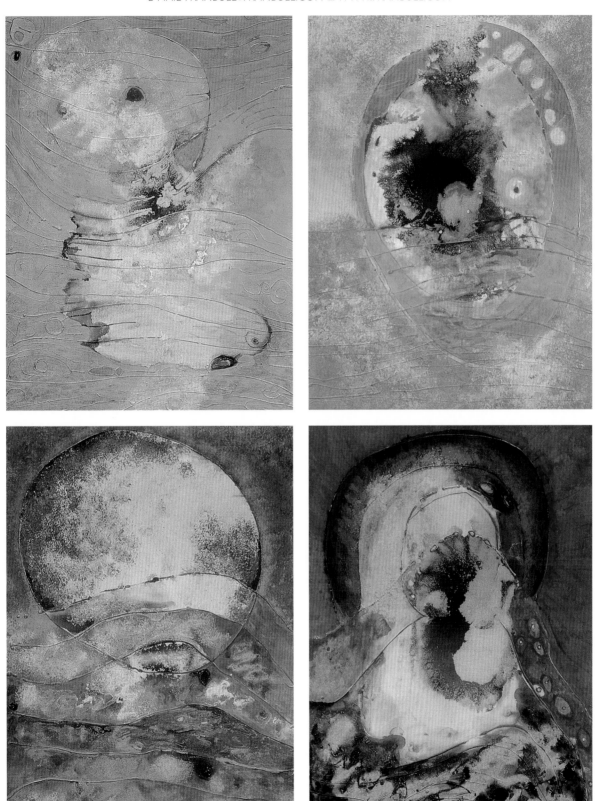

251

Top left: *Syzygy Series: Shekhinah*, 2002, mixed media on canvas, 48" × 36". Top right: *Syzygy Series: Sun in Earth*, 2002, mixed media on canvas, 48" × 36".
Bottom left: *Syzygy Series: Untune the Sky*, 2002, mixed media on canvas, 48" × 36".
Bottom right: *Syzygy Series: Sublime Disguise*, 2002, mixed media on canvas, 48" × 36". Photographs: David Allison.

GINNY KRUEGER

PO BOX 7174 ■ GRAYSLAKE, IL 60030 ■ TEL 847-899-3676
E-MAIL GINNY@GINNYKRUEGER.COM ■ WWW.GINNYKRUEGER.COM

252

Top: *Reconciled With the Rain V,* 2003, encaustic on wood panel, 32" x 56". Bottom: *Burgeonburn V,* 2002, encaustic on wood panel, 32" x 56". Photographs: Tom Van Eynde.

KAREN SCHARER

SCHARER FINE ART, INC. ■ 1150 SOUTH PEAKVIEW DRIVE ■ CASTLE ROCK, CO 80109
TEL 303-660-9037 ■ FAX 303-688-0367 ■ E-MAIL KAREN@SCHARERFINEART.COM ■ WWW.SCHARERFINEART.COM

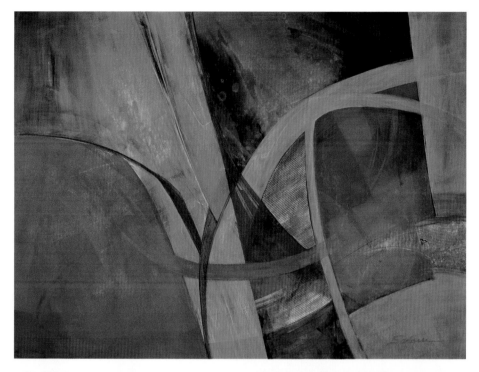

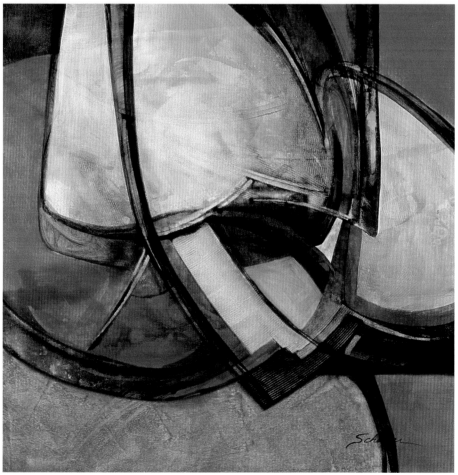

Top: *Microcosm*, 2003, acrylic on canvas, 36" x 48". Bottom: *Still Waiting*, 2003, acrylic on canvas, 36" x 36". Photographs: Brian Birlauf.

JOAN SKOGSBERG SANDERS

3156 STEVELY ▨ LONG BEACH, CA 90808 ▨ TEL 562-421-5369 ▨ FAX 562-435-2209
E-MAIL SKOGSBERG@AOL.COM ▨ WWW.GUILD.COM

Top: *Emmental*, 2003, acrylic, 24" x 24". Bottom: *Long Beach*, 2003, acrylic, 24" x 24".

254

MARY BURKE

MARY BURKE PAINTINGS ■ 723 SYCAMORE COURT ■ LINDENHURST, IL 60046
TEL 847-356-4133 ■ FAX 847-249-7171 ■ E-MAIL MEB12@ATTGLOBAL.NET ■ WWW.MARYBURKEART.COM

Top: *Units,* 2003, acrylic and pencil on canvas, 15" x 30". Bottom: *Frame Arranged,* 2003, acrylic and pencil on canvas, 24" x 30".

MICHELLE LINDBLOM

MICKART STUDIO ■ 3316 HACKBERRY STREET ■ BISMARCK, ND 58503 ■ TEL 701-258-1456 ■ FAX 701-258-2992
E-MAIL MICKART@BIS.MIDCO.NET ■ WWW.MICK-ART.COM

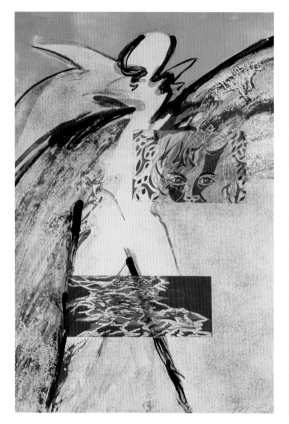

256

Top left: *Childhood Muse*, 2002, metal lithography and relief, 23" x 15". Top right: *Unresolved Dialogue*, 2003, mixed-media monotype, 24" x 18".
Bottom left: *Execution IX I I*, 2002, mixed-media monotype, 24" x 18". Bottom right: *Musical Dialogue—Strings*, 2002, acrylic on BFK Rives, 40" x 30".

BARBARA KELLOGG

304 MOTT ROAD ▥ FAYETTEVILLE, NY 13066 ▥ TEL 315-637-4743
E-MAIL DKELLOG1@TWCNY.RR.COM

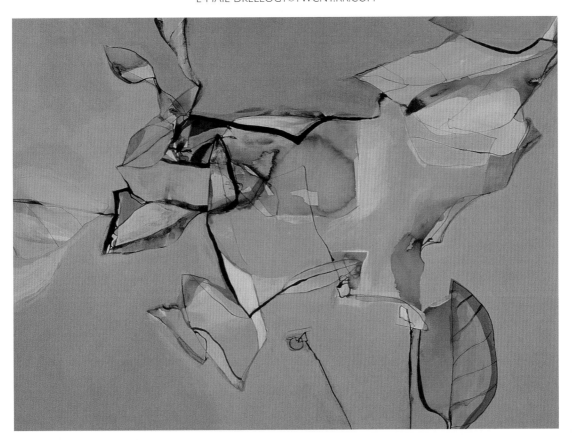

257

Top: *Citron,* 2002, acrylic, 21.75" × 29.25". Bottom: *Counterpoint,* 18.5" × 25.5". Photographs: Industrial Color Labs.

TERESA McCUE

75 ORCHARD STREET ▨ PORTSMOUTH, NH 03801 ▨ TEL 603-433-5331
E-MAIL TERESA@TMCCUEPASTELS.COM ▨ WWW.TMCCUEPASTELS.COM

258

Top: *Afternoon Light*, pastel on paper, 24" × 36", giclée also available, 20" × 30".
Bottom left: *Summer Reverie*, gouache and pastel on paper, 12" × 18".   Bottom right: *August Morning*, pastel on paper, 24" × 24".

MARLENE LENKER

MARLENE LENKER STUDIO ▦ 13 CROSSTREES HILL ROAD ▦ ESSEX, CT 06426 ▦ TEL 860-767-2098
E-MAIL LENKERART@PRODIGY.NET ▦ WWW.MARLENELENKER.COM

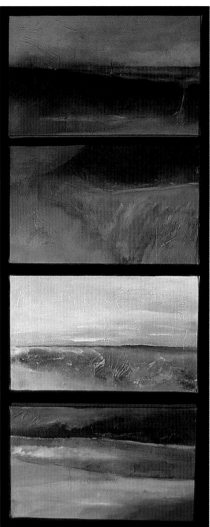

259

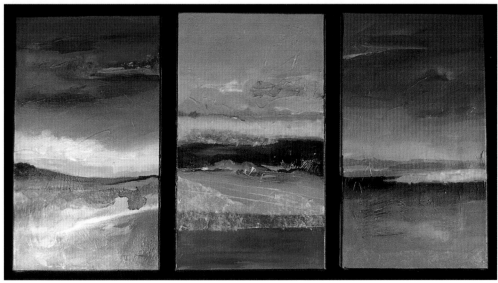

Top left: *River* series, 2003, acrylic and mixed media on canvas, each: 12" x 20".
Top right: *Island Vistas*, 2003, acrylic and mixed media on canvas, each: 12" x 20". Bottom: *Trio*, 2003, acrylic and mixed media on canvas, each: 20" x 12".

CLAIRE BURKE

CLAIRE BURKE FINE ART ■ 606 PINEVIEW DRIVE ■ SAN JOSE, CA 95117 ■ TEL 408-551-0606 ■ FAX 408-395-6563
E-MAIL CLAIRE@DIABLOGATO.COM ■ WWW.CLAIREBURKEART.COM

Top: *Skyline Ridge*, oil on canvas, 40" × 30". Bottom left: *Into the Forest*, oil on canvas, 40" × 36". Bottom right: *Tree Study*, oil on canvas, 16" × 22".

STEWART WHITE

STEWART WHITE STUDIOS ■ 1121 TYLER ■ ANNAPOLIS, MD 21403 ■ TEL 410-263-7465
E-MAIL STEWHITE30@EARTHLINK.NET ■ WWW.STEWARTWHITESTUDIOS.COM

261

Top: *Tree and Stone Fence with Power Lines*, oil on panel, 16" × 20". Bottom: *RR Crossing, The Plains, VA*, oil on panel, 16" × 20". Photographs: Gregory R. Staley.

CATHERINE A. MAHONEY

COLORFUL BRUSHES ■ 1058 OLD STONEHILL HIGHWAY ■ HERMANN, MO 65041
TEL 573-486-2444 ■ FAX 573-486-8919 ■ E-MAIL CAMAHONEY@KTIS.NET ■ WWW.COLORFULBRUSHES.HOMESTEAD.COM

262

Top: *Sequence Stands Below*, 1999, Forest Park, St. Louis, MO, oil, 12" × 36".
Bottom: *Laumeier Lilly Pond #II*, 2003, St. Louis, MO, acrylic, 5' × 7'. Photographs: Allied Photo: Mark McIntyre.

MICHAEL IRELAND

THE WATERCOLOR STUDIO OF MICHAEL IRELAND ▧ 7816 NEWBOLD ROAD ▧ CARY, IL 60013 ▧ TEL 847-516-4419
E-MAIL MI@IRELANDWATERCOLORS.COM ▧ WWW.IRELANDWATERCOLORS.COM

263

Top: *Against the Wind*, 2002, watercolor, 13" x 29". Bottom: *Prairie Path #3*, 2002, watercolor, 26" x 30".

STEPHEN HENNING

INSPIRATION PEAK PUBLISHING COMPANY ■ 22399 OAK HILL ROAD NW ■ EVANSVILLE, MN 56326
TEL 218-948-2288 ■ E-MAIL HENNING@GCTEL.COM ■ WWW.STEPHENHENNING.COM

264

Top: *River's Edge*, acrylic on canvas, 36" x 60".
Bottom: *Maple Creek*, acrylic on canvas, 20" x 64". Photograph: Jerry Mathiason.

NIKI GULLEY

6421 LARMANDA STREET ■ DALLAS, TX 75231 ■ TEL 214-803-5812 ■ FAX 214-823-8866
E-MAIL NIKI@NIKIGULLEY.COM ■ WWW.NIKIGULLEY.COM

265

Top left: *Golden Treetops,* 2003, oil, 60" × 48". Top right: *White Tulips,* 2003, oil, 40" × 30".
Bottom: *Hill Country Bluebonnets,* 2002, pastel, 18" × 24". Photographs: Scott Williams.

ANN MOTTERSHEAD BETAK

BLUE KUDZU STUDIO ■ 5710 INVERNESS PLACE ■ NORTHPORT, AL 35473
TEL 205-339-6524 ■ E-MAIL HBETAK@COMCAST.NET

266

Top: *In the Company of Clouds*, 2003, oil on canvas, 27" × 55". Bottom left: *Sansevieria*, 2003, oil on canvas, 50" × 52"
Bottom right: *Corn Plant*, 2003, oil on canvas, 48" × 48". Photographs: Rickey Yanaura.

LISA AMBLER

GRACE CREATIONS ■ 69 FALCON HILLS DRIVE ■ LITTLETON, CO 80126
TEL 303-683-0537 ■ E-MAIL ARTGLEE@AOL.COM ■ WWW.ARTISTSREGISTER.COM

Top left: *Warm and Dry*, oil on linen, 16" x 20". Top right: *Lilies and Bells*, oil on linen, 18" x 24".
Bottom: *Parade of Roses*, oil on canvas, 24" x 48". Photographs: Max Styles.com

KERRI LAWNSBY

PROLIFIC MUSE INC. ■ 59 WASHINGTON STREET SUITE 242 ■ SANTA CLARA, CA 95051
TEL 408-280-6960 ■ E-MAIL KERRI@PROLIFICMUSE.COM ■ WWW.PROLIFICMUSE.COM

268

Top: *Relaxing in the Garden*, 2003, pastel, 16" × 20". Bottom left: *Tulips in a Blue Vase*, 2003, pastel, 6" × 9".
Bottom center: *Rose-Ensconced Arbor*, 2003, pastel, 20" × 26". Bottom right: *Velvet Purple Iris*, 2003, pastel, 16" × 20". Photographs: Richard Johns.

CAROL CANNON

CAROL CANNON & CO. ▧ 32-45 37TH STREET ▧ ASTORIA, NY 11103
TEL/FAX 718-956-9334 ▧ E-MAIL CANNON33@EARTHLINK.NET ▧ WWW.CAROLCANNON.COM

269

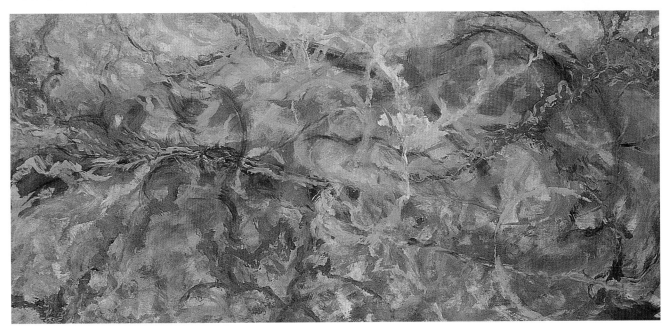

Top: *Breakthrough*, 2003, acrylic on canvas, 6.5' × 5'. Bottom: *On a Full Moon*, 2002, acrylic on paper, mounted on canvas, 5' × 2.5'.

ROBERT BISSELL

1572 62ND STREET ■ EMERYVILLE, CA 94608
TEL 510-547-1622 ■ E-MAIL ROBERTBISSELL@EARTHLINK.NET ■ WWW.ROBERTBISSELL.COM

Top: *Am*, oil on canvas, 46" x 64". Bottom: *The Dilemma*, oil on canvas, 28" x 40".

COLETTE ODYA SMITH

HOLLOW REED ARTS ▨ 2471 NORTH 81ST STREET ▨ WAUWATOSA, WI 53213-1012
TEL 414-476-7367 ▨ E-MAIL COLETTEODYA@SMITH.NET ▨ WWW.COLETTEODYA.SMITH.NET

271

Top: *Cave Point*, 2002, pastel over watercolor, 30" x 40". Bottom: *Field in Half Light*, 2003, pastel over watercolor, 20" x 30".

YVETTE SIKORSKY STUDIO

YVETTE SIKORSKY ▨ PO BOX 146 ▨ MOHEGAN LAKE, NY 10547-0146 ▨ TEL 914-737-5167

272

Top: *Summer Breeze*, 2003, Westchester, NY, acrylic, 30" × 40". Bottom left: *Crystal Ice*, 2003, Westchester, NY, acrylic, 18" × 24".
Bottom right: *Joy*, 2003, Westchester, NY, acrylic, 24" × 36". Photographs: Howard Copland, Peekskill, NY.

STEPHEN YATES

YATES ARTS ■ PO BOX 744 ■ PORT TOWNSEND, WA 98368
TEL 360-385-4330 ■ E-MAIL YATESART@OLYMPUS.NET ■ WWW.YATESARTS.COM

273

Top: *Water,* from *The Four Elements* suite, 36" × 80", 2002. Center: *Spring,* from *The Four Seasons* suite, 48" × 120", 2002.
Bottom: *Air,* from *The Four Elements* suite, 36" × 80", 2002. Three of ten oil on wood panels, University of Washington
and Cascadia College co-campus library, Bothell, WA. Giclée prints available. Photographs: Frank Ross.

CYNTHIA ROOT

VALHOLLOW STUDIO ▦ 192 G L MANOR ROAD ▦ MORRISONVILLE, NY 12962
TEL 518-561-6597 ▦ E-MAIL CINROOT@TOGETHER.NET

274

Top: *Firelight*, 2002, watercolor, 31"x 42". Bottom: *Light in the Forest*, 2001, watercolor, 22"x27". Photographs: Neal Keach.

GLENDA DIETRICH

CREATION ENERGY ART STUDIO ■ 5401 FRANKLIN STREET ■ LINCOLN, NE 68506 ■ TEL 402-483-5308 ■ FAX 402-483-5930
E-MAIL CREATIONENERGY@ALLTEL.NET ■ WWW.GLENDADIETRICH.COM

Top left: *Into the Depths*, watercolor, 26" x 16". Top right: *The Painted Wall, Black Canyon of the Gunnison, CO*, watercolor, 36" x 24".
Bottom: *Falls in Autumn*, watercolor, 18" x 26".

STEVEN BOONE STUDIO

STEVEN BOONE ▪ 124 LEAPING POWDER ROAD ▪ SANTA FE, NM 87508
TEL/FAX 505-992-8221 ▪ E-MAIL SB@STEVENBOONE.COM ▪ WWW.STEVENBOONE.COM

276

Top: *God's Land*, 2003, oil on linen, 54"H × 46"W. Bottom: *River Song*, 2003, oil on linen, 46"H × 54"W. Photographs: Donald Gregg, Hawthorne Studio.

STEVEN BOONE STUDIO

STEVEN BOONE ■ 124 LEAPING POWDER ROAD ■ SANTA FE, NM 87508
TEL/FAX 505-992-8221 ■ E-MAIL SB@STEVENBOONE.COM ■ WWW.STEVENBOONE.COM

Triumphant Light, 2001, mixed media on paper, 18" × 24". Photograph: Kim Kurian Photography.

277

SHANNON S. BUEKER

NOT NOW, KATO! FINE ART STUDIO ▨ 167 EDDIE PERRY ROAD ▨ PITTSBORO, NC 27312
TEL 919-542-0136 ▨ E-MAIL SHANNON@NOTNOWKATO.COM ▨ WWW.NOTNOWKATO.COM

278

Top left: *Pele Woman*, 2002, acrylic on canvas, 48" × 48". Top right: *Astro Scratching*, 2003, acrylic on canvas, 36" × 48".
Bottom: *Circus Horses*, 2002, acrylic on canvas, 48" × 60". Photographs: Diane Amato.

PAULA DES JARDINS

2400 KETTNER BOULEVARD STUDIO 213 ▨ SAN DIEGO, CA 92101 ▨ TEL 858-204-2636 ▨ FAX 619-231-1111
E-MAIL ART@PAULADESJARDINS.COM ▨ WWW.PAULADESJARDINS.COM

279

Top left: *It's All There*, 2003, oil on canvas, 24" × 30". Right: *Breath Inside I*, 2003, oil on canvas, 36" × 60".
Bottom left: *Rise Up*, 2003, oil on canvas, 24" × 36". Photographs: Gary Conaughton.

280

Red Sea #2, 2003, oil on canvas, 30" x 30".

PRINTS & DRAWINGS

ARTHUR STERN

ARTHUR STERN STUDIOS ■ 1075 JACKSON STREET ■ BENICIA, CA 94510 ■ TEL 707-745-8480
E-MAIL ARTHUR@ARTHURSTERN.COM ■ WWW.ARTHURSTERN.COM

282

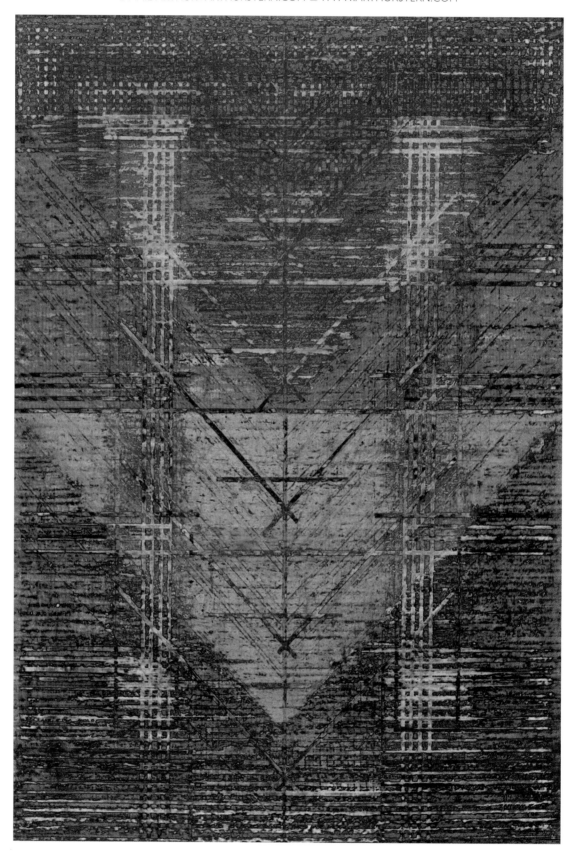

Prayer Sticks #3, mixed media on Arches paper, 46.5"H x 34"W.

ARTHUR STERN

ARTHUR STERN STUDIOS ■ 1075 JACKSON STREET ■ BENICIA, CA 94510 ■ TEL 707-745-8480
E-MAIL ARTHUR@ARTHURSTERN.COM ■ WWW.ARTHURSTERN.COM

283

Top: *Prayer Sticks # 2*, mixed media on Arches paper, 34"H x 46.5"W. Bottom: *Exotic Birds #16*, mixed media on Arches paper, 34"H x 46.5"W.

BJORN SJOGREN

STUDIO SKANDINAVA ▪ N4946 LEE ROAD ▪ ELROY, WI 53929
TEL 608-562-3722 ▪ E-MAIL INFO@STUDIOSKANDINAVA.COM ▪ WWW.STUDIOSKANDINAVA.COM

284

Top: *I'm Leaving.* Bottom: *Fragrance.*

HOLLY A. HEBEL

SUNSHINE ENTERPRISE ■ 823 CROOKS STREET ■ GREEN BAY, WI 54301 ■ TEL 920-437-6833

285

Top: *Purple House*, 2001, pastel, 22" × 30". Bottom: *Fire House*, 2003, pastel, 22" × 30".

YOUR ARTFUL HOME
Tips From the Artist

ARTIST: Kelly L. Fitzgerald

PROJECT: *Trees, Southern Italy* (left); *Ogliastro Marina, Italy* (right)

MEDIUM: Black-and-white gelatin silver prints

DIMENSIONS: 16" x 20" each

These photographs were purchased by some of Kelly Fitzgerald's longstanding clients for their Italian-themed home. Photograph by Cheryl Ramsay.

Photography is an increasingly collectible and popular art form. A photograph is typically not as expensive as other work for the wall, and is unique in its ability to capture an exact moment in time and place. You can collect photography according to theme (such as Italian architecture), or simply because the image appeals to you. The versatility of this medium allows for a wide range of artistic styles—from traditional black-and-white landscapes to digitally altered abstracts in bright colors. Photographer Kelly Fitzgerald prints her black-and-white photographs in numbered editions, and provides a certificate of authenticity with each piece.

Fitzgerald recommends the following tips for the care and placement of photographs in a home:

- Choose a frame that complements the subject matter of your photograph. Fitzgerald suggests simple black, silver or wood frames for black-and-white images. Frame your photographs behind glass. Plexiglass or acrylic alternatives tend to scratch easily.
- Do not display your photographs in direct sunlight or in settings that are very humid. These conditions can cause your photograph to fade or ripple.
- A bright wall treatment often helps set off a black-and-white photograph. Alternately, try displaying several smaller photographs as a group, or place a photograph on a shelf instead of hanging it on a wall.

BARBARA ZINKEL

BARBARA ZINKEL EDITIONS ■ 333 PILGRIM ■ BIRMINGHAM, MI 48009
TEL 248-642-9789 ■ FAX 248-642-8374

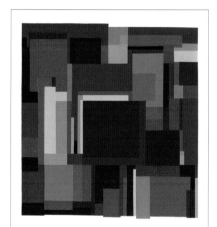

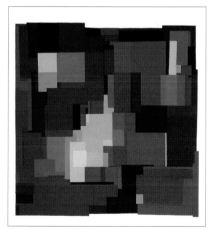

Top left: *Sunrise*, silkscreen print, 30" x 30". Center left: *Midday*, silkscreen print, 30" x 30". Bottom left: *Sunset*, silkscreen print 30" x 30".
Top right: *A San Francisco Night*, silkscreen print, 60" x 40", edition of 250. Bottom right: *BZ-R104*, custom wool area rug, available in 7' x 9', 9.6' x 12' and larger custom sizes.

288

Kyoto, limited-edition giclée print on watercolor paper, 24" x 24".

TIMOTHY DUFFIELD

LANDSCAPE IMAGES ■ 1551 JOHNNY'S WAY ■ WEST CHESTER, PA 19382 ■ TEL 800-368-1909 ■ FAX 610-431-4261
E-MAIL TIMD@TIMOTHYDUFFIELD.COM ■ WWW.TIMOTHYDUFFIELD.COM

289

Top: *Rio Grande Valley 2*, archival giclée print, 12.1" × 21.5".
Bottom: *Storm, Haweswater 1*, archival giclée print, 10.4" × 17.7".

SLICES OF LIFE BY G. BUTEYN

G. BUTEYN ■ 435 WEST MAIN STREET ■ BRANDON, WI 53919
TEL 920-346-5891 ■ E-MAIL GBUTEYN@CHARTER.NET

290

Top: *Neither Do They Reap*, 2001, canvas giclée, 12" x 40", framing by Vintage Works.
Center: *They Sow Not*, 2002, canvas giclée, 11" x 36", framing by Vintage Works.
Bottom: *Self-Disciplined*, 2003, canvas giclée, 12" x 40", framing by Vintage Works. Photographs: David Hornung.

ANNE ELLIOTT

ZIPPITY-DOO-DAH PRODUCTIONS ■ 7 CLEVELAND LANE ■ PRINCETON, NJ 08540
TEL/FAX 609-924-1911 ■ E-MAIL ELLIOTT_ANNE@HOTMAIL.COM

291

Top: *Her Bedroom*, archival digital print, 22" x 22". Bottom: *Mangroves #3*, archival digital print, 22" x 28". Photographs: Christopher Burke.

STEVE SMULKA

BROADBRUSH STUDIO ▪ 40 TRUESDALE LAKE DRIVE ▪ SOUTH SALEM, NY 10590 ▪ TEL 914-763-6824 ▪ FAX 914-763-0043
E-MAIL BROADBRUSHSTUDIO@HOTMAIL.COM ▪ WWW.BROADBRUSHSTUDIO.COM

Top: *Summer Solstice*, signed archival giclée print on canvas, 26" x 30", edition of 100. Bottom: *Porch Rail*, signed archival giclée print on canvas, 22" x 38", edition of 295.

PHOTOGRAPHS

GLEN WANS

WANS STUDIO ▩ 4001 BROADWAY ▩ KANSAS CITY, MO 64111 ▩ TEL 816-931-8906 ▩ FAX 816-931-6899
E-MAIL WANSSTUDIO@AOL.COM ▩ WWW.WANSSTUDIO.COM

294

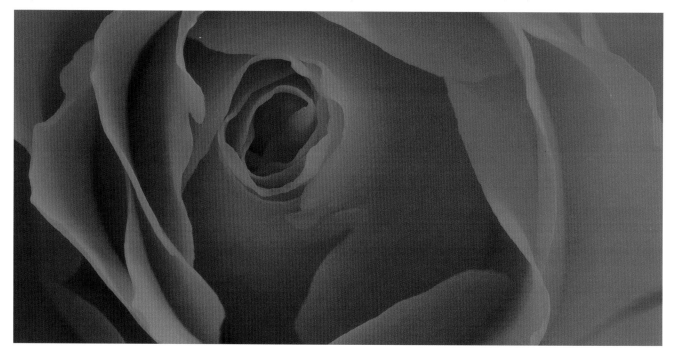

Top: *Four Pears*, limited-edition giclée print. Bottom: *Red Rose*, limited-edition giclée print.

TALIAFERRO JONES

TALIAFERRO JONES STUDIO ▨ 442 DUFFERIN STREET UNIT N ▨ TORONTO, ON M6K2A3 ▨ CANADA
TEL 416-538-3304 ▨ FAX 416-538-8272 ▨ E-MAIL TALIAFERRO@TALIAFERROJONES.COM ▨ WWW.TALIAFERROJONES.COM

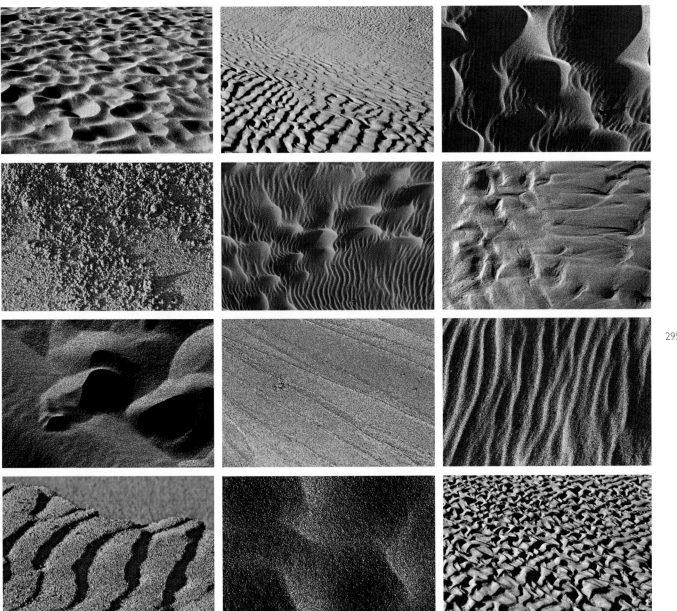

295

Sand, 2003, giclée print, 32.5" × 34".

LEN MORRIS

LEONARD MORRIS, INC. ■ TEL 917-992-3313 ■ E-MAIL LENMORRIS@EARTHLINK.NET ■ WWW.LENMORRIS.NET

From the *Lily* series: *Cloud Dancer*, photograph of a lily on paper, 16" x 20", limited edition of 125.

ADAM JAHIEL

ADAM JAHIEL, PHOTOGRAPHER ▓ 90 NORTH PINEY ROAD ▓ STORY, WY 82842
TEL 307-683-2862 ▓ FAX 307-683-2730 ▓ E-MAIL AJAHIEL@VCN.COM ▓ WWW.ADAMJAHIEL.COM

Top left: *Remuda, Spanish Ranch*, 1995, platinum print, 14" × 14". Top right: *Part of His String*, 1993, platinum print, 14" × 14".
Bottom left: *Top Hand*, 1996, platinum print, 14" × 14". Bottom right: *Remuda #1*, 1995, platinum print, 14" × 14".

RICHARD LA MARTINA

EARTHTONES PHOTOGRAPHY ▪ 43188 GUTHRIE DRIVE ▪ GAYS MILLS, WI 54631 ▪ TEL/FAX 608-872-2302
E-MAIL RICKSPIX@MWT.NET ▪ WWW.LAMARTINAPHOTOS.COM

298

Top left: *Calla Lilies*, 2002, photograph. Top right: *Petalscape*, 1998, photograph. Bottom: *Gatherings*, 2000, photograph.

MORGAN MILLER

MORGAN MILLER GALLERY ■ 650 MULLIS STREET SUITE 100 ■ FRIDAY HARBOR, WA 98250
TEL 360-378-3011 ■ FAX 360-395-7958 ■ E-MAIL MORGAN@MMGALLERY.COM ■ WWW.MORGANMILLERGALLERY.COM

299

Irish Jug, 2003, giclée print from digital photograph, image size: 26" × 42".

ALLAN BRUCE ZEE FINE ART PHOTOGRAPHY

ALLAN BRUCE ZEE ■ 2240 SE 24TH AVENUE ■ PORTLAND, OR 97214 ■ TEL 503-234-3211 ■ FAX 503-236-2973
E-MAIL ABZ@SPIRITONE.COM ■ WWW.ALLANBRUCEZEE.COM

300

Left: *The Red Door*, Marvau, Portugal. Right: *The Yellow Roses of Burano*, Burano, Italy.

ROB HYNER

HYNER PHOTOART ■ 30 ST. ANDREWS DRIVE ■ AVON, CT 06001
TEL/FAX 860-673-7502 ■ E-MAIL HYNERPHOTOART@AOL.COM ■ WWW.HYNERPHOTOART.COM

301

Top left: *Coal Yard Shovels*, 2001. Top right: *Scale with Pears*, 2002. Bottom: *Walk in the Park*, 2001.

DON HOUSE

HOUSE PHOTOWORKS ■ 16609 OLIVE ROAD ■ FAYETTEVILLE, AR 72701 ■ TEL 800-793-7229
E-MAIL DON@DONHOUSEPHOTOWORKS.COM ■ WWW.DONHOUSEPHOTOWORKS.COM

302

Top left: *Dickson Street*, limited-edition giclée print, 10" x 10". Top right: *Glenda's Garden, Zinnia*, limited-edition giclée print, 5" x 5".
Bottom left: *Denise and Wolf*, traditional chromogenic print, 10" x 10". Bottom right: *Sunset #1*, limited-edition giclée print, 10" x 10".

KELLY FITZGERALD PHOTOGRAPHY

KELLY L. FITZGERALD ▨ 1357 MONUMENT TRAIL DRIVE ▨ CHULA VISTA, CA 91915
TEL 619-934-6608 ▨ E-MAIL KELLY@KLFPHOTO.COM ▨ WWW.KLFPHOTO.COM

303

Top left: *Old Mine*, Bodie, CA. Top right: *Old Door*, Bodie, CA. Bottom: *Swan*, Ireland.

ALESSANDRA DeClARIO

ILLUMINATING REALITIES ■ PO BOX 2534 ■ MALIBU, CA 90265 ■ TEL 800-966-9646 ■ FAX 310-457-0458 (CALL FIRST)
E-MAIL DOCTORDADC@EARTHLINK.NET ■ WWW.ILLUMINATINGREALITIES.COM

304

Top: *By the Sea, By the Sea, By the Beautiful Sea, One, Malibu, CA*, 2003, giclée, 16" x 10.12". Bottom: *View From Zumirez Beach, Malibu, CA*, 2003, giclée, 15" x 9.88".

WOODLAND STUDIOS

GARY WALKER ■ CINDY LOU HOESLY ■ 4378 JORDAN DRIVE #4 ■ McFARLAND, WI 53558
TEL 608-576-6868 ■ FAX 608-835-8006 ■ E-MAIL GWALKER@WOODLAND-STUDIOS.COM ■ WWW.WOODLAND-STUDIOS.COM

305

Top left: *Spirit of the Forest*, mixed media on giclee print. Top right: *Hotel California*, mixed media on giclee print. Bottom: *Fall Calm Lake*, mixed media on giclee print.

KIRK L. WELLER

3439 NE SANDY BOULEVARD, PMB695 ■ PORTLAND, OR 97232 ■ TEL 503-230-9241
E-MAIL KWELLER@GORGEOUSPLANET.COM ■ WWW.GORGEOUSPLANET.COM

Top: *Christopher's Pond, Sauvie Island*, OR, 2000. Bottom: *Colorado River at Mouth of Blacktail Canyon*, Grand Canyon, AZ, 2001.

MURALS, TILES & WALL RELIEFS

MARY DENNIS KANNAPELL

5200 CHERRY VALLEY ■ PROSPECT, KY 40059
TEL 502-228-7750 ■ FAX 502-228-9515 ■ E-MAIL MDKART@AOL.COM

308

Top: *Emergence*, hand-painted ceramic tiles, bas-relief, each: approximately 12" × 12".
Bottom left: *Emergence* (detail). Bottom right: *Madonna*, hand-painted ceramic tile. Photographs: Geoff Carr.

KEVIN ALBERT YEE

TERRATHENA ▪ 41661 SIERRA DRIVE ▪ THREE RIVERS, CA 93271 ▪ TEL 559-561-2928 ▪ FAX 559-561-0122
E-MAIL TERATHEN@INREACH.COM ▪ WWW.TERRATHENA.COM

309

Top left: *T'ai Ye*, 2003, ceramic tile with copper mantel, 66"W × 12"D × 129"H.
Right: *The Sequoia*, 2002, ceramic tile, 66"W × 212"D × 22"H.
Bottom left: *The Pacifica*, 2001, ceramic tile with limestone, 70"W × 40"D × 65"H. Photographs: Jean Roy.

MARCIA JESTAEDT

13300 FOREST DRIVE ■ BOWIE, MD 20715-4391 ■ TEL 301-464-8513
E-MAIL FJESTAEDT@BOO.NET

310

Top: *Tropical Memories*, 2003, raku-fired clay tiles, 18"H x 36"W x .75"D.
Bottom left: *Jewels/Rubys*, 2003, raku-fired clay tiles, 38"H x 28"W x .75"D. Bottom right: *Windows of My World*, 2003, raku-fired clay tiles. Photographs: PRS Associates.

CHRISTOPHER GRYDER

METAMORPHEUS ■ 2718 CUMBERLAND STREET NW ■ ROANOKE, VA 24012 ■ TEL 540-366-9839
E-MAIL CHRIS@CHRISGRYDER.COM ■ WWW.CHRISGRYDER.COM

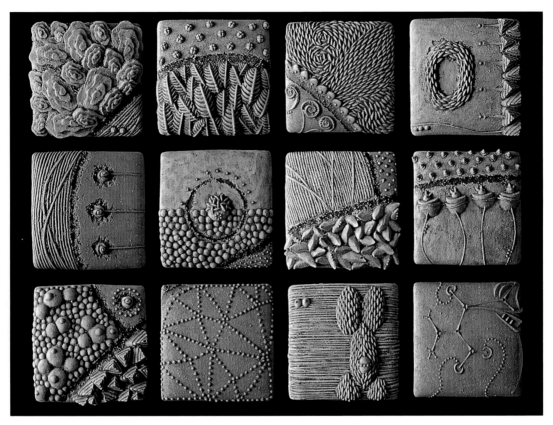

Top: Zuckoff commission, 2002, ceramic relief tiles, 12 tiles at 12" each.
Bottom: *Gyrus Meridian*, 2003, collection of corporate office, Ann Arbor, MI, ceramic relief tiles, 60 tiles at 12" each. Photograph: DC Goings.

BIG BANG MOSAICS

CYNTHIA FISHER ■ RFD BOX 87B ■ CHARLEMONT, MA 01339 ■ TEL/FAX 413-625-8204
E-MAIL BIGBANGM@BIGBANGMOSAICS.COM ■ WWW.BIGBANGMOSAICS.COM

Top: *Green Fox, Red Fox*, 2002, mosaic, 45" × 16.5".
Bottom left: *Tree of Life*, 2002, mosaic, 24" × 36". Bottom right: *Cardinals and Doves* (detail), 2001, mosaic, 68" × 22.5". Photographs: Ben Barnhart.

MERRYWOMAN STUDIOS

CHRISTINE MERRIMAN ▥ 7076 US ROUTE 4 ▥ PO BOX 153 ▥ BRIDGEWATER, VT 05034
TEL 802-672-2230 ▥ E-MAIL MERRYWOMAN@VERMONTEL.NET ▥ WWW.VERMONTEL.NET/~MERRYWOMAN

313

Left: *My Meiko*, 2001, handmade raku-fired tiles, 48"H × 32"W, mounted for hanging, weight is 40 lbs. Photograph: Don Ross ©2001.
Top right: *Dancing Samurai*, 2002, handmade raku-fired tiles, 36"H × 36"W, mounted for hanging. Photograph: Don Ross ©2001.
Bottom right: *Raging Samurai*, 2002, handmade raku-fired tiles, 54"H × 38"W, mounted for hanging, weight is 70 lbs. Photograph: David Siegle ©2002.

LISA BAILEY

1100 NE 99TH STREET ■ MIAMI SHORES, FL 33138
TEL 305-756-1724 ■ E-MAIL LBAILEY303@AOL.COM

314

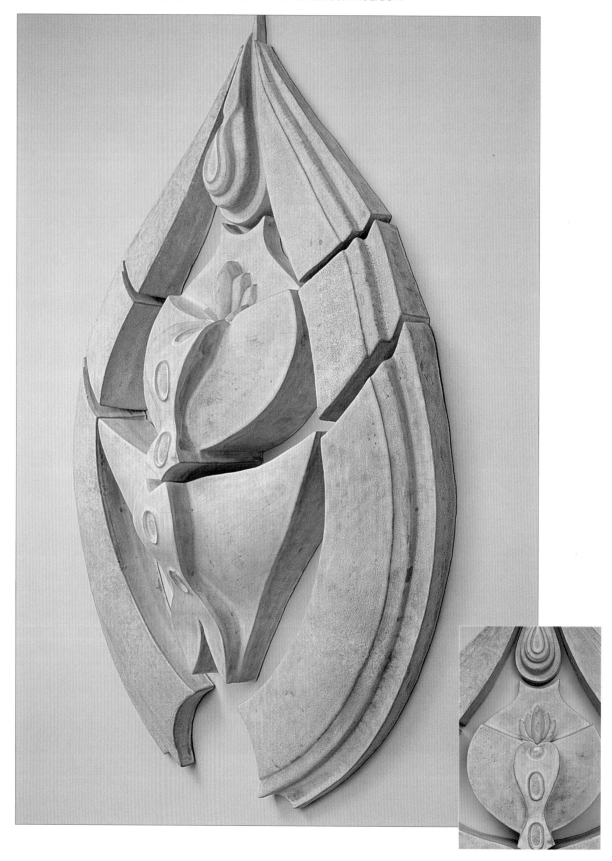

Lotus Heart Center, 2003, Ron Porter residence, glazed and sandblasted stoneware, 60"H × 36"W × 12"D.

BETTS ART

TODD BETTS ▥ 591 TOSCANNA COURT ▥ BRENTWOOD, CA 94513
TEL 925-803-0463 ▥ FAX 925-240-1426 ▥ E-MAIL TBETTSART@AOL.COM ▥ WWW.BETTSART.COM

315

Top left: Italian-themed garage, 2003, trompe l'oeil murals on limestone veneer. Top right: Interior fireplace, 2003, limestone veneer over existing firebox.
Bottom left: Chimney, 2003, limestone veneer over existing brick. Bottom right: Interior staircase, 2003, limestone veneer over interior drywall.

TIMOTHY HAGLUND STUDIO

TIMOTHY HAGLUND ■ 427 EAST STEWART STREET ■ MILWAUKEE, WI 53207
TEL 414-481-7007 ■ FAX 414-481-7006 ■ E-MAIL HAGLUND@TICON.NET ■ WWW.TIMOTHYHAGLUNDSTUDIO.COM

Trompe l'oeil mural and decorative painting, private residence foyer, oil paint on interior walls and ceiling, 600 sq. feet. Photograph: Steve Prost.

MIXED MEDIA

JOHN SEARLES

SEARLES SCULPTURE ■ 642 SOUTH LOMBARD AVENUE ■ OAK PARK, IL 60304
TEL 708-445-8711 ■ E-MAIL JOHNSEARLES@SEARLESART.COM ■ WWW.SEARLESART.COM

318

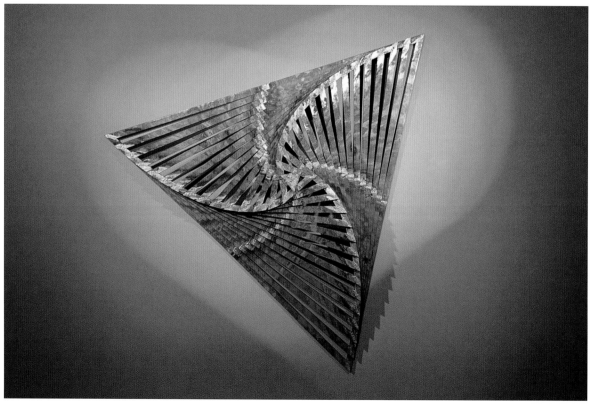

Top: *Wavy Weaving*, copper with fire colors, 36" x 60" x .5".
Bottom: *Rotating Triangles*, copper with brass and flame patina, 55" x 55" x 55" x 8".

LINDA LEVITON

LINDA LEVITON SCULPTURE ◼ 1011 COLONY WAY ◼ COLUMBUS, OH 43235
E-MAIL GUILD@LINDALEVITON.COM ◼ WWW.LINDALEVITON.COM

319

Patterns of Nature, etched copper, patina, each square 14" × 14" × 3" deep. Photograph: Flashback Photography.

YOUR ARTFUL HOME
Tips From the Artist

ARTIST: Lauren Camp

PROJECT: *Verde Que Te Quiero,* wall hanging

MEDIUM: Threadwork and ribbon on dyed and layered cotton and silk

DIMENSIONS: 39" x 72"

Fiber artist Lauren Camp created this piece for a client's bedroom. The wall hanging was made specifically to match the color scheme of the room and the dimensions of the wall space above the bed.

Fiber wall hangings can add warmth and softness to a space in ways that many other mediums cannot. From a distance, a fiber wall hanging can be viewed as a beautiful, formal piece of artwork, ranging in style from figurative to abstract and color from subdued to bright. When viewed up close, layers of various materials, stitching and other embellishments add another element of interest to the piece. Lauren Camp says that the detail of fiber wall work encourages the viewer to approach a piece and can be appealing on a very human and familiar level. Fiber wall hangings can also alter the acoustics of a space, absorbing some of the resonating sound—another way in which the medium adds to the coziness of a space.

Below are Camp's suggestions for the care and placement of fiber works for the wall:

- Keep your piece hanging, and though it may be tempting, don't handle it too often. Vacuum occasionally using a gentle attachment to keep the fiber free of dust.
- Consult the artist about the best way to hang your piece. Camp uses a wooden slat that slides into a fabric sleeve on the back of her pieces for wall hanging. She also suggests suspending fiber pieces from the ceiling with fishing wire to give the piece added depth and a nice drop shadow.
- If you're commissioning a fiber piece, you may want to provide the artist with paint chips, a theme or photos of the other pieces of artwork in the room. The medium is so versatile that it can be created to complement your room or stand out in beautiful contrast.

GLASSIC ART

LESLIE RANKIN ▦ 5850 SOUTH POLARIS #700 ▦ LAS VEGAS, NV 89118
TEL 702-658-7588 ▦ FAX 702-658-7342 ▦ E-MAIL GLASSICART@GLASSICART.COM ▦ WWW.GLASSICART.COM

321

Fusion glass with embellished elements and painted frame. Photograph: Sampsell & Preston Photography of Nevada.

ORKA ARCHITECTURAL ART GLASS

SHARON ROADCAP-QUINLIVAN ■ 1181 JENSEN DRIVE ■ VIRGINIA BEACH, VA 23451
TEL 757-428-6752 ■ FAX 757-428-6750 ■ E-MAIL LROADCAP@ORKA.COM ■ WWW.ORKA.COM

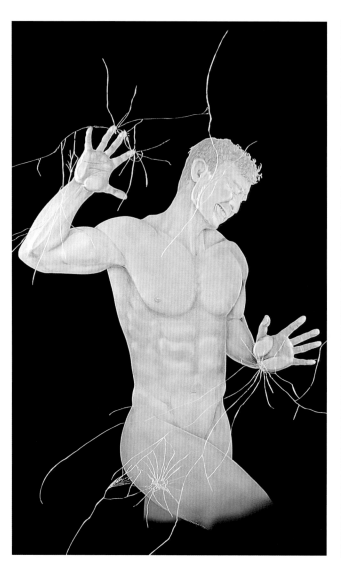

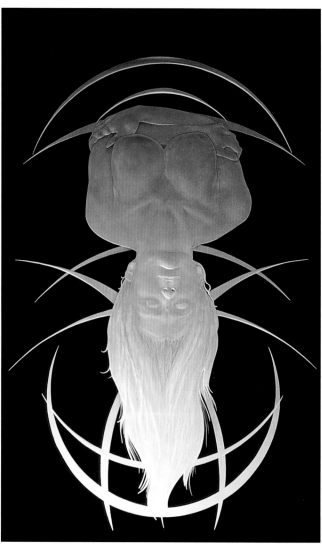

322

Left: *Male Bust Study*, .5" thick × 30"W × 47"H, starfire annealed glass, deep sculpture carved second surface with first surface details.
Right: *Female Bust Study*, .75" thick × 24"W × 31"H, clear annealed glass, deep sculpture carved second surface.

ORKA ARCHITECTURAL ART GLASS

SHARON ROADCAP-QUINLIVAN ▨ 1181 JENSEN DRIVE ▨ VIRGINIA BEACH, VA 23451
TEL 757-428-6752 ▨ FAX 757-428-6750 ▨ E-MAIL LROADCAP@ORKA.COM ▨ WWW.ORKA.COM

323

Female Portrait, .75" thick × 24"W × 36"H, clear annealed glass, deep sculpture carved second surface.

ZINGARA YULI GLASS STUDIO

39 LINCOLN PLACE ■ BROOKLYN, NY 11217 ■ TEL/FAX 718-857-1015
ZINGARA@ZYGLASSTUDIO.COM ■ WWW.ZYGLASSTUDIO.COM

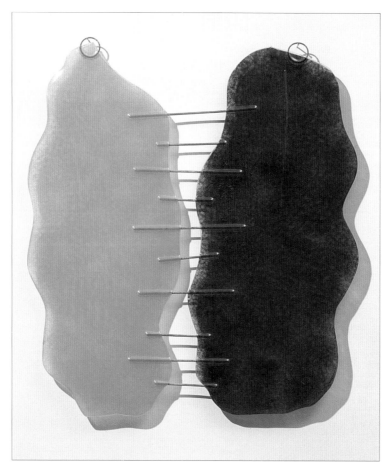

324

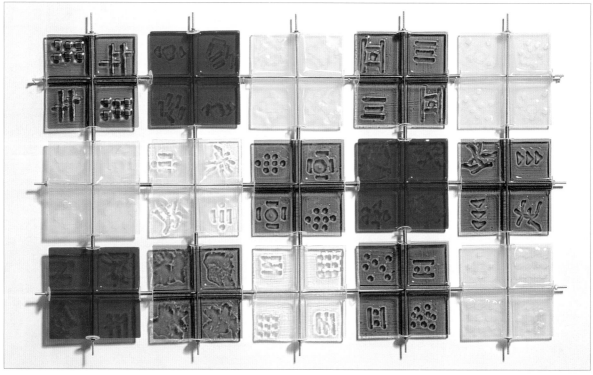

Top: *Lovers*, 1999, private residence, fused glass, 22" x 27". Bottom: Red and gray glass panel, private residence, fused glass, 48" x 30". Photographs: D. James Dee.

MEKO DESIGNS

MEG BRANZETTI ▨ VICKY KOKOLSKI ▨ 34-11 255 STREET ▨ LITTLE NECK, NY 11363
TEL/FAX 718-224-8078 ▨ E-MAIL MEKODESIGNS@YAHOO.COM ▨ WWW.MEKODESIGNS.COM

325

Shamshuni, 2003, fused glass and metal, 36" x 21".

STEPHEN J. DALY

31350 RANCH ROAD 12 SUITE C ■ DRIPPING SPRINGS, TX 78620
TEL 512-858-1995 ■ E-MAIL STEVE@DALY-STUDIO.COM ■ WWW.DALY-STUDIO.COM

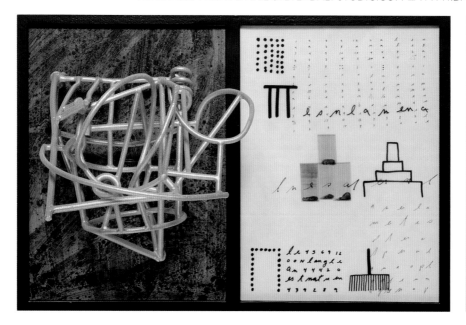

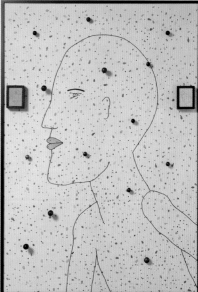

326

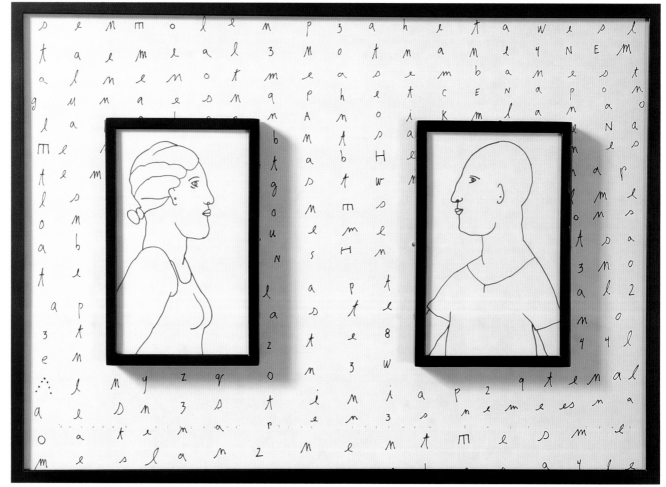

Top left: *Energy and Theory*, 2002, ink on Mylar, dye on cast aluminum and enamel on steel, 12" × 18" × 9".
Top right: *Afterthought*, 2002, ink on Mylar, dye on cast aluminum and enamel on steel, 66" × 45.75" × 4.5".
Bottom: *Encoded Dialogue*, 2002, ink on paper and Mylar, and enamel on steel, 20" × 28" × 2". Photographs: Brian Birlauf, Birlauf Steen Photo, Denver, CO.

L.P. GREGORY

1025 OAK VALLEY ROAD ■ SEDALIA, CO 80135 ■ TEL 303-663-4185 ■ FAX 303-663-4187
E-MAIL LP@LPGREGORY.COM ■ WWW.LPGREGORY.COM

327

Top: *Three Tenors*, 2003, copper, ceramic and fiber, 42"H × 39.5"W. Top right: *Flight of Fancy*, 2003, copper and ceramic, 36" × 36".
Bottom: *Sacred Plains*, 2003, copper, ceramic and fiber, 37"H × 49"W. Photographs: Chris Perez.

ALONZO DAVIS

5812 SIXTH STREET NW ▧ WASHINGTON, DC 20011 ▧ TEL 301-454-0433
E-MAIL ALONZODAVIS@YAHOO.COM ▧ WWW.ALONZODAVIS.COM

328

Iraq and You, bamboo with mixed media, 80"H x 40"W x 7"D. Photograph: Arron Levine.

ART QUILTS

LYDIA B. JOHNSTON

2375 SKIPAREE ROAD ▨ NORTH POWNAL, VT 05260 ▨ TEL 802-823-7713
E-MAIL ART@LYDIAJOHNSTON.COM ▨ WWW.LYDIAJOHNSTON.COM

330

Top: *Flash Point*, textile collage, 26" x 30". Bottom: *Didn't We Have Fun*, textile collage, 24" x 38". Photographs: Arthur Evans.

MICHELE HARDY

147 ACADIAN LANE ▦ MANDEVILLE, LA 70471 ▦ TEL 985-845-0792
E-MAIL MHARDY@MICHELEHARDY.COM ▦ WWW.MICHELEHARDY.COM

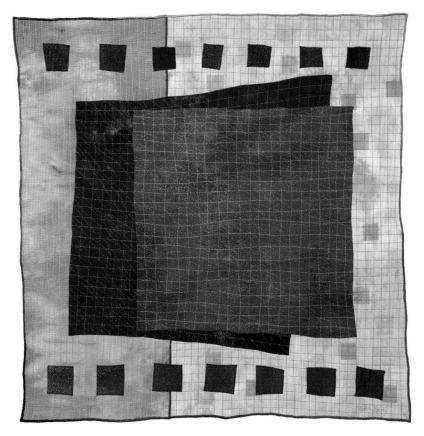

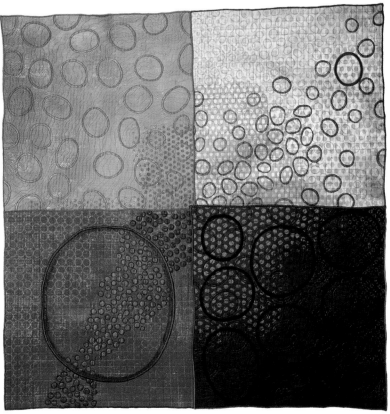

331

Top: *Colorfields: Carnelian*, 2002, 40" x 40". Bottom: *Geoforms: Porosity #6*, 2003, 48" x 48". Photographs: Jackson Hill.

MARILYN MERKT FELBER

COLLECTED WORKS—THE FINE ART OF FIBER ■ 1935 CEDAR STREET ■ BERKELEY, CA 94709
TEL 510-548-7129 ■ E-MAIL PFELBER@MINDSPRING.COM

332

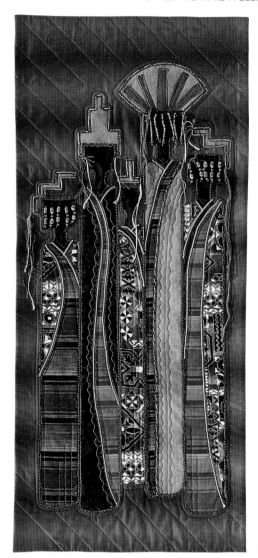

Top left: *Guardians II,* 1999, couched, beaded and quilted seven-layer appliqué, 39"L x 17"W.
Top right: *Beginner's Mind IV: Spring,* 1999, hand-painted and stenciled canvas with appliquéd, pieced and quilted hand-painted and commercial fabrics, 29"L x 14"W.
Bottom: *Beginner's Mind VII: Searching #170,* 2003, pieced and quilted composition with hand-dyed, batik and commercial cottons. Photographs: Don Tuttle@photography.com.

KIM RITTER

18727 POINT LOOKOUT ■ HOUSTON, TX 77058
TEL 281-333-3224 ■ E-MAIL KIM@KIMRITTER.COM ■ WWW.KIMRITTER.COM

Top: *Spark*, 16" x 16". Bottom: *Night Ponies*, 43" x 44".

DARCY YOUNG

DARCY'S DESIGNS ■ 12506 COUNTRY ARBOR LANE ■ HOUSTON, TX 77041 ■ TEL 713-983-9506 ■ FAX 713-983-9398
E-MAIL DARCY@DARCYSDESIGNS.COM ■ WWW.DARCYSDESIGNS.COM

334

Top: *Adrift*, 2002, silk, cotton, lame and crystal organza with metallic and silk threads, 25"W × 13"H.
Bottom: *Fireworks in a Black Hole*, hand-dyed and painted silk crepe with hand-beaded embellishments, 40"W × 31.5"H. Photographs: Mike McCormick.

BETH CASSIDY

BETH CASSIDY, LLC ▓ 4510 171ST AVENUE SE ▓ SNOHOMISH, WA 98290
TEL 360-563-0698 ▓ FAX 360-563-0697 ▓ E-MAIL BC@BETHCASSIDY.COM ▓ WWW.BETHCASSIDY.COM

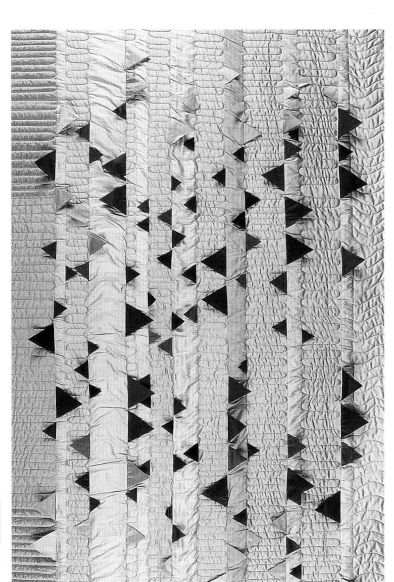

335

Top left: Embroidered metallic silk tissue pillows and comfort quilt, 1998. Photograph: Tom Collicott. Bottom left: King-size silk crazy quilt, 2002, 102" x 115". Photograph: Ron Sawyer. Right: Queen-size silk dragon-back quilt, 2003, 89" x 102". Photograph: Ron Sawyer.

JOY SAVILLE

244 DODDS LANE ▪ PRINCETON, NJ 08540 ▪ TEL/FAX 609-924-6824
E-MAIL JSAVILLE@PATMEDIA.NET ▪ WWW.JOYSAVILLE.COM

336

Top: *Lago di Como*, pieced cotton, linen and silk, 57" × 67".
Bottom: *Dogwood*, collection of Roger and Caroline Ford, pieced cotton, linen and silk, 62" × 79". Photographs: William Taylor.

BERRI KRAMER

BERRI KRAMER FIBER ART ■ FOUR EAST AVENUE ■ KENNEBUNKPORT, ME 04046
TEL 207-967-0118 ■ FAX 207-985-6333 ■ E-MAIL BERRIKRAMER_2000@YAHOO.COM ■ WWW.BERRIKRAMER.COM

337

Top left: *Random Order*, 2000, fiber, 27" × 31". Top right: *Hot Perspective*, 2002, fiber, 26" × 24".
Bottom: *African Jazz*, 2001, fiber, 38" × 24".

THERESE MAY

651 NORTH FOURTH STREET ■ SAN JOSE, CA 95112 ■ TEL 408-292-3247 ■ FAX 408-292-5585
E-MAIL MAYQUILTER@AOL.COM ■ WWW.THERESEMAY.COM

338

Tulip, 2003, puzzle interchange, machine appliqué with paint, 8' × 8', machine quilted by Jenny Michael. Photograph: Richard Johns.

TAPESTRY, FIBER & PAPER

JANNA BERNHEIM BERNSTEIN

CR8IVE PRODUCTIONS ▧ 319 FERNWAY COVE ▧ MEMPHIS, TN 38117
TEL 901-680-0812 ▧ FAX 901-722-4494 ▧ E-MAIL CR8IVEART@AOL.COM

340

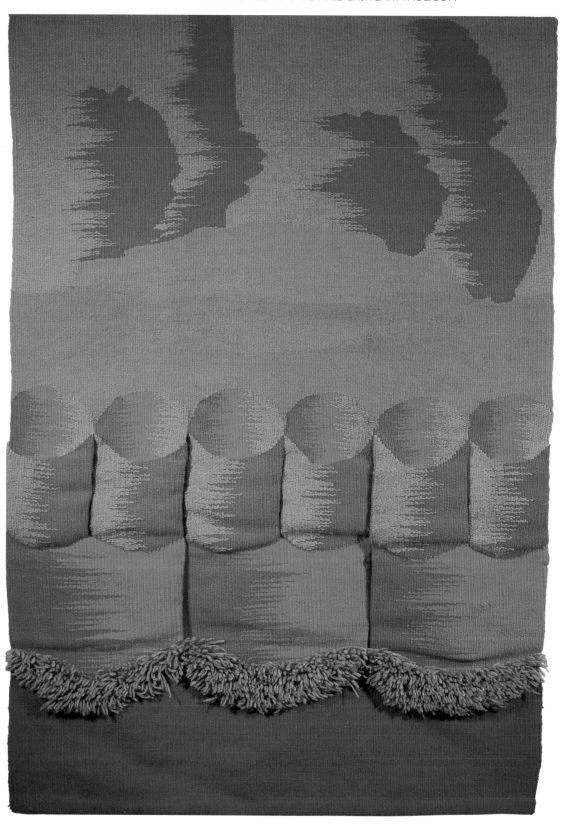

Windswept, collection of the artist, tapestry and double-weave tapestry, 5'H x 3'W. Photograph: Rod Long.

HOLLIE HELLER RAMSAY

1318 BIRCH DRIVE ■ BASKING RIDGE, NJ 07920
TEL 908-304-9155 ■ E-MAIL HOLLARTIST@AOL.COM

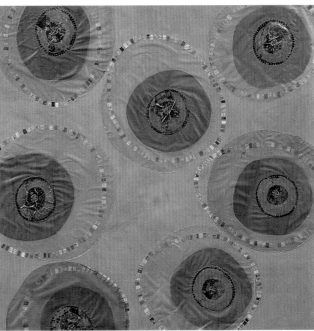

341

Top left: *Cellular Structures*, 2003, commission for Johnson & Johnson Ortho Biotech division, NJ, collaged stitched paper and fabric, paint and stretched canvas, 48" × 48".
Top right: *Surrounding*, 2003, commission for Johnson & Johnson Ortho Biotech division, NJ, stiffened and stitched fabric, stretched canvas and paint, 48" × 48".
Bottom: *New Directions*, 1993, painted paper, 36" × 46". Photographs: D. James Dee.

ELINOR STEELE

1345 PEARSON ROAD ■ NEW HAVEN, VT 05472 ■ TEL 802-545-2665
E-MAIL ESTEELE@GMAVT.NET

342

Top: *Reflections–San Jose*, handwoven tapestry, 27" x 44".
Bottom left: *Hay Barns 2*, handwoven tapestry, 21" x 15". Bottom right: *Composition with Barns*, handwoven tapestry, 36" x 18".

MYRA BURG

6180 WEST JEFFERSON ■ LOS ANGELES, CA 90016
TEL 310-399-5040 ■ FAX 310-399-0623 ■ WWW.MYRABURG.COM

343

Top left: *Sleeves of a Kimono*, wrapped fiber on copper, 4'W x 6'H. Top right: *Evie People*, wrapped fiber on burnished aluminum, 4'W x 6.5'H.
Bottom left: *Eclipse*, wrapped fiber on burnished aluminum, 5'Dia. , 3.8'Dia. and 2.3'Dia. Bottom right: *Jenny*, wrapped fiber on burnished aluminum, 3'W x 12'H.

BARBARA BARRAN

CLASSIC RUG COLLECTION, INC. ■ 1014 LEXINGTON AVENUE, 2ND FLOOR ■ NEW YORK, NY 10021
TEL 212-249-6695/888-334-0063 ■ FAX 212-249-6714 ■ E-MAIL INFO@CLASSICRUG.COM ■ WWW.CLASSICRUG.COM

344

Medallion, from Gee's Bend Quilt Collection, 2003, hand-tufted New Zealand wool, 70" x 87". Photograph: Hossein Montazaran.

LAURENCE BRANESCO

ART & DESIGN ▪ 6851 NORTH NW HIGHWAY
CHICAGO, IL 60631 ▪ TEL/FAX 773-631-1682

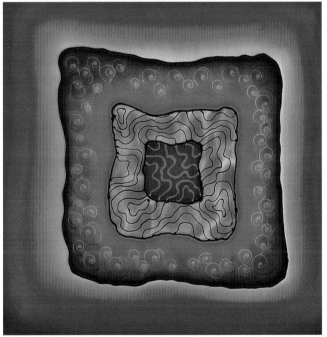

345

Top left: *Genesis*, 45" x 45".
Right: *Metamorphose*, 45" x 74". Bottom left: *Genesis* (detail).

LAUREN CAMP

25 THERESA LANE ■ SANTA FE, NM 87507 ■ TEL 505-474-7943
E-MAIL LAUREN@LAURENCAMP.COM ■ WWW.LAURENCAMP.COM

346

Top: *Interlude #4*, 2002, threadwork on dyed and layered cotton, 22" x 21", framed with suede mat.
Bottom: *Interlude #14*, 2003, threadwork and paint on layered cotton, 22" x 21", framed with linen mat. Photographs: Hawthorne Studio.

GRETCHEN ROMEY-TANZER

TANZER'S FIBER WORKS ▓ 33 MONUMENT ROAD ▓ ORLEANS, MA 02653
TEL 508-255-9022 ▓ E-MAIL ROMEYTANZER@COMCAST.NET

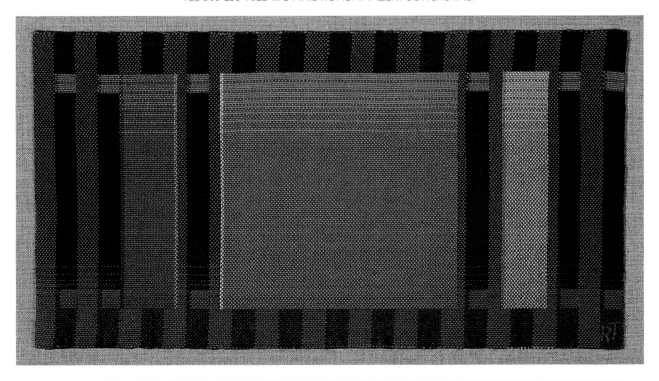

Top: *Blue Note*, 2003, woven cotton thread, 8" x 15". Bottom: *Regular Beat*, 2003, woven cotton thread, 20" x 27". Photographs: Rodney Whitelaw.

OUT OF THE MAINSTREAM DESIGNS, INC.

CHRISTINE L. KEFER ■ 107 SOUTH SECOND STREET ■ GENEVA, IL 60134
TEL 630-232-2419 ■ FAX 630-232-2491 ■ E-MAIL C.KEFER@WORLDNET.ATT.NET

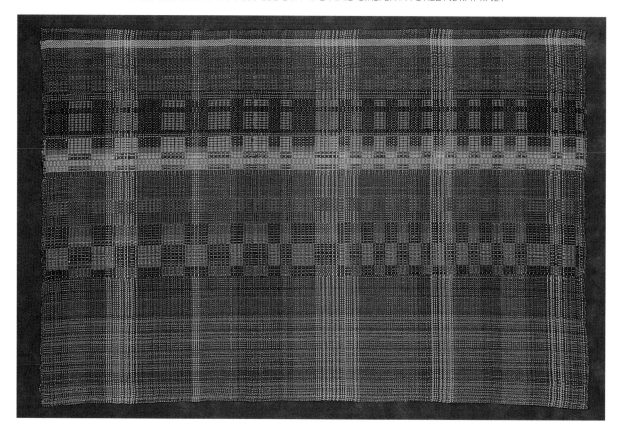

348

Top: Handwoven, multi-colored panel, 100% cotton, framed and matted. Bottom: Horizontal wall piece, handwoven, bias-cut fabric strips, 32" x 60".

PAVLOS MAYAKIS

4015 MATCH POINT AVENUE ■ SANTA ROSA, CA 95407 ■ TEL 707-578-4621 ■ 866-629-2547 (TOLL FREE)
E-MAIL PAVLOS@PAVLOSMAYAKIS.COM ■ WWW.PAVLOSMAYAKIS.COM

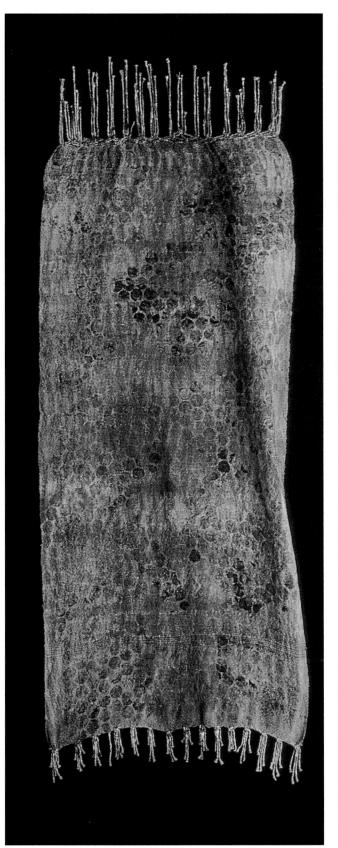 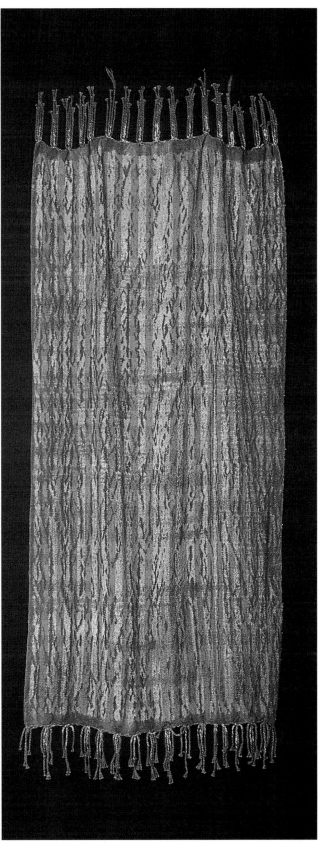

349

Left: *Shibori Bingo*, 2001, handwoven, dyed and stamped, 28" x 60". Right: *Ethno Shibori*, 2002, handwoven, dyed and over-dyed, 28" x 60". Photographs: Black Cat Studios.

LISA AND LORI LUBBESMEYER

LUBBESMEYER FIBER STUDIO ■ 550 SW INDUSTRIAL WAY STUDIO #47 ■ BEND, OR 97702
TEL 541-330-0840 ■ FAX 541-330-0841 ■ E-MAIL LUBBESMEYER@LUBBESMEYERSTUDIO.COM ■ WWW.LUBBESMEYERSTUDIO.COM

350

Top: *Savoring the Summer*, 2002, private collection, fiber appliqué, 24" × 26".
Bottom: *Cobblestones and Alleyways*, 2002, private collection, fiber appliqué, 24" × 26". Photographs: Petronella J. Ytsma.

NANCY EGOL NIKKAL

22 DOGWOOD LANE ▩ TENAFLY, NJ 07670 ▩ TEL 201-568-0159 ▩ FAX 201-568-0873
E-MAIL NANCY@NIKKAL.COM ▩ WWW.NIKKAL.COM

351

Top: *Dream Painting*, 1995, collage and acrylic on paper, 22" × 30". Bottom: *Boys and Girls*, 2000, collage and acrylic on paper, 14" × 18". Photographs: John Ferrentino.

MARILYN FORTH

BAYBERRY ART STUDIO ■ 7658 HAYLAGE CIRCLE ■ BALDWINSVILLE, NY 13027
TEL 315-638-3666 ■ FAX 315-458-0913 ■ E-MAIL WFORTH@TWCNY.RR.COM

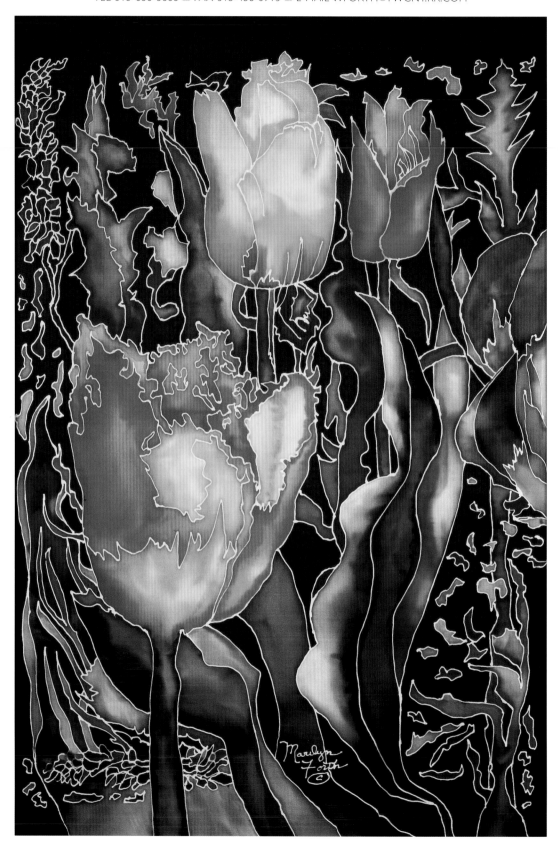

352

Tulips, painted batik, 25" x 35". Photograph: Anthony Potter.

KATE MILLER STUDIO

KATE MILLER ■ PO BOX 803 ■ LAKE OSWEGO, OR 97034 ■ TEL 503-534-1010
E-MAIL INFO@KATEMILLERSTUDIO.COM ■ WWW.KATEMILLERSTUDIO.COM

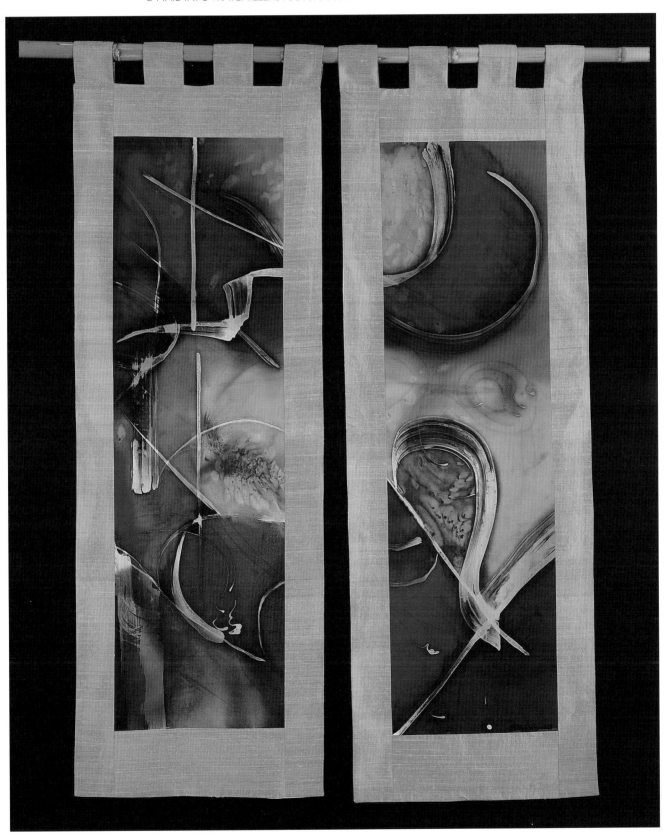

353

Persephone's Journey, 2003, batiked silk fiber art, total diptych: 54"H × 40"W. Photograph: Keith Krumbein.

ELLEN MEARS KENNEDY

6500 BROXBURN DRIVE ▨ WEST BETHESDA, MD 20817
TEL 301-320-9014 ▨ E-MAIL EMEARSKENN@AOL.COM

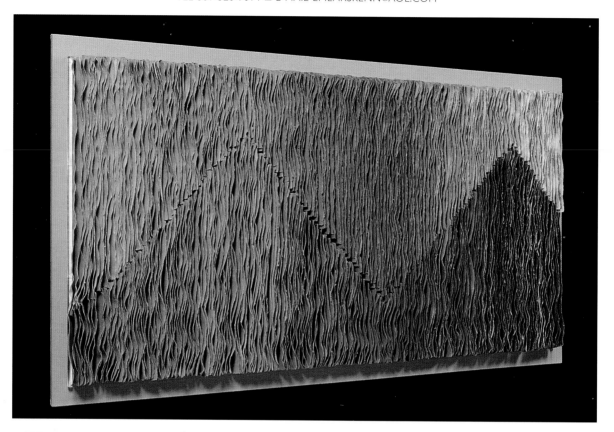

354

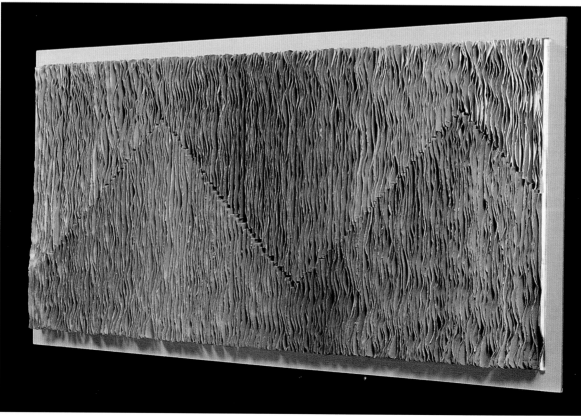

Top: *Two Peaks* (left view), 2003, handmade paper, 66"W × 36"H × 3"D. Bottom: *Two Peaks* (right view). Photographs: PRS Associates.

MEG BLACK HANDMADE PAPER PAINTINGS

MEG BLACK ■ 48 PROSPECT STREET ■ TOPSFIELD, MA 01983
TEL/FAX 978-887-8670 ■ WWW.MEGBLACK.COM

355

Top: *Seaside Garden*, 2003, handmade paper, 20" × 40".
Bottom: Untitled (house portrait), 2002, handmade paper, 40" × 55" (unframed). Inset: House depicted in the portrait. Photographs: Eric Roth Photography.

ALICE VAN LEUNEN

VAN LEUNEN STUDIOS ▪ 9025 SE TERRACE VIEW COURT ▪ AMITY, OR 97101
TEL 503-835-7717 ▪ FAX 503-835-7707 ▪ E-MAIL AVANLEUNEN@MSN.COM ▪ WWW.ALICEVANLEUNEN.COM

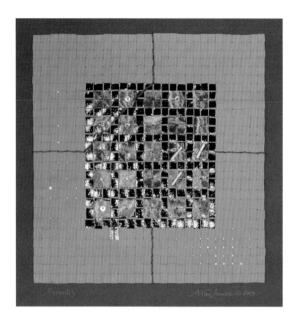

356

Top left: *Mementos*, 2003, woven paper with paint, metallic foil, metallic fabric, collage, mother-of-pearl, bone and stitchery, 21" × 20".
Right: *Mihrab*, 2001, woven paper with paint, metallic foil, fabric, collage and stitchery, 40" × 26".
Bottom left: *Log Cabin Study #2*, 2003, woven paper with paint, metallic foil, fabric, collage and stitchery, 23" × 22".

NANCY A. GEZELLA

847 BASEL STREET ■ DE PERE, WI 54115
TEL 920-336-7102 ■ E-MAIL GIZ4G@AOL.COM

Top: *Birds' Nests*, handmade paper, colored pencil and mixed media, 30"H × 42"W. Photograph: Larry Sanders.
Bottom: *Triple Leaf*, handmade paper and mixed media, 26"H × 42"W. Photograph: Michio Sano-Giles.

RESOURCES

Helen Vaughn, *Pears and Lemons*, pastel still life. Photograph: Doug Brewster.

ARTIST STATEMENTS

AEOLIPILES
Sculpture
Page 196

Tiara is one of a number of kinetic steam-driven glass sculptures called aeolipiles by their inventor, Hero of Alexandria (1st century, BC). They are also called Hero's Engines, though they weren't used as mechanical labor, but to create magical effects for temple worship. The Alexandrians used boiling water under pressure and fuel to make bronze snakes appear to hiss, or thrones appear to levitate; my pieces use distilled water and denatured alcohol to create the same effect. To me they are beautiful, contemplative sculptures in which cause and effect are visible as familiar processes.

AKYROS DESIGN
Furniture/Garden Sculpture
Pages 99, 209

In 1988 I met George Pratt, a sculptor who was preparing to fly to Baffin Island to train ten Inuit master carvers. I hitched a ride to the North Pole and carved my first marble sculpture there. I spent six months with George in Vancouver before going to Italy in search of my own place in the sculpting community. While pedaling my Cannondale in Pietrasanta, searching for a chance to carve with the masters, I found the Giuseppe Giannini Studio. The Giuseppe brothers said, "No beginners", until Steffan saw my bike. Two hours later I had traded my Cannondale for a 100-pound block of marble and a home for four months. My art is the art of nature. My tools are the spirit of the earth. My freedom is in each piece that I create.

ALLAN BRUCE ZEE
FINE ART PHOTOGRAPHY
Photographs
Page 300

When I was 18 months old, my brother lifted me up to the window to see a magnificent rainbow over Lake Michigan. At that moment, my passion for color was imprinted upon me. Photography has been my vehicle for exploring that passion and sharing it with others. It has taken me around the globe for the past 34 years, interpreting landscapes, architecture, textures and abstractions. I have been blessed with an enthusiastic response that finds my prints in homes, offices, medical facilities, and corporate and public collections on six continents. Prints, signed and numbered, range from 10" x 14" to 40" x 60" and are priced from $250 to $1,500, depending on size and paper type. Slide, color copy or electronic portfolios are available upon request.

ROBERT E. ALLEN
Objects
Page 150

Ancient technology has always been a fascination of mine; it has truly inspired this latest evolution of my work. Classical craftsmanship and timeless, innovative design have been my foremost goals in a 30-year career that has encompassed jewelry design, detailed naturalist bronze sculpture, and functional art and craft. I feel that technology is the conduit between my concepts and their tangible realization. I handcraft each piece utilizing a variety of methods, including metal casting and fabrication, glass casting, original patinating and woodworking.

LISA AMBLER
Paintings
Pages 9, 240, 267

Shades of blue with yellow and white: a flutter of daisy petals against swirls of cobalt and ultramarine. Beige, black and brown: plumes of pampas grass at midnight. Distracted realism: paintings with recognizable forms that are neither entirely realistic nor completely abstract, a new style of art I've invented to satisfy my desire for creativity and the decorative needs of clients. Given a specific size and color scheme, I can create commissioned works for any decor. It is my equal joy to paint and then to see my work at home in another's environment. Whether a children's portrait or "playscape," a scriptural allegory or distracted realism, it gives me the greatest satisfaction to fashion unique works of art that will become a part of life.

ROBIN ANTAR
Sculpture
Page 187

I carve common American objects out of stone, "freezing" them in time and creating a visual record of our culture. The life-size stone carvings are highly realistic, confounding the eye and defying the viewer to discern the sculpture from the original object. I use tints from custom-made stains and incorporate paints, plastics, gold leaf and other materials into my work. Projects include: DIESEL Jeans show, 2002, Soho, NY. Commissions include: Sketchers Boots USA, Inc.; Chateau Haut-Brion. Exhibitions include: *The Really Big Shoe Show*, 2000, City Museum, St. Louis, MO; *More Artistic License*, 1999, Nabisco Corporate Gallery, East Hanover, NJ. My work has been featured in previous GUILD sourcebooks.

STACIE ANTHONY
Objects
Page 153

I am inspired by the beauty of nature, and also by the human form and emotions. The tree, which is one of my favorite subjects, holds much significance for me as a vital, vertical force of life; my work with the tree form focuses on the interconnections in nature. Because I draw on my own experiences of being a human, an artist and a woman, I often explore themes of motherhood, creation and freedom, utilizing the female form in varying degrees of abstraction. Sculptures include stylized works in stone, wire, cement and mixed media. Preparatory sketches are available as finished drawings in charcoal on paper.

KATHLEEN ASH
Objects
Page 138

Glass has always fascinated me. As a girl growing up in New England, I played in the colored light from church windows. In my work now, I love combining clean, modern design with the very old techniques of fusing glass. We've worked in many techniques in glass: etched, leaded, fused, laminated and painted. My studio makes everything from small dishes to 90' walls to scores of light fixtures. We have a large production line, but most of our work is custom commissioned. I am president (we say Queen) of the Architectural Artisans Collaborative. We are dedicated to bringing beauty into the fabric of architecture that we all live in every day. I love that idea. We live in Austin, Texas. Yee-Haw!

MARJORIE A. ATWOOD
Paintings
Page 224

My unique vision is expressed in my widely recognized fine art pieces. My diverse work ranges from large wall paintings and murals to small, three-dimensional multimedia pieces. In many of my creations, I start with the tradition of the figure, then proceed to incorporate a rich vocabulary of surface patterns and textures to re-orient an appreciation of that tradition, as in my multimedia treatment of the myth of Icarus. My color palette can be brilliant and vital with its rich, unashamed reds and golds, or can achieve a quiet intensity by means of softly chiming pale blues and soft silvers. Commissions are welcome. My work is found in both private and corporate settings. Pricing and additional visuals are available upon request.

ARTIST STATEMENTS

GWEN AVANT
Paintings
Page 247

I believe that art has a job: to transform us, soften and comfort us, give us cues and encourage us to notice who we are. Through painting, I wrestle with what I don't understand, what is difficult to accept, what is unknown and will remain unknown. My process is intuitive. Decisions about form or meaning are not made beforehand but evolve as the work progresses. My paintings are abstract. I may use some representational images, but then I mess with them, float them, erase them. I don't want to force the viewer into a solid place or time. I want to provide a visual space for contemplation. Hopefully, the viewer's own meanings and questions will emerge through the exchange. And so the creative process continues.

CHAD AWALT
Sculpture
Page 179

I was inspired by my grandfather to pursue woodcarving from an early age. I studied anatomy at the University of Colorado and have spent the last 20 years expanding my knowledge of classical design and traditional art. My abilities range from classical woodcarving to traditional oil painting, with a specialty for rendering the human figure. My flowing lines and light edges bring life and emotion to these spectacular life-size human forms. For over ten years, I have been producing beautiful furniture and creating works of art that are sought after by clients and galleries all over the country. My work can be found in many corporate and private collections.

ARYA AZADI
Sculpture
Pages 16, 177

It is my love for Nature and my reverence for Spirit that guide me through the process of melting marble and metal. May my work lead to more true beauty in this troubled world. May it instill desires within man to be quiet, still and silent. May our architects and designers realize their power and influence, their overwhelming significance in the lives of today's turbulent world. May they truly realize their responsibility to design sacred areas in our homes, inner sanctums in our workplaces, areas for reflection, tranquility and stillness ... where one may go to gaze upon glistening stone and listen to trickling waters, allowing for that quiet inner voice of wisdom and truth to come through. My art is that which leads me through it all.

BADMAN DESIGN
Furniture
Page 85

Badman Design specializes in custom design items. All our work is created by hand in our 5,000-square-foot design studio in Grand Forks, ND. In business since 1988, I now have commercial, residential and liturgical pieces across the United States. Pieces range from cabinets, mirrors, benches, tables and lamps to wine racks, bar tops and light switch plates. My work is constructed from metal and sometimes also incorporates wood and/or clay. Since every piece is built according to the wishes of the client, the result is work that can fit into any contemporary space—and is typically the focus of the room for which it was designed. Each piece reflects, therefore, a one-of-a-kind statement from the client.

LISA BAILEY
Murals, Tiles & Wall Reliefs
Page 314

My ceramic wall sculptures have a dynamic visual presence, while simultaneously expressing energies of the heart. They are created with the intention of uplifting and inspiring all who view them. Undulating, pneumatic forms with graceful lines and fluid movement have been essential elements in my work. Using organic, abstract forms, combined with an architectural approach, I can express content of a mythical nature. I currently attend graduate school, selling my work out of regional galleries and completing commissioned pieces for the Cultural Council. My work is suitable for home, corporate, indoor and outdoor settings, and ranges vastly in scale. I am open to alternative conceptual impetus, keeping in mind that aesthetics are the enduring signature of my heart.

BARBARA BARRAN
Tapestry, Fiber & Paper
Pages 9, 124, 344

Featuring bold designs, strong colors, exciting textures and a sense of whimsy, my rugs are created in collaboration with my clients, so the finished piece reflects my design vision and complements the installation site. To achieve just the right look for each commission, the rugs are hand-tufted, hand-knotted, hand-hooked, hand-fabricated or flat-woven. I work in all styles, although quilt-patterned, American primitive and children's designs are among my favorites. In addition, I have the exclusive right to translate the Gee's Bend Quilts (currently touring museums throughout the U.S.) into rugs. *Elle Dcor, American Farmhouse, The New York Times* and *Country Living* have featured my work. The Whitney Museum's Store Next Door, the American Folk Art Museum, the Smithsonian and other fine museum stores have all carried my designs.

LYNN BASA
Floor Coverings
Pages 13, 123

Whether displayed on the floor or on the wall, I want my rugs and tapestries to tell a story. Take, for example, the two pieces shown in this book: *Formation* uses symbols to commemorate the marriage of the couple who commissioned the piece, as well as their ties to Hawaii and their four children. *Portal* was created for a Jesuit university law school; the word "justice" appears in the piece in 17 different languages. The cave motif refers to St. Ignatius' epiphany in Manresa, which encouraged spiritual enlightenment through knowledge. Each rug and tapestry is hand-knotted of wool and silk in Nepal by a team of artisans I have worked with since 1986. I've also created a few suites of limited-edition tapestries. Please visit my website to see these and other examples of my work.

KEN BECKLES
Paintings
Page 241

My art is abstract in both approach and execution. It is very vivid and dynamic in nature, and the colors I use run the gamut from rather dark to extremely brilliant. I typically use acrylic paint on either wood and canvas surfaces. Rarely do I rely on standard squares or rectangles; most pieces are shaped to reflect a mood, scene or an expression that is personal, not a trend. My art is the linear descendent of the great abstract paintings of the past. As an abstract painter and an accomplished photographer, my art reflects the combination of a variety of skills. My unique perspective comes from my sense of both color and shape. My paintings are shown around the world in museums, art galleries and homes.

BELLOZAR STUDIO
Home Accessories
Page 116

My pillows are hand-painted original designs, created on recycled bank money bags and stuffed with polyfiber fill. The paint is a washable fabric paint. The pillow sizes vary from 5.5" x 11" to 17.5" x 34.5", and prices range from $45–$250. I love to use color and texture, along with humor, in creating images. My themes include animals (especially cats and dogs) and ethnic or wild people. All designs are one-of-a-kind since I draw each pillow individually; while I do re-create images, your pillow will always be unique.

ARTIST STATEMENTS

NANCY BENEDICT
Home Accessories
Page 119

My idea to make mirrors with painted frames originated from my experience as a child, when I helped my father in his woodworking shop. There I developed an appreciation for the craftsmanship of decorative and functional objects. I focus on mirrors because they engage the viewer on a personal level. I paint each mirror in stages by skillfully blending and layering transparent and opaque paints, and sometimes collaging with readily found materials. Intriguing compositions with rich tactile surfaces are achieved by harmonizing geometric and organic shapes, as well as motifs from nature. My limited-production mirrors are sold nationally through fine craft galleries. Custom work is available, if the client provides color reference materials. One-of-a-kind and other types of work are available; please see my website portfolio. My most recent exhibition was at the Smithsonian Craft Show.

BETTS ART
Murals, Tiles & Wall Reliefs
Page 315

For over a decade, I have been known as a master of trompe l'oeil murals and old-world painted finishes. In recent years I have fallen in love with the creativity allowed through crushed limestone veneers and plasters. This allows me to take projects to the next level, to a real third dimension that you can see, touch and feel. Whether used in interior or exterior applications, stone walls, floors, fireplaces and exterior facings are just some of the possibilities. Clients are pleasantly surprised when their vision, combined with my background in painting, sculpture and design, becomes more than they could have ever imagined. My work has been featured on national television and in various publications.

SUSAN BLOCH
Sculpture
Page 198

While manipulating glass by cutting, kiln-forming, pâte de verre and sandblasting, I'm compelled by the belief that a glass garden creates joy. Everyone who collects a glass flower sculpture loves flowers. Their stories imbue my work. Gloria Gaynor, the late Frank Sinatra and ex-mayor of New York Robert Wagner are among notables who have owned my art. Collected internationally, it is in private, corporate and public spaces. My art glass includes sculptures and windows, in both large and small scale. Commissions, special and custom orders are accepted. Please see my website for examples of other work.

JANNA BERNHEIM BERNSTEIN
Tapestry, Fiber & Paper
Page 340

Using ancient tapestry techniques, rich colors and evocative textures, I create contemporary woven designs inspired by the discoveries and experiences of my life and travels. My wall installations vary in color and texture, creating lush, vibrant spaces; and often combining such diverse materials as Mylar, metals, and Plexiglas with various thicknesses of wool, cotton, and silk. Incorporating symbols, colors and textures, these tapestries and wall pieces are installed in public, corporate and residential spaces throughout the South. Commissions include Baptist Hospital Radiation and Oncology; Christian Brothers University; and Bruce School, Barge Wagner, Architects

BIG BANG MOSAICS
Murals, Tiles & Wall Reliefs
Page 312

One of my goals at Big Bang Mosaics is to put a contemporary spin on the classic mosaic art form. Each mosaic I create is an original, unusual, one-of-a-kind work of art. After I finalize a sketch and color scheme, vitreous glass tiles are carefully cut, positioned and grouted into place. Mosaic panels may be hung like paintings; I also do on-site custom installations for a variety of interior and exterior surfaces, including walls, tabletops, benches and floors. My ability to work collaboratively on creative design solutions is at the core of my work process. Ultimately, I am committed to providing every client with a unique, high-quality mosaic that will inspire, delight and wow its viewers.

JOEL D. BLOOMBERG
Lighting
Page 113

Since opening my studio in the early 1980s, I have created a wide variety of functional and sculptural works. Throughout this time I have sought to design objects that expand the vocabulary of art glass, and to use materials in new and unexpected ways. This latest series of *Jellyfish Lamps* reflects these goals as tabletop-and-chandelier-illuminated sculptures. Each piece requires a combination of blown forms, coldworking, polishing and a lamination process that I have developed over the years. The density of colors can range through a whole spectrum depending on the time of day, direction of light or its own internal illumination. My work is found in private and corporate collections in North America, Europe and Japan.

ANN MOTTERSHEAD BETAK
Paintings
Page 266

My work is oriented toward natural phenomena. My approach is Romantic, whether I am focusing on the fragility of a sunset or the nobility of a common houseplant. I try to dramatize the mystery and elegance of my subject. I attempt to express the disturbing aspects of beauty and therefore signify a larger presence. In true Romantic fashion, I celebrate my independence as reflected in my choice of genre. Collections include: Phifer Wire Corporation; Southern Progress Corporation; Delaware Art Museum; The University of Alabama Permanent Collection; The Arts Council of Tuscaloosa, AL; and numerous private installations throughout the United States. I work in oil, acrylic and oil stick. My current paintings range in size from 10" x 12" to 62" x 235".

ROBERT BISSELL
Paintings
Page 270

My narrative paintings are, in fact, animal allegories that reflect the human disposition. I paint the animals we all knew as children in a realistic, somewhat naive way so that the effect is both real and unreal at the same time. Ideas for my work come from travels in the Western United States and my native England. I paint in oil color, using numerous glazes for maximum brightness and radiance. I studied at The Royal College of Art in London and have exhibited extensively. Paintings are in private and corporate collections throughout the United States. Current sizes range from 18" x 24" to 80" x 48". More information and gallery representation can be found at www.robertbissell.com.

BLUE STAR DESIGN COMPANY
Furniture
Page 71

Bodacious, yet functional. My passion for fabrics and color becomes obvious as you cast your eye on my fanciful benches. Traditional joinery and upholstery techniques, combined with myriad fabrics, beads and tassels, define my signature style, which includes uncompromising craftsmanship and attention to detail. My one-of-a-kind and limited-edition benches are shown at national craft shows and in fine craft galleries in North America. As a full-time, award-winning artist, I invite you to visit my studio in a restored turn-of-the-century distillery in historic Cumberland, Maryland. Let's work together to define a look that embraces your own vibrancy and spirit in a custom bench for your home or office! Rosen Group's Niche Award Winner, 2003; and member, American Craft Council.

ARTIST STATEMENTS

BORSHEIM ARTS STUDIO
Sculpture
Page 182

Art, like mathematics, is simply determining relationships between things. My passion is the human form. Whether painting from a live model or creating sculptures in stone or bronze, I am interested in the personal moments of our lives. I am also fascinated by the duality of our nature, especially the idea that two opposing concepts exist in a strange kind of balance. The tactile quality of sculpture allows me to explore coexisting opposites in an additional way; for example, a soft curve created from a hard material. I love it when people are drawn to one of my works and reach out to touch it, since touch is the most intimate and universal sense we have.

LAURENCE BRANESCO
Tapestry, Fiber & Paper
Page 345

My work's intent is to create a visual sanctuary about life and simplicity. I design one-of-a-kind pieces with guaranteed quality for many private and corporate collections. Each design is on original piece of art, unique in its own color, character and whimsical style. The art is suitable for framing and hanging on a wall, as you would a tapestry. More than 25 years of experience in painting with dye helps me to create my own combination of colors for my work. Colors are fade proof. Sizes range from 15" x 15" to 4' x 8'. Prices range from $150 to $4,000, based on size and complexity. For special-order custom pieces, prices will vary.

BRIAN WEIR, WOODWORKER
Furniture
Page 66

Inspired by the natural beauty of wood, I have evolved professionally from a boat carpenter to a fine furniture creator and designer. My furniture is contemporary in nature, but firmly rooted in the past. Woods are carefully chosen to enhance each design and create harmony within a client's home. A balance between aesthetics and function is achieved while meeting the needs of the individual buyer. Traditional joinery and modern woodworking techniques are employed to assure both beauty and quality construction. Often, one may feel the subtle characteristics left by a hand plane, chisel or spoke shave, all of which are the mark of the craftsman. These qualities culminate in the creation of elegant furnishings that will last for generations.

BRUCE ANTHONY & COMPANY
Garden Sculpture
Page 205

We live in the Toutle Valley by Mount Saint Helens in Washington. Our sculptural birdbaths and fountains were inspired by the landscape when we moved here in 1995. The work is about simplicity in design and the function of art in everyday life. The excitement is in the creation and design, which I work on until I have a piece that is aesthetically pleasing to me. The creativity is in the development of an idea to the manifestation of the structure. Each fountain and birdbath is carefully handcrafted with the greatest attention given to detail. The copper bowls are handspun on a 1950s metal spinning lathe. This technique of metal spinning was first developed by the ancient Egyptians approximately 4,000 years ago. The birdbaths and fountains can live outside year round. Rocks are hand picked from the Mount Saint Helens Toutle River. The handspun copper bowls will become more beautiful with age.

SHANNON S. BUEKER
Paintings
Page 278

I have been drawing since my beginning—in books, on my shoes and now on most any surface. I paint and draw animals, people and things on the move. Gesture is the backbone of my approach. I am fascinated and challenged by how I can express shape and power with the simplest of lines. Watercolor, ink, acrylics and charcoal are my tools of choice, and I work on canvas, board and paper in all sizes. I often begin with an observation from my sketchbooks, or I let the paintings make themselves initially, mixing water and ink on paper or paint, gesso and charcoal on canvas. Art being what it is, I see reflections of my own life, memories and dreams in the resulting shapes and blurs. I have a B.F.A. from the University of Texas-Austin in painting, drawing and sculpture.

FRAN BULL
Paintings
Page 251

The belief of some primitive cultures was that the sun descends into the earth at the end of each day. It was imagined that the sun, for some hours, dwelt in darkness, illuminating the dark matter with its brilliance. This notion of light in darkness exists for me as a provocative and poetic image, and as a powerful metaphor for awakening, or consciousness. My *Syzygy* series is a meditation on the sun's daily descent into darkness, the image of an underground sun, of light in matter and the metaphor of dark matter illuminated, alive and even sacred. Our world, which we seem to ravage and sacrifice so easily these days, comes alive as a gleaming, luminescent entity.

MYRA BURG
Tapestry, Fiber & Paper
Page 343

Wanting a change from practicing architecture and realizing my didgeridoo at home was more an art piece than musical instrument, I wrapped a companion piece and named it *Quiet Oboe*. I fell in love with the warmth of wrapped fiber on the cylindrical form. Laid side by side, a series of wrapped tubes allows me to express images. These tubes are held to the wall via the aluminum structure that becomes an integral part of the artwork. Sizes range from tabletop to monumental, prices from $150 to $30,000 and styles from individual *Oboes* to large corporate commissions. It is architecture. It is jewelry. It is my passion.

CLAIRE BURKE
Paintings
Page 260

I paint landscapes depicting rural California in the tradition of the modern masters. My oil paintings reflect not only my own experiences, but as a native of the Bay Area and a fifth-generation Californian, they also express the shared experience of living in California with all who embrace the uniqueness of the land. I spent much of my childhood visiting Napa Valley and rural areas of Northern California. My paintings are influenced by those travels, and my technique is inspired by artists like Edward Hopper. My work is found in private collections from the United States to Norway. Prices range from $400 to $4,000.

MARY BURKE
Paintings
Page 255

The balance of play and careful analysis are in mind when I work. I enjoy using the accidental mark along with the intended mark and relish being entertained by what paint can do. I work in acrylic paint and graphite. Formally, my work manifests the play of design elements such as line, pattern and texture, intermingling nonfigurative, gestural marks with those that reference reality. Utilizing a kind of visual free association, I put marks on the canvas with an eye to flat composition. My images reflect the intimacy of a simple garden. Less grand than the untamed wilderness, the garden is friendlier and, like art, surrounds us with proof of what one person can do.

ARTIST STATEMENTS

JEFF BURNETTE
Objects
Page 143

I am as intrigued with glass now as I was when I was a kid, wondering how they got the color in those marbles. Seeing a film in high school on glass and glassblowing literally changed my life. Working with some of the top glass artists in the world has taught me how to design and complete the pieces that I dream up, such as my *Ray Gunz*. Today, the ability to work in my own studio, Joe Blow Glassworks, allows me the freedom to create the work I love, which is found in private collections internationally. Joe Blow Glassworks is always working on new ideas and welcomes commissions.

CAROL CANNON
Paintings
Page 269

My intention as an artist is to uplift the viewer and his or her environment, whether it be through a painting or on the walls of a home. A painting begins with a brush stroke "from the void," while my rooms begin with an understanding of the client's color schemes and life themes. I hold degrees in illustration and art therapy; my intuitive process is guided by my desire to reach the hearts of my viewers and to elevate their states of mind. I have attended school, worked and taught in New York City for 25 years. I am lucky enough to have worked across the country, in the Middle East and Hong Kong, and have integrated the natural elements and cultural motifs of these countries in my work. To see more examples of my work, please visit www.carolcannon.com. Read a review of my work at www.franklinreport.com.

BETH CASSIDY
Art Quilts
Page 335

I make textiles for the home using a variety of fabrics and colors. Designing with the client in mind, I create pieces to enhance beds, tables, seating arrangements, walls and floors. Soft sculptural elements combine with the wild abandon of color, moving across the pieces like flowing water to create a work that is abstract as well as an homage to the rich history of quilting. Custom work is my forte. If a client is not completely happy, I will gladly exchange the piece for one that will be treasured in his or her home. My work is currently showing at the Renwick Museum gallery store, the Seattle Art Museum store, the Toledo Art Museum store, New Morning Gallery and Abacus Galleries, as well as many others. I have pieces in the American embassies in Thailand and Armenia and in many private and public collections worldwide. I show my work at American Craft Council Shows and other fine craft shows across the country.

MARY ELLEN BUXTON
AND KEVIN KUTCH
Objects
Page 139

Kevin and I are versatile artists who have worked together in partnership for over 25 years. During the last ten years, we have collaborated in our designs to create blown and cut sculptures. One reason we create gem-like sculpture is because we are fascinated with glass's ability to reflect, refract and magnify light. A variety of blowing techniques helps us to realize this fascination and manipulate the glass into each visualized sculpture. Recently, we have pursued our individual ideas with other glass technologies and mixed media. These include kiln-formed woven structures and sand-cast cubist figures. Our work is exhibited in national and international galleries. Commissions are on display in private homes, as well as the public sector.

KENNETH CARLL
Furniture
Page 69

I have sculptured stone and wood on and off for over 30 years; however, most of my past full-time working life was spent as a teacher and engineer. After leaving engineering I began making up for a considerable amount of lost shop time. I have added furniture to my repertoire, with a focus on Asian-influenced tables and accessories. I view and design furniture as sculpture and strive to use very simple forms—to which I often add stone or wood carvings and free-form edges to create reflective facets and vivid contrasts. Game tables, marine-themed tables and various types of occasional tables have been my favorites. Accessories include stone Ikebana vases, display easels and sculpture.

FRANK CAVAZ
Lighting
Pages 6, 112

I met my wife, Julie, at the Rhode Island School of Design while we were pursuing our M.F.A. degrees in glass and painting. We established our studio in Sonoma, California, in 1996 out of our love for design and my desire to blow glass. Bacchus Glass creates decorative and functional blown glass for tabletops, as well as sculptural vases. My current body of work, *The Botanicals,* is an exploration of three-dimensional surface patterns, mixing a modern aesthetic with organic elements. Because we have fine art backgrounds, Julie and I are eager to work with artists and designers on one-of-a-kind pieces or production runs, as well as custom lighting projects.

LAUREN CAMP
Tapestry, Fiber & Paper
Pages 8, 320, 346

The bold, musical *Interludes* shown in this book are my way of doodling—with fabric. I start with a series of hand-drawn designs and then combine several to make the full-size cartoon. I choose fabrics of different weights, patterns, colors and textures and then layer the shapes, much like a collage. The threadwork adds another dimension of interest upon closer inspection. The pieces measure 21" × 22" with frame and mat, and can be grouped together or hung singly. My work has been collected by hospitals, community centers, museums and many individuals. Notable exhibitions include Johnson & Johnson corporate headquarters, the JVC Jazz Festival and the Fiber Art Biennial in Chieri, Italy. Other works can be seen on my website. Commissions are accepted. Santa Fe, New Mexico, studio open by appointment.

ANDREW CARSON
Garden Sculpture
Page 206

My interest is not in metal itself, but what it can become if assisted by the wind or the environment. All the materials in my installations are intricately cut, forged, hammered and patinated by hand. With bearings, balance and color, I like to craft these sculptures to work not only within a chosen landscape, but to elaborate on its artistic energy. My large kinetic sculptures range from frenetic to serene. I graduated from the University of Washington in 1986. My sculptures can be found in public and private collections throughout the United States, with a wide range of high-profile clients among them. Smaller works range from $2,000 to $6,000. Larger works range from $7,000 to $60,000. Special commissions are welcomed.

CHAJO
Furniture
Page 56

Our mission is to create functional pieces of art that inspire both conversation and everyday use. We are drawn to clean forms that command attention by virtue of their subtle elegance and grace. Each of our furnishings has a unique personality, and we build with an equal emphasis on design, materials and craftsmanship. Our work showcases the natural characteristics of our materials, including fossilized limestone, petrified wood, ammonites, hard woods, metals and select textiles. Shown in residential and corporate collections in the United States and abroad, our work ranges from pedestals to modular cocktail table systems to conference tables and chairs. We welcome custom work and enjoy creating pieces to meet clients' individual needs.

ARTIST STATEMENTS

LAURIE REGAN CHASE
Paintings
Pages 24, 233

In my paintings I have made a study of coastlines, harbors and the boats that inhabit them, and have become known for my handling of light and reflections. I was recently juried into the prestigious American Society of Marine Artists. Today my paintings capture the bold colors and rugged yet proud character of functional wooden workboats from around the world—from the day-fishing boats of the Black, Aegean and Adriatic Seas, to the large shrimpers of Key West. My medium is oil on canvas; where I combine detailed brushwork with the soft, impressionistic use of the palette knife, creating images radiant with intense color and rich, realistic textures. My paintings bring the viewer to another place and time. Prices for originals range from $2,000 to $20,000.

MARCIA CHRISTENSEN
Sculpture
Page 176

My stone sculptures, described as sensuous and graceful, yet powerful and elegant, are influenced by intensive study in Italy. I rarely use models, but carve from intuition and emotion to capture the beauty, strength and grace of the human form. I especially enjoy working on commissions with clients to create personal, unique and timeless pieces. Sizes range from tabletop to monumental. Bronze limited editions are available on select pieces. My work has recently been featured in *Sculptural Pursuit* magazine and on KCNC Channel 4 News, Denver, CO. Commissions include Larsen-Juhl Frame Company and Boulder Community Hospital, CO.

JEREMY R. CLINE
Sculpture
Page 202

My glasswork reflects my love for the medium, my fine craftsmanship and an ongoing endeavor to better my working processes. I started working with glass in 1987 at Santa Monica College, then furthered my education at the California College of Arts and Crafts and Pilchuck Glass School. In 1991 I apprenticed with Pino Signoretto, master glass artist, in Murano, Italy. I opened Incline Glass in 1992. My work examines the vessel as an art form, taking cues from the glass itself, as well as from antiquity and contemporary sources. In addition to creating my own work, I also use my facility to produce various pieces for other artists and designers, including custom lampshades for the lighting industry, Venetian-style stemware, sculptures and various prototypes. I continue to expand my abilities, techniques and methodology in pursuit of excellence in glass.

TOM CHENOWETH
Furniture
Page 80

My work is formal and structural. Energy and balance are primary concerns. Every piece is a conversation in material and stems from the physical experience of manipulating metal, achieving an organic grace and intuitive expressiveness while maintaining the integrity of the man-made structural materials. I began my work 30 years ago while earning my B.F.A. and M.F.A. in sculpture. In the beginning my work was about learning all the things I could do with the material and acquiring the technical expertise necessary to give form to my ideas. Later I began borrowing design elements from my large-scale sculpture, creating practical objects for creative environments. I currently offer furniture, lighting and sculpture. I have work in private and public collections and accept custom requests.

CITY JOINERY
Furniture
Page 65

I design new furniture that brings the best of traditional craftsmanship together with adventurous contemporary design. My studio, City Joinery, makes limited-edition and custom-designed pieces, utilizing the finest solid hardwoods and other natural materials. From dining tables, desks and armoires to couches, chairs and beds, I strive for my work to be vital, meticulous and rigorously original. Designs are born out of a thoughtful process in which I continually push boundaries to discover new forms. The furniture possesses subtleties that continue to impress their owners long after they are first used. In the choice of materials and the manner with which we join and finish them, I intend for our furniture to become the sought-after antiques of the next centuries, long outlasting their makers.

DAVID CODDAIRE
Furniture
Page 82

I was born in Massachusetts in 1945 and studied painting and art history in Italy. I continued my studies with the Kansas City Art Institute, focusing on sculpture. I currently live and work in California. The works shown in this publication are created in my studio and are generated from some of the many drawings I create on a regular basis.

L.T. CHEROKEE
Garden Sculpture
Page 208

I have expressed my vision of artistic form for more than 20 years. My works in bronze, stone and wood are represented by galleries internationally and are widely held in private collections. I am most known for my ability to breathe the emotional gamut into my medium, thereby impacting the living environment, bringing fluidity and substance together through graceful, lyrical forms. Many pieces can be scaled to site-specific requirements, integrating well within a variety of spaces. I prefer close collaboration with architects and designers to achieve optimal impact. Brochures are available upon request.

CLARKSON McGIBBON
Furniture
Page 95

I trained as a furniture designer/craftsman at Humber College in Toronto, Ontario. I have collaborated with interior designers and architects for over 26 years to help bring their designs to fruition. I use this experience in designing furniture with function and high style in mind. Our furniture reflects a neo-minimalist style with a twist by using the unique textures and colors of exotic woods and geometric forms. Our experience also brings a refined sense of proportion and detail to our fine contemporary furniture. Custom furniture designed to suit your individual style is always welcome. Our furniture has been shown at the Philadelphia Furniture and Furnishings Show and is represented in select galleries.

ROBERT L. CRECELIUS
Objects
Page 149

I have been working as a blacksmith for over 20 years. All of the pieces within my current body of work are created from steel. The raw material is forged at temperatures ranging from 1,500 to 2,000 degrees. The work is shaped by hammer and anvil in the traditional manner. Pieces are then wire brushed and treated with a clear rust-resistant finish. The bronze accents are the result of a patina process that is done while hot. As an artist I am interested in craftsmanship and how traditional techniques relate to the overall form of a completed piece. My studio is located 80 miles south of St. Louis along the St. Francois river valley, within the foothills of the Ozarks. I employ no assistants, preferring to work alone in the solitude of my surroundings.

ARTIST STATEMENTS

PATT DALBEY
Paintings
Page 243

My abstract paintings reflect my vision of the cities and countryside of the Midwest lake country where I grew up, as well as places I have visited. Using distinct line, rich colors and graphic form, I bring a rhythm and play of patterns to the canvas. I first started showing my art through a women's co-op in Minneapolis, Minnesota. Currently my paintings are available through Art Holdings Consulting or by contacting my studio directly. I have shown my work at the Minnetonka Center for the Arts and am represented on the web by www.artspan.com. Pieces are generally in the mid-size range, but because of the bold, graphic style, I can put two or more together to create a larger visual impact.

DANIEL LOTTON STUDIOS
Lighting
Pages 109–110

I have enjoyed glassmaking ever since I was a young boy, when I looked on in my father's studio. During the last several years, I have found myself exploring different styles of chandeliers. The chandeliers featured in this book are Victorian in style, but the majority of my work is contemporary. Whatever the décor, I enjoy meeting the challenge of designing light fixtures for the home. My work can be found in many galleries across the country, as well as in private collections.

ALONZO DAVIS
Mixed Media
Page 328

As I weave my way through Ghana, Togo, Hawaii, Mexico and the Southwest, my art does its own traveling—into new territories and old—resulting in several new series, including *Power Poles, Woven Ladders* and *Bamboo Constructions.* The bamboo constructions evolved from mixed-media paintings, which incorporated sweat lodge poles, branches, arrows and twigs. I now work with the bamboo as its own medium. The lengths of bamboo are variously embellished. Most are textured with burned-in, patterned designs, which alternate with various wrappings. Wrappings include twisted and painted canvas, wire bracelets and cowhide.

STEPHEN J. DALY
Mixed Media
Page 326

As a sculptor, I appreciate the immediacy of drawing, which stands in contrast to the process of creating sculpture. I prefer a working methodology that allows for both chance and predication. When appropriate to an artistic idea, I will frame and mount drawings on top of each other or attach cast metal sculptural elements to the surface. The physicality of these elements creates another dimension and, as fixed components, can halt the action of the more gestural and atmospheric drawing just below. Mimicry can also be used to question the "reality" of a drawn form versus a sculptural form. I seek a universal visual language that combines recognizable images with more abstract or symbolic forms, establishing context while allowing the viewer's imagination to enter.

DANIEL MAHER STAINED GLASS
Windows, Doors & Railings
Page 169

Light is my medium. In my work I use a variety of blown, pressed, machine-rolled and prismatic glass to bend and control the light entering an environment. I am most drawn to the transparent qualities of glass, which give my windows an interactive effect as the viewer moves or the sun moves throughout the day. Interspersing the creation of new works with the restoration of masterworks by Tiffany, LaFarge and Connick motivates me to respond to the intrinsic stylistic quantities of glass and various construction materials. My design influences are rooted in Gothic and Art Deco traditions, but often come from the glass itself.

ALESSANDRA DeCLARIO
Photographs
Page 304

As a true multimedia artist, I use many different media and plunge into many different projects. Being born and raised in New York City—and then moving to California—has affected my art considerably. In California I developed my interest in film and photography. However, my love of nature led me toward plein air watercolors, where I could really see the yellows and blues that made the greens of the trees! I also began printing my own giclées. I credit my reading of ads (while riding on New York buses and trains) with my current use of illuminating display boxes for my art. A special photo process creates a dramatic backlighting effect. The finished piece can be placed in a classically designed display illuminator or used as a ceiling panel.

DAN RIDER SCULPTURE
Garden Sculpture
Page 216

Over 20 years of sculpture design and mold-making experience have culminated in my latest series of garden sculpture, *Spirit Markers.* These modern, abstract totems featuring layers of varying materials, such as rock, reinforced concrete, brass and copper, have been my primary focus. As a result each piece resonates with its own unique character. Since I have always favored large, bold statements for outdoor sculpture, my pieces begin at six feet high and head skyward from there. I begin with sketches, which allow me the freedom of unlimited imagination. Then I proceed to the fabrication, beginning with the top of the sculpture. Once I have the crowning element completed, I continue construction on the chosen site, utilizing molds, rock and concrete. The final touches may include patinas, staining or sealing. These organic pieces range from soaring and curving, to jagged and angular.

HOLLYE DAVIDSON
Paintings
Page 234

I look to capture the sensual, subtle energies and mystic truth of my subjects through light and vibrant color. I use techniques of the old masters in modern form to bring intense luminescence and depth to my pastel drawings and oil canvases. My work, which ranges from 8" x 6" to over 8' x 6', is found in international collections, both corporate and private. Exhibits include Mayfair Galleries and the Lowe Art Museum. Works include one-of-a-kind pieces and limited editions. I am available for commissions, including portraits and murals.

PETER F. DELLERT
Furniture
Page 68

My college degree is in biology. I was planning to be an oceanographer and then a lichenologist. Since then I have worked as a cook, a shipwright, a potter, a builder, a cabinetmaker and finally as a furniture maker. My work continues to change and evolve from functional tables and wall cabinets to pieces that are more sculptural, and often narrative. The boxed constructions began as wall-mounted jewelry cabinets. I have always loved doors, arches and entries. I have photographed them in my travels, and they serve as focal points for many of the pieces. When opened these pieces further reveal themselves through the scrutiny and personal involvement of the viewer. There is no one key or meaning to my work, although many reflect my continued, profound respect for and wonder of the natural world.

ARTIST STATEMENTS

PAULA DES JARDINS
Paintings
Page 279

Passion drives my art. I paint for the pure love of color, texture and light, as well as the ability to bring something to life that never existed before. I thrive on the challenge of attaining the next level—always taking risks and moving forward. The ability of the human spirit to rise above adversity is a source of constant inspiration; I search for it in history, literature, music and particularly in the lives of those around me. Through my work I hope to share this spirit of optimism with the viewer. My work is found in many private and corporate collections, including ABN AMRO Bank, IBM, Hyatt Regency Hotel, Ritz Carlton Hotel and Xerox. Commissions welcomed.

SIMONE DeSOUSA
Paintings
Pages 228, 250

My paintings evoke architectural elements through a combination of geometric forms, structural lines and color fields, an abstract universe containing layered fragments of either landscapes or interiors. The root of my expression comes from my Brazilian heritage and is marked by a sensibility resulting from the harmonious fusion of different references. The colors emphasize the combination of deconstructed elements, creating a visual language that serves both as a record of my experiences and an invitation to share my observations of the multiple facets of our human spirit. I have exhibited in galleries around the country. Current paintings range from 12" x 9" to 96" x 48". A detailed portfolio is available upon request. Latest corporate collection in 2003: Compuware Corporation headquarters, Detroit, MI.

GLENDA DIETRICH
Paintings
Page 275

I choose to use a vibrant, rich, deeply hued palette in my energetic watercolor paintings, which are executed on white watercolor paper or board. Subject matter includes landscape, still life, figures and personal interpretations. My style ranges from traditional, representational work to pieces that are contemporary and abstract (as seen on the website). Commissions are welcome. Existing sizes range from 6" x 6" to 32" x 40". Prices for existing original paintings range from $175 to $1,200, and giclée reproductions range from $60 to $200. I have a B.F.A. in painting from the University of Nebraska and have studied watercolor painting beyond my degree work. My paintings have been widely accepted in juried group and solo exhibitions, and are part of private and public collections. My work has been published frequently in *The Other Side* magazine and *The Upper Room Devotional Guide,* among others.

MICHAEL DOERR
Furniture
Page 63

I began my career as a wooden shipwright; my love of workmanship has evolved into furniture making with a focus on comfort, function and an eye for clarity of line. I am nationally known for my sculptural chairs, which are represented in the Parson School of Design/Smithsonian Institute lecture series, "Contemporary American Crafts." Since the founding of Doerr Woodworking in 1989, a national and international clientele has developed. All furniture is handmade by commission—collaboration between myself and the client creates the opportunity to select sizes, wood type and grain that will best enhance a quality piece of furniture. My shop is a place where the soul of the tree meets the spirit of the craftsman.

GLENN DONOVAN
Sculpture
Page 188

Using balance, springs and dead machinery, I recycle both metal and energy to create sculptures that come to life when touched. My kinetic assemblage sculptures include found object and wire metals of steel, stainless steel, brass and copper. I heat-shape and weld my sculptures using a MIG welder and gas welder and finish with a metal lacquer. My sculptures evolve from my artistic inclinations, a personal fascination with technical challenges and a sense of humor. Nearly 30 years as an artist has brought me satisfaction and a good sense of accomplishment as I continue to improve and transform my artwork. I create all my pieces, start to finish. Commissions are welcome. My largest outdoor work ranges from 5'–12'H and $5,000–$15,000. My 20"–48"H kinetic work generally ranges from $300 to $1,500. My smaller wire "story sculptures" are 6"–14"H and $60–$150.

TIMOTHY DUFFIELD
Prints & Drawings
Pages 25, 289

Archival giclée prints in limited editions. I am a sculptor and landscape architect. I have returned to my first love: printmaking. The land informs all my work. I reflect it in my sculpture; I work with it—and heal it—in my landscape design. My prints explore an understanding of the earth as an active force, not as a passive stage for human activity. My working metaphor is that I am not changing the appearance of the scene before me, but that the land is working on me, changing the way I look at the scene. It is I who change. My images are modest pictures. They are also heartfelt expressions of the physical and spiritual sustenance that the land bestows.

ANNE ELLIOTT
Prints & Drawings
Page 291

I think of landscape as that which we see around us, as well as that which we feel within us. My external landscapes explore extraordinary geologic formations that I have encountered. My internal landscapes present dramatic situations that are painful, humorous, frightening or revelatory, moments that transform one's emotional life. I use my computer as a compositional tool, manipulating scanned images, placing figures in new contexts or relationships. After I print the image, I paint it with acrylic paint because the brush strokes enhance the intimacy. My prints are limited editions of these paintings. I have exhibited my work in museums and galleries in New York, Chicago, Pittsburgh, Philadelphia and Long Island. I have received a Fellowship from the Pennsylvania Council of the Arts.

ERNEST PORCELLI / ART GLASS
Windows, Doors & Railings
Page 164

The challenge of creating a stained glass window that will last 100 years is just one of the elements that makes me so passionate about my art. The available and ever-shifting light in a stained glass window is my canvas; the line, color and texture are my paints. My work naturally lends itself to commissions. I see each commission as an opportunity to collaborate with others, while exploring new ideas and design possibilities. I have been creating original designs for over 30 years. Working mostly through commissions, I create custom glass installations in homes, churches and landmark buildings. My unique line of kiln-formed glass has been featured at the American Craft Museum, the Whitney Museum's Store Next Door and Gump's in San Francisco, CA.

ETCETERA, COUTURE
FOR THE HOME BY SOLOMONIC, INC.
Objects
Page 152

At Solomonic, Inc., we offer original home décor items made of clay, ceramics, wood and Norwegian moss. Our group of talented professionals creates unique pieces of art that are inspired by our past experiences, diverse tastes and perspective of the ultimate home. Our founder was born in Uzbekistan, educated in Europe as a mathematician and, after spending a decade in New York financial services, started a home decoration business that has recently gained significant momentum. The works of Solomonic can be found in offices, lobbies and homes around the country. The pieces generally range in price from $50 to $1,000. We hope you will see the simple beauty of nature, richness of color, originality, honesty and passion, and will enjoy a unique and emotional connection with our work.

ARTIST STATEMENTS

ROBIN EVANS
Furniture
Page 88

As an award-winning glass artist, I am often asked to categorize my contemporary glass mosaics. I classify the majority of my work as functional glass mosaic sculpture. In the last several years I have added a range of materials, including steel, onyx, granite, kiln-formed glass and lighting, to my widely collected commission work and limited-edition series. Color, movement and meticulous attention to detail are a vital part of my work. Growing up, I was greatly influenced by accomplished parents (one of whom is a brilliant visual artist; the other encouraged culture and creativity in her children). My upbringing continues to be a gift to me and my work like no other. I remain grateful for those unusually early art-drenched days, and I honor those memories with my mission: to add beauty, balance and harmony to any environment.

MARILYN MERKT FELBER
Art Quilts
Page 332

My passion is art. My medium is fiber, mainly quilt art. My interests include traditional Asian and contemporary Native American art and the universal geometric harmonies found in art and nature worldwide. I notice images of "Listening Woman" wherever they appear. It is key to my process. I'm attracted to very focused imagery, like that of the early 20th-century abstractionists—especially the Bauhaus artists—and wish to express a kind of simplicity through elegant color, striking composition and an Amish-like clarity. Yet I find life rich and complex, mysterious and interrelated; it's always a challenge to express this depth and beauty in a simple way. My work is owned by private collectors companies and institutions.

ANNE LEUCK FELDHAUS
Paintings
Page 242

My bold, high-contrast paintings are simple reflections of my life, surroundings and dreams. These light-hearted, whimsical images appeal to adults and children alike. I paint a broad range of subjects, including dogs, cityscapes, roadways, flying people and the occasional still life. Often these are simple, decorative iconic paintings, but on occasion they develop into more narrative compositions. My original works are collected worldwide. I've also illustrated greeting cards, a book and a line of two-dimensional wall art for the home furnishings market. Public works include a full suite of dog-themed painted furniture, which was commissioned through the Chicago Public Art Program and displayed prominently on Michigan Avenue. In addition to originals, I offer giclée prints and commissioned paintings of dogs and other subjects.

SANDY AND BILL FIFIELD
Windows, Doors & Railings
Page 168

We have worked together for over 36 years on collaborations and separate projects in stained glass and wood. Sandy: "The intricacy of my stained glass is facilitated by my background as a jeweler and my use of the copper-foil method of construction. This is combined with my technique of beveling *dalles de verre* glass to produce a sculptural effect depicting birds, flowers and landscapes." Bill: "My work has been influenced by folk art from around the world and was featured in *The Artful Home*, 2002." Over 95% of our work is commissioned. We love the challenge of new projects that incorporate wood and/or glass. Please visit www.macfifield.com to see more of our work.

MARILYN FORTH
Tapestry, Fiber & Paper
Page 352

My batik paintings light up a room with nature's wonder. Add natural foliage to the mix and inside merges with outside. I have exhibited for the past 20 years and have created paintings for corporate and residential clients. I have also taught fiber courses at Syracuse University. Satisfied clients are a must for me. Photos of completed commissions are sent to the client for final approval. The art is light fast and guaranteed. My work has been featured in previous GUILD sourcebooks.

TOBY ATTICUS FRALEY
Paintings
Page 238

My work focuses largely on common everyday places or subjects. I often feel these airports, laundromats, children's toys, etc., are sometimes overlooked as great sources of composition for painting. For the most part, I render these subjects in the architectural styles of the 1950s, '60s and '70s. What's left in this style is rapidly being torn down to make room for progress; I record it on canvas for future generations to enjoy. In addition to my originals, I have also expanded into making limited-edition giclée prints on acid-free paper and canvas. These prints are available in a variety of sizes to fit into your space. My work has been featured in over 30 national and regional group and solo shows, and is found in university and private collections.

DAN FREEMAN
Sculpture
Page 194

As a child I played on construction sites and created with what I found there, making buildings, figures and families. As an adult my wife and I created a real family, and I continue to make sculptures with salvaged and elemental materials. I like the idea of reclamation—giving new life to found materials by combining them with the energy of natural elements such as wood and stone. I make markers, totems and talismans, and sometimes tell stories with my sculptures. My sculpture ranges in size from 3" tabletop pieces to standing sculptures up to 8' tall. My work can be found in public and private collections on the West Coast. To see more examples of elemental sculpture, please visit my website: www.elementalartwork.com.

GAIL McCARTHY STUDIO
Objects
Pages 128, 392

Glowing lusters were prized above gold itself by 12th-century Persian caliphs. I have been enchanted by the elusive radiance of lusterware and have spent years of research reclaiming the antique firing techniques. When most potters are done, I am just beginning, resubmitting emergent forms to the smoldering kiln. Between perilous margins I search out the unique moment when precious metal glazes bloom into living light. I produce one-of-a-kind vessels, luster paintings, site-specific installations and custom tiles. My graduate work in architecture has enhanced my ability to work with spatial concepts, and I invite commissions and special projects. I've exhibited widely, with work in numerous U.S. collections, museums and galleries, and internationally in Istanbul, Turkey; Faenza, Italy; and Mino, Japan.

GALAZZO GLASS
Objects
Page 141

My contemporary fused glass work is a celebration of color. It is the play of color, shape and light reflected in and through the glass that intrigues and inspires me. My work is in numerous private collections throughout the United States and has been exhibited in a wide variety of galleries and museums, including the Bullseye Glass Connections Gallery, 2002, Portland, OR; the Art Institute of Chicago Museum, IL; and the American Craft Council Retail and Wholesale shows. Recently my work was auctioned at The National Liberty Museum, Philadelphia, PA; as well as Urban Glass, Brooklyn, NY. In 2002 the American Craft Council awarded me the Emerging Artist Mentor Program Recipient, and in 2003 I was nominated for a Niche Award. Commissions and custom orders are welcome.

ARTIST STATEMENTS

GARTNER/BLADE
Objects
Page 136

We combine our individual ideas, techniques and experiences to create original works in blown and sculpted glass. Since 1995 we have been developing a series of pieces that explores our interpretation of objects of ritual and worship. Through these pieces we hope to convey a reverence and understanding of the value of our natural resources. The inspiration for these pieces began with our fascination with the use of found objects in the rituals of primitive cultures. Elements such as bone, antler, wood, vines, fossils and rock formations have informed our work, which includes covered vessels, chalices and lidded bowls.

GLASSIC ART
Mixed Media
Pages 317, 321

For over 20 years, Glassic Art has been creating innovative and intriguing works of art that are both functional and decorative. Using a combination of techniques (including painting, sandblasting, etching and fusing), types of glass (dichroic, iridescent, plate, smoked, stained and streamed) and materials from all over the world, our talented team will create anything imaginable. Bring your vision, and we'll make it a reality. Recent Projects: MGM Grand Casino, Las Vegas, NV; Turnberry Towers penthouse residence, and Park Towers residence, Las Vegas, NV. Commissions: Golden Door Spa, 2002, Puerto Rico; Street of Dreams, 2002, Las Vegas, NV. Publications: "Modern Masters," HGTV; *American Style* magazine, 2003.

HERB GOLDMAN
Garden Sculpture
Page 204

I take pride in my flexibility as a sculptor to work in a full range of materials and styles. Monumental sculptures cast in stainless steel and bronze are now available for indoor and outdoor placement. Featured pieces are also available in 13" and 30" heights for interiors. Price range for medium sculptures is $1,500 to $5,000. Ninety-four of my commissioned works are registered with the Smithsonian Institution's Inventories of American Painters and Sculptors. My work has been placed in libraries, churches, synagogues, banks, schools, universities, hotels, zoos, municipal parks, shopping centers and commercial office buildings. Works have been featured in many publications. One large environmental project appeared in *Time* magazine, another was featured in *Art in America* and *Arts and Architecture* (and was the cover image for this publication). Please visit my website: www.herbgoldman.com

BLAISE GASTON
Furniture
Pages 15, 54

Creating furniture inspired by the things I find beautiful—the trunk of an elephant, the wing of a bird, the legs of a woman—motivates me as much today as it did 30 years ago when I began making furniture. I'm looking for ways to bring the shapes of nature into our homes, wending my way between tradition and often playful innovation. Over the years, my designs have become more alive, richer in movement and feeling. I want those who meet my work to feel better for it—revived and inspired in some way.

GLOCKE'S GLASS
Objects
Page 144

We welcome you to the world of cold fusion glass. For the last ten years, we have used glass to make art that makes you smile. What have evolved are creations that have become participatory art; that is, where the piece is viewed determines what is seen. This is accomplished by using only clear optical glass, with color added through dyes. We are currently creating three series of work. The first, our *Vase* series, consists of representational vase shapes with the illusion of a second shape, or interior design. The *Cube* series uses geometric designs to elicit creations with dramatic movement of color. Finally, our *Sculptural* series, new for 2004, is a series of nonrepresentational pieces that will help make anyone's home an artful home.

AMY GRASSFIELD
Furniture
Page 79

My earthy and eccentric vision finds poetry in a whimsical and leguminous fantasy world of oversized peapods, tendrils and foliage, which are masterfully fashioned into functional objects such as furniture, garden fixtures, lanterns, fountains and sculpture. First trained at Tiffany's and Cartier, Inc., I exploit jewelry-making techniques to fabricate large-scale objects from hand-tooled, patinated copper and steel elements. I have created installations for retails stores, public spaces, restaurants and residences, and I relish every unique opportunity to spread "Peas-on-Earth." Commissions have been completed for: Blue Fish Inc., Taos, NM; Dandelion Green Restaurant, Bellerica, MA; Barnsider Restaurant, Albany, NY; Bernadette Peters and Dudley Moore. My work has been published in *Victoria*, *Home & Garden* and *Sunset* magazines.

NANCY A. GEZELLA
Tapestry, Fiber & Paper
Page 357

I incorporate a variety of materials into my work to achieve an interesting and creative mix of textures and depth. An important aspect to achieving the richness of my work is the layering of color and texture. My love for gardening and nature strongly influences my work, which is created from handmade paper made of 100% acid-free, white cotton pulp. To this I add a variety of other materials such as metal, beads, yarns and my own colored pencil sketches, which are applied with an archival, acid-free adhesive. My work can be found in galleries across the country and is part of public and private collections including The American Craft Museum, NY; SAS Institute, NC; Marshfield Clinic and Marshfield Public Library, WI.

LAURIE GODDARD
Paintings
Page 229

My work combines traditional gilding on gessoed wooden panels with contemporary patinas. The abstract landscapes are reflections of time spent in Italy, Japan and Western Massachusetts. Painted from memory, they are the result of a long look. The gilding and patinating requires quiet deliberation, while the over- and underpainting is bold, gestural and expressive. The result is a travelogue of modern and antique imagery. The paintings are often produced in a diptych or triptych format, with the empty space between the panels an integral part of the piece. They are meant to float on a wall. I hold a B.F.A. in printmaking from the Moore College of Art, Philadelphia, PA. My work is included in the collections of the Museum of Fine Arts, Boston, MA; Eli Lilly Corporation; and Claude Picasso, among others.

CAROL GREEN
Objects
Page 151

Like yours, my heart catches in my throat when I encounter scenes of great natural beauty. It's a feeling we've shared with our ancestors throughout the world and over the millennia. Artists have always created works celebrating the natural world. Artists have also created objects for utility, pleasure and symbolic meaning. My goal is to combine the beauty of the natural world with objects that serve.

ARTIST STATEMENTS

GREG AANES FURNITURE
Furniture
Page 92

Take an initial design, knead it and let it rise to perfection. I sharpen and mature my designs through the reiteration of chairs, which add to our lives. Grace and balance emphasize the natural grain and colors of the wood, with echoes of our long furniture design history as a foundation. Building furniture professionally since 1980, I have studied with James Krenov, Sam Maloof and Isaburo Kawada, all of whom were undoubtedly a great influence. Yet motivated by my own visions, I consider myself self-taught. Exhibits include American Craft Council shows in Baltimore, Chicago (second place, 2001), San Francisco and St. Paul (honorable mention, 2002); The Philadelphia Furniture Show; and Santa Monica Contemporary Crafts. My chairs are also shown in 15 galleries nationwide.

NIKI GULLEY
Paintings
Page 265

My oil paintings and pastels convey a sense of serenity to the viewer by utilizing warm, vivid colors and representing the natural beauty of the American and European landscapes. My clientele ranges from young professionals to retirees, first-time collectors to established galleries, and high-tech corporations to prestigious hospitals. I am happy to work on special projects in a variety of sizes. Some previous commissions include New York Presbyterian Hospital, Baylor Medical Center, Nayna Networks, North Star Bank of Texas and Moore Disposal. Giclées and prints on canvas are also available. Please call for pricing and a catalog of my work.

GUTZWILLER STUDIOS
Furniture
Page 89

Twenty years ago I graduated from the Cleveland Institute of Art with a B.F.A. in sculpture. In a "disposable, do-enough-to-get-by society," I am still driven to produce objects of lasting integrity. Design and craftsmanship are predominant forces in my furniture, and I use these elements to create a visual language in my sculpture. All pieces are one-of-a-kind. I work in steel, stainless steel, bronze and aluminum, occasionally adding marble, granite or wood. Tables and chairs start at $1,800, cabinets at $3,000 and bedroom sets at $6,500. My work has been shown in *Craft, Architectural Record* and *Colorado Homes and Lifestyles*. Representation includes Woodlot Gallery in Sheboygan, WI, and Shidoni Gallery in Tesuque, NM.

L.P. GREGORY
Mixed Media
Page 327

I am a classically trained sculptor who tests the boundaries of relief by drawing on the unique potential of mixed media. As a repeat director of the board for the La Scuola Classical Sculpture School, I keep one eye on the masters and the other on the present. Many of my pieces incorporate sculpted ceramic and patinated sheet metals, such as copper, brass, bronze and steel. To expand my palette, I often include specialty fabrics. These combinations provide vast potential for unique colors, textures and feelings. My work—figurative, environmental, and abstract—has been represented by galleries across the United States. Prices range from $300 to $3,000 and up.

JEANINE A. GUNCHEON
Furniture
Page 70

My life has always been dominated by the visual, but I did not know I was an artist until I started my own work in 1986. I taught myself to draw and paint when I discovered a process that fascinated me: painting on wood with dyes. The medium is technical and unforgiving, but produces a beautiful, luminescent look. Each piece is finished with many coats of lacquer. I do no preliminary drawings on paper, but draw directly on the wood with no preconceived plan. The unfolding of the picture is what interests me. My work can be found in the homes of many collectors. I do not think anyone is as fascinated with my work as I am; I consider it the ultimate form of entertainment and self-indulgence.

MICHELE HARDY
Art Quilts
Page 331

My mixed-media fiber art incorporates elements of collage, surface design, quilting and embroidery. I use a variety of dyed and painted fabrics, many of which are transformed by extensive stitching or silkscreen printing prior to construction. Vibrant color, energy, texture and graphic appeal are all important energies in my images. My lifelong love of geology and nature is the inspiration for my current work. My works can be interpreted as landscapes, cross-sections or maps of our world, or they can be viewed as purely abstract forms. I actively show my art in national juried exhibits and galleries and have received numerous awards, including several best of show. My art is collected and featured in many private, corporate and public collections throughout the United States.

CHRISTOPHER GRYDER
Murals, Tiles & Wall Reliefs
Pages 307, 311

The lineage of my hand-carved ceramic relief traces back to the tradition of organically inspired terra cotta architectural panels, which formed the intricate facades of buildings around the world. My work reinterprets natural objects and processes into a new language of form. The tiles, suitable for both indoor and outdoor applications, have been installed in residential and corporate settings, including the headquarters of a corporate office in Ann Arbor, Michigan. My skills as an architect allow me to seamlessly integrate the unique needs of each client and space with my own artistic sensibilities. From the production of detailed study drawings and images to the creation of one-of-a-kind tiles, I have perfected a process that leads to artwork of extraordinary beauty.

CARRIE GUSTAFSON
Objects
Pages 16, 147

I first discovered glass while completing my B.F.A. in printmaking at the Rhode Island School of Design. Following graduation I carried a printmaker's fascination with pattern and texture into the glassblowing studio of Martha's Vineyard Glassworks, where I continue to exhibit every summer. Further studies have taken me to Murano, Italy, the Penland School of Crafts, Pilchuck Glass School and the Corning Museum of Glass. My work has been featured in national shows and international publications, including *Neus Glas, This Side Up!* and, most recently, the Smithsonian Craft Show. I continue to find inspiration in the patterns and rhythms of organic life and have come to see glass (formed with the heat of fire and breath of man) as a potent metaphoric tool for exploring the spiritual undercurrent of the natural world.

MARY HATCH
Paintings
Page 227

I love color and creating stories that are mysterious like childhood memories, resonating feelings just beyond my grasp. Sometimes a painting arrives almost fully formed in my mind, but mostly it begins with a tiny bit of information and evolves until finally it seems to have always existed. The figure captured me at an early age, and I have rarely strayed from that focus; however, exploring different mediums has always interested me, and new archival print technology has led me to experiment with digital art. My work has been shown in over 30 one-person exhibits and is included in more than 300 public and private collections throughout the United States and Canada. Prices range from $300 for digital prints to $6,000 for a 48" x 60" painting.

ARTIST STATEMENTS

BOB HAWKS
Objects
Pages 3, 127, 156

I have been turning wood for 16 years. The joy in turning comes from being able to combine different species of wood or use the characteristics of a log to create a pleasing design. Much of the wood that I use comes from trees destroyed by storms or cleared to make way for a highway or commercial construction. My pieces have been accepted in over 30 juried exhibitions and are owned by collectors and museums in the United States, as well as Germany, Colombia, Venezuela and Japan. In 1993 my piece *Longitudinal* was selected for the White House Collection of American Crafts.

HOLLY A. HEBEL
Prints & Drawings
Page 285

To me, color is powerful; it is the driving spirit of my work. When people see my art, I want them to feel like they are seeing fireworks for the first time. I use vibrant colors to evoke those feelings of awe and wonder. My desire is that people grasp the emotion and energy that permeate the passionate bursts of color in my drawings. Prices and resume are available by request.

DALE HEFFERNAN
Objects
Page 137

My odyssey into the world of glass began in September 1979, when I took glassblowing as an elective class in college. A week into that semester I changed my major from geology to art and have not looked back since. I have spent over 20 years working for some of the West Coast's most prominent glass artists, while honing my skills to develop designs in a style of my own. I lit the furnace in my own studio on January 1, 2003. With the advent of my own studio has come the opportunity to further explore my ideas, as well as the good fortune to enjoy the company of my wife, Corky, who works alongside me to execute designs of her own creation.

STEPHEN HENNING
Paintings
Page 264

I was an award-winning graphic designer and creative director for over 15 years before I took up the brush on a full-time basis. Since the early 1990s, I have developed a distinctive style of American impressionism. My original paintings hang in private, corporate and public collections across North America. Mentored since childhood by Ernest Oberholtzer (co-founder of The Wilderness Society), I strive to paint the landscape in its untamed state. I am essentially an introvert. I enjoy people, but part of me is always hungry for wide-open spaces and the beauty of nature; painting is my means of escape. Honors include: Arts Leadership Award, 1999, the Minnesota State Arts Board; Featured Artist, 1998, Minnesota Porcelain Artists Teacher's Guild Expo; Minnesota Percent for Art Purchase Award, 1997; and the People's Choice Award, 1996, New York Mills Regional Cultural Center Invitational Exhibit.

KAREN HEYL
Garden Sculpture
Pages 203, 211

I use Indiana limestone to carve stylized figurative, natural and organic forms to enhance a garden setting. My relief carvings are custom commissions and reflect ideas shared between client and artist. Works include monolithic shapes carved in the round, as well as one-sided flat stones that can be mounted on a base, pedestal or wall. I create aesthetic sophistication with simplified, sensual forms suitable for the home garden, memorial garden, patio, courtyard or entryway. I have been creating stone sculpture for 20 years and have large-scale relief carvings throughout the United States in parks, churches, hospitals, corporate buildings, convention centers, universities and housing developments. My work has been featured in previous GUILD sourcebooks.

HOLMAN STUDIOS
Furniture
Page 72

I am a custom furniture maker; accordingly, the range of my work is as diverse as my clientele. I build reproduction pieces. I build funky new pieces. I even build giant golf clubs (well, once). The constant in all of this furniture is that it is well crafted. While I enjoy stretching my own creative process beyond established idioms, all my work is firmly planted within the craftsman's tradition. Even my most whimsical work is meticulously well made. In my personal lexicon, function defies craft, and my work is always functional, even when it's not traditional. My designs are generally collaborative; I work with residential and corporate clients (and their designers and architects) to create a piece that excites us all.

DON HOUSE
Photographs
Page 302

Photography is an abstract medium, and I try to make the most of it. Whether I choose to use traditional black-and-white or alternative approaches, the goal is always the same: capture the essence. Producing unique imagery for over 20 years, my work has appeared in numerous publications, from *Forbes* to *American Forests*, and in solo and group exhibitions around the country. Recently, I co-authored *Buffalo Creek Chronicles*, a collection of essays and photographs of the Southern Plains. For an extensive catalogue of color and black-and-white photographs and limited-edition prints, as well as descriptions of the various photographic processes I use, please write, call, e-mail or access the website. Special projects and commissions are welcome.

HUGH C. CULLEY ART DESIGN
Windows, Doors & Railings
Pages 166, 174

Born in Derby, England, I immigrated to the U.S. in 1958. Since childhood it has been natural for me to imagine and create art. Through the years I have refined my techniques in drawing and applied my metalworking skills to create an array of art objects in steel, stainless steel, bronze, aluminum and copper. Having worked in metals for over 30 years (10 of them in business for myself), I have been able to combine design and engineering with hot metal forging and fabrication to create objects that are artistic yet practical, meeting all building codes. My award-winning works are in homes throughout the United States. I am a member of several national metalworking organizations and am fully licensed and insured.

REBECCA HUNGERFORD
Objects
Page 148

For 20 years I accepted the norm and created traditional functional pieces from fine pewter. But since 1995 I've taken a contemporary approach and experimented with form, surface treatment, materials and color. My goal is to pull pewter away from its stereotype and demonstrate its decorative versatility. Often inspired by nature, I have used leaves to create etched designs. Sometimes I color these imprints with subtle metallic paints and pencil or add semiprecious gems, foil, wood and antler. My pieces have received recognition in international exhibitions. Recent commissions include communion sets, decorative pieces and funerary urns.

ARTIST STATEMENTS

ROB HYNER
Photographs
Page 301

I have been interested in photography since college, but could only pursue it as a part-time hobby. Recently, after 30 years in the business world, I decided to follow my dream and enter the realm of fine art photography. My photographs tend to be simple and uncluttered. Some are created with props; others are as I find them in the field. No matter what creative method is used, an artist should be comfortable with the result of his labors. What it takes to achieve this satisfaction surely changes over time and that, to me, is the beauty of the adventure. All digital images are created using the latest archival inks and papers. All framing is to museum standards.

INNES COPPER LIGHTING
Lighting
Page 104

When creating my copper lamps and lighting designs, I avoid bending to current design trends, periods or styles. Old or new copper is warm and everlasting, leading to a multitude of surface finishes and design possibilities. Guided by the principle of form following function, I create lamps and lighting fixtures that satisfy varied tastes and styles. Copper brings a glowing warmth to indoor and outdoor living environments. Quality and integrity are never compromised as I work towards simplicity, ease and comfort in each design.

MICHAEL IRELAND
Paintings
Page 263

After over 25 years of participating in the creative process, my love for painting has never subsided. Working in my primary medium of watercolor, I have discovered a certain transcendentalism that has emerged from the painting process itself. From my point of view, I know a painting succeeds when I become so immersed in the process that I am actually standing in the scene I have painted. That is when I know the viewer will perhaps have an opportunity to feel the wind, smell the earthen path and be warmed by the light that moves across the scene itself. Most recently, I have been working in a relatively large-scale format for transparent watercolor; new pieces average 80" x 18". Quite exciting!

KATHRYN JACOBI
Paintings
Page 226

Classically trained as a realist painter and printmaker, I create oil portraits, still lifes, figurative narratives and editioned prints. I have been working professionally for over 35 years and have exhibited in galleries throughout the United States, Canada, and Europe; my credits include over 50 solo shows. I accept only six portrait commissions per year, working from sittings or, in the case of children or the deceased, from photographs. For further information, to view my resume and to see a comprehensive overview of my work, please visit my website at www.kathrynjacobi.com.

EILEEN JAGER
Furniture
Page 75

I'm endlessly fascinated by the dance between glass and light. This has been my passion since a magical moment at Chartres Cathedral, when I was struck by the ability of light and color to transform a space. I am inspired by my world travels, the cycles of nature and the balance between form and function. Each piece I create is a journey revealed through vision, trust and perseverance. My luscious glass mosaic furniture and "aquatiture"—or tablefountains—are multidimensional sculptures, a sensory delight to see, hear, touch and experience. Iridescent glass shimmers while water gently flows, creating a soothing and energizing ambiance. I am moved by the power of art to enhance our lives, and I welcome private and public commissions for site-specific projects for both home and garden. Prices range from $2,800 to $18,000.

ADAM JAHIEL
Photographs
Page 297

For years I have been photographing the cowboys of the Great Basin, perhaps one of the most inhospitable regions of the already-rugged West. I try to give an honest, fresh account of what is clearly an authentic—but vanishing—American subculture. My images and portfolios are found in the collections of the Nevada Museum of Art, the Joslyn Museum, the Amon Carter Museum, the Buffalo Bill Historical Center, the Ralph Lauren Collection and the Raytheon Corporation, as well as many private international collections. My work has also been honored with two NEA awards. Limited-edition print prices range from $750 to $3,300. Prints are available as platinum and silver gelatin prints. Image size ranges from 14" x 14" to 30" x 30". Each print is meticulously hand printed using traditional photographic methods.

MARCIA JESTAEDT
Murals, Tiles & Wall Reliefs
Page 310

I have been working with clay since 1970 and raku firing since 1972. My work is characterized by rich, lustrous glazes and designs that are inspired by the Orient. This work consists mostly of hand-formed tiles, which are etched with geometric and floral images, then glazed in a painterly manner. I am a graduate of the University of Maryland, where I majored in studio art and taught for a number of years. My work has been exhibited in galleries and shows throughout the country, including the Smithsonian Institution. I have received numerous grants and awards and have been featured in *Handbuilt Ceramics* and *Surface Decoration*, both published by Lark Books, and in *Ceramics Monthly*. Prices range from $1,250 to $3,600.

JIM MILLAR STUDIO
Sculpture
Page 189

For the past 35 years, my goal has been to create an aesthetic relationship between form, movement and sound. For me, a successful sculpture is one that appears as if it has grown into its composition and is compatible with the environment for which it was created. My work is made from sheet bronze and is formed with various hammers and anvils. I work much like a silversmith, only on a larger scale. Most of my self-contained fountains range in size from 2'H to 8'H and can be placed either indoors or outdoors. My work is shown in numerous galleries and private collections nationwide. Over the years I've shipped my pieces all over the world. I gladly accept custom work.

LYDIA B. JOHNSTON
Art Quilts
Pages 329–330

My work expresses color and movement, balance and harmony. Subtle interactions between one color block and another make each piece sing. In my studio I search for just the right combination of color to captivate. I work primarily with fine cotton broadcloth, as well as silk. Color blocks are individually hand dyed, then layered upon each other as a collage. My designs are simple yet elegant, with an asymmetry that draws the eye around the piece. The designs are purely abstract, but often evoke a sense of the world around us. My work has been exhibited throughout the country and hangs in many private collections. Prices for wall hangings range from $1,100–$3,600; a series of smaller framed pieces ranges from $375–$650. Please visit www.lydiajohnston.com to view all available work.

ARTIST STATEMENTS

JULIANN JONES
Paintings
Page 246

I paint vivid, colorful images on archival board with the milk-based paint, casein. The subject matter of my pieces tends to be nature or animal based, but the subject is not the driving force behind the images. My mission is to make each painting a jewel of its own, layering and placing color in exciting ways. The properties of casein allow me to layer and texture in ways that other paints do not. Casein has a chalky finish, which adds to the textural and striking look of the piece. I work out of my studio in downtown Livingston, Montana, and accept commissions. Visit my website to see hundreds of drawings, as well as current paintings.

TALIAFERRO JONES
Photographs/Sculpture
Pages 197, 295

Utilizing texture, form and light, I explore the essence of balance from the physical to the spiritual in my glass sculptures and giclée prints. My sensual photographs of macro patterns of sand, water, grass and other natural elements carry on a dialogue with my minimal glass sculptures. My photographic prints range from single images to multi-image prints, while my vibrant glass sculptures vary in size from 1'L to 9'L. Both the glass and the photography come in a variety of textures and vivid colors. I enjoy working with clients to create dynamic commissions. Some recent projects include: CordeValle, CA; Georgina Fantoni, England; Northwater, Toronto, Canada. My work can also be viewed in these books: *International Glass* by Richard Yelle and *The Craft of Northern California* by Alcove Books.

CINTHIA JOYCE
Sculpture
Pages 180–181

Through my bronze sculptures, I hope to inspire peace and bring beauty and serenity into the world. I love working with the figure, exploring the endless possibilities of emotions conveyed through body language. In addition, I often portray the spiritual relationship between animals and humans. My foundation as an artist was strengthened by my B.A. in art history from UCLA, studies under nationally recognized masters, travels in Europe and a childhood spent surrounded by animals in rural Malibu, California. I am unusual in that I often explore the same model or pose through both abstract and realistic interpretations. My sculptures vary from miniature to life sized. I have won numerous awards in juried exhibitions nationwide.

MARY DENNIS KANNAPELL
Murals, Tiles & Wall Reliefs
Page 308

Creating art, for me, is a way of knowing. It is a gestalt experience consisting of observation, sensory knowledge, body knowledge, emotion, intuition, imagination, deliberation and play. It is a form of dialogue I enter into with my subject, though I feel the most important thing I'm doing is listening—listening to the sound of ideas percolating, to my own responses and to the ripeness of a medium. I am immensely attracted to a wide range of mediums and feel they are as sounds moving at different speeds or rhythms, a river of motion. The investigation of nature, dreams and language is my current creative river. To know something in my head, hands and heart allows me an integrating experience that I find dimensionally challenging and evolutionarily rewarding.

KATE MILLER STUDIO
Tapestry, Fiber & Paper
Page 353

I use the batik method of painting on 100% silk crepe de chine to make wall hangings of layered, sparkling colors and rhythmic contemporary designs. Inspired by ancient myths of transformation, I explore how layering colors creates unique variations in depth and texture. The result is a triptych or diptych that hangs from bamboo poles mounted on a wall, each a banner of its own world. I work by playing the colors off one another, as if the hues themselves were having a conversation. Many viewers see musical expression in my work. Among my raw materials are life's polarities and contradictions—Exploration of paradox is in the spirit of everything I do. The movement and drama of my pieces mirrors the complexities I see in the human heart. In each of my pieces, I seek an edge, a defining moment when harmony arises out of complexity and chaos swirls into beauty.

BARBARA KELLOGG
Paintings
Page 257

My paintings are semi-abstract and motivated by my love of nature. I use acrylic paint, watercolor, casein and ink. Oftentimes, I will monoprint textures on the piece of watercolor paper as a first step. Line, movement and careful attention to design are important features in my work. Collage is sometimes used as a subtle and integral part of the painting. Unframed images vary in size from smaller than 15" x 11" to 30" x 40". Prices range from approximately $300 to $1,600. My work has been exhibited in several national water media exhibitions, and in 2002 my painting, *Fishing for Fun*, was awarded the Loa Ruth Spring Award for best nonrepresentational painting in the National Watercolor Society Annual Exhibition in Fullerton, California.

KELLY FITZGERALD PHOTOGRAPHY
Photographs
Pages 286, 303

I love traveling to different parts of the globe and documenting images from my photographic adventures, capturing the images, faces and landscapes of our ever-changing world. I have an excellent reputation for producing uniquely creative and quality images within the field of black-and-white photography. I have received top honors in *Photographer's Forum* magazine and the Canon Photography Contest series and have been featured every year in the *Best of Photography Annual* since 1998. My photographs have appeared in numerous exhibits in various art galleries around the world. This past year my work was exhibited alongside photographers Linda McCartney and Cecil Beaton. I make my gelatin silver prints with only the finest museum-quality materials available.

ELLEN MEARS KENNEDY
Tapestry, Fiber & Paper
Page 354

My artwork is constructed of hundreds of double-sided papers, all handmade in my studio from pigmented pulp. Each paper has a left and right side that displays a unique shade. When the paper is folded, one color shows on the left side and a second color shows on the right. As viewers walk past each construction, the colors subtly change as they see alternating sides of the design. My work has been featured in previous GUILD sourcebooks.

BERRI KRAMER
Art Quilts
Page 337

My love of color, combined with my travels to different cultures, brings continued inspiration to the creation of my abstract art quilts. The process of completing my master's degree in color and design at Lesley University allowed concentrated studio time. My current work is the culmination of that endeavor. My interest in color relationships leads to intricate work with complementary and tertiary color families. Travels to South America and the Philippines on humanitarian missions brought me new palettes, new emotions and new visions that became my studio companions. My asymmetrically pieced works are made from a vast array of fabrics, which come from all over the world. Sizes range from 22" x 28" to 48" x 60" ($600–$3,000). Many are also available as giclée prints ($60–$335).

ARTIST STATEMENTS

GINNY KRUEGER
Paintings
Page 252

As a child I catalogued my environment through painting and drawing: indigenous trees, fish, flowers and birds. Later, I became fascinated by the work of the Abstract Expressionists—their spontaneous, gestural mark-making and their emotive use of color. I work with encaustics, a form of paint created from molten beeswax, pigment and damar, a highly sensuous, physical substance. I apply the molten layers and burn in, or fuse, each successive layer with a propane torch. I pay homage to the images that were important to me as a child and strive to honor the innate tendencies that each painting dictates, for this yielding to the unknown is what is ultimately important to me. I was recently awarded the prestigious Illinois State Visual Arts Fellowship Award; my work is found in private and corporate collections nationwide.

CHRISTINE KUHN
Paintings
Page 248

I create mixed-media talismans intended for use as meditative aids. These talismans help individuals and communities focus on goals both material and spiritual. The talismanic images arise out of a process of meditation in which I consider the desired problem or goal and envision the most positive outcome. The visualization and meditation techniques used to create the talismans are derived from tantric Buddhist practice. While painting a talisman, I recite mantra to infuse it with the appropriate spiritual energies; thus, the creation of a talisman is a ritual geared toward the desired outcome. Situations appropriate for the use of talismans include births, weddings and other new beginnings, as well as the memorialization of loved ones, conflict resolution and commitment to business and personal goals.

L. BALOMBINI
Sculpture
Page 186

When I open the door to my studio in the morning, I am greeted by a colorful menagerie of dancers, acrobats and playful friends. I hand-weave steel wire into basket-like vessels, skirted figures and long-legged birds, with much attention paid to detail. I show my work nationally and have been featured in both polymer and wire art publications. I will gladly discuss commissions, gallery representation and opportunities to teach workshops in your area. See my website for show and workshop schedules, and for prices. Or come visit me at my studio on the beautiful coast of Maine.

LH POTTERY
Furniture
Page 94

I started making tiles for tables in 1997 as Christmas presents for friends and family. I soon realized that the size and shape of tiles are limited only by an artist's imagination. I began experimenting with nontraditional tile shapes and discovered that I could make the abstract design ideas floating around in my head a reality. Today every tile is hand cut and trimmed; each table is custom made for the client. It is a collaborative process from start to finish, from the shape and size of the table, to the kind of wood used in the frame, to the color of the tiles. I work with the client to ensure his or her complete satisfaction.

RICHARD LA MARTINA
Photographs
Page 298

Most of my photographs are created in the field, where I meet my subjects in a natural and comfortable environment. I believe this creates a less-contrived look to my photographs and gives the impression that the composition was happened upon. In fact, I spend hours working with the details, using my 35mm like a large-format camera. Every detail is contemplated before the composition is recorded on slow speed slide film. I then digitally scan these images to be printed as limited-edition archival giclée prints. My work has been published, exhibited or sold to private and corporate collectors around the world, including the State of Wisconsin, the Milwaukee Public Museum, *Popular Photography*, Amphoto publishing and the Carnegie Museum of Natural History, among others.

LaCASSE STUDIOS
Sculpture
Page 185

My work strives—through the medium of bronze—to transform the boundless world of imagination into reality. My admiration for classical and contemporary artwork, combined with my extensive knowledge of anatomy, metal fabrication and the foundry arts, allows me to physically illuminate my thoughts. My ideas begin with a combination of things, ranging anywhere from a childhood experience to a series of harmonious musical notes. The mélange of sensory stimuli is then translated into metal using the lost wax process, along with other techniques. Ultimately, each sculpture is unique in conception, subject matter, meaning and execution, while maintaining a common thread that plays to the human spirit and emotion.

LAKESIDE FIBERS
Floor Coverings
Page 126

Our fine artisans at Lakeside Fibers in Madison, Wisconsin, have extensive experience in knitting and weaving. Our work includes home furnishings, as well as apparel and art pieces. We have designers on staff and consultants from the University of Wisconsin–Madison, who collaborate on our custom-designed pieces. We have completed commissions for Temple Beth El, Madison, WI; The Washington Hotel and Restaurant, Washington Island, WI; and for private individuals. We specialize in wool and linen rugs (up to 24'L), as well as other household furnishings. Our custom-designed shawls and scarves feature all types of fibers, from silk and Tencel to wool and alpaca.

KERRI LAWNSBY
Paintings
Page 268

I create artwork that captures the natural inner luminosity of flowers, landscapes, still life subjects and people. My artwork has been described as emotionally rich, intensely colorful and vibrant, and evocative of the experience of the subject. My style is influenced by the rich, intense colors of Degas pastels, and the powerful close-ups of flowers painted by Georgia O'Keeffe and Vincent van Gogh. As a painter my goal is to enrich the lives of those who view and collect my artwork by creating images that evoke positive emotions. I enjoy meeting collectors and welcome commissions of any size and subject. My work has been displayed in juried exhibitions nationwide, including the elite Amsterdam Whitney in Chelsea, New York, and the Farmington Museum in New Mexico.

ERIC DAVID LAXMAN
Garden Sculpture
Pages 212-214

I am a sculptor and furniture designer working in a wide range of materials, including steel, bronze, stainless steel, wood, marble and granite. I explore the abstract and realistic by assembling welded metal and stone fragments into intricate compositions. I find my inspiration in both Eastern and Western art traditions, using themes that express balance, transformation and movement. With Anahata Arts I have extended my sculptural sensibility into the realm of metal furniture and functional art. I work closely with clients on location to create designs that fit harmoniously within a particular environment. I was awarded best of show for the exhibit *Made in NY—2003* at the Schweinfurth Memorial Art Center in Auburn, New York. Recent commissions include decorative metal designs for Ashford and Simpson's Sugar Bar Restaurant in New York City and a bronze fountain for an estate in New Canaan, Connecticut.

ARTIST STATEMENTS

MARLENE LENKER
Paintings
Page 259

My work reflects my response to nature and time. This year I began a new concept of stacked and series group paintings, which express my love for landscape, light and mood. I am governed by my intuition and instinct, capturing a moment felt using acrylic, mixed media and collage on canvas paper and board. Commissions are welcomed. Collections include: Arthur Young, Oppenheimer Fund, Lever Bros., PepsiCo, Kidder Peabody, Warner-Lambert, Merrill Lynch, Horcht, Pfizer, Hoffman-Laroche and Johnson & Johnson. Publications include: *Bridging Time and Space,* 1999; *Who's Who in America; American Artists; Women Artists; World Women* and *International Art.* My work has been featured in previous GUILD sourcebooks. The international art publisher Winn Devon Art Group will publish my work in limited editions and open-end editions.

MITCH LEVIN
Furniture
Page 83

My work generally tends to be a marriage of materials; I enjoy juxtaposing dissimilar materials against one another. I will use almost any material and often include recycled elements in my work. Since 1984, my passion has been creating one-of-a-kind and limited-edition furniture and sculpture. My work has been exhibited nationwide in numerous private and corporate collections, and has appeared in major publications. I feel education is an important part of an artist's life, and I have had the opportunity to teach while working on my master's degree. I have also established several internship programs within my own studio. I constantly challenge myself creatively in areas that are unfamiliar so as to learn and grow from these experiences.

MICHELLE LINDBLOM
Paintings
Page 256

My work is a challenging and psychological examination of my internal conflicts, thoughts and perceptions. These internal dialogues have their basis in the spontaneous reactions and personal relationships I experience on a daily basis. It is where my most passionate and mystifying dialogues exist. My work has become the visually tangible result of these examinations and ultimate revelations. I received my undergraduate degree from the University of Louisiana–New Orleans and my M.F.A. from the University of North Dakota. Besides working as a professional artist, I teach full-time at Bismarck State College in the Visual Arts department and direct the campus galleries. My work has been exhibited in the United States, England and Norway and has received numerous awards. Price range: $650–$2,500.

LEPOWORKS, INC.
Furniture
Page 90

Our studio is composed of a family of artists who use their individual talents to create work that reveals the one-of-a-kind philosophy of LepoWorks. For 30 years, we have designed private, public and corporate art to match our clients' particular aesthetic preferences. Our artwork enhances interior and exterior architectural elements and spaces, offering artistic solutions while meeting budget and deadline demands. We express our diversity through a multitude of materials used in traditional and contemporary styles. Our line of signature studio pieces are shown in this book.

LINDA LEVITON
Mixed Media
Page 319

Creating modular wall sculpture that evokes the color and texture of nature is central to my art. These designs can be hung to form one large piece or mounted as smaller separate units, creating ease and flexibility for large installations as well as changing interior spaces. Using etching, dyes, patinas and paint, I can texture and color metal to form subtle or vibrantly colored designs. My techniques come from many disciplines, including blacksmithing, sheet metal construction, welding, silversmithing and printmaking. My work includes large metal quilts, etched three-dimensional wall-hung constructions and woven forms. I've been profiled on HGTV's "Modern Masters" and was the recipient of the 2003 Individual Artist Grant from the Ohio Arts Council. Commissions include: Northwest Airlines, State of Ohio, University of Southern California and Northeastern Utilities.

LISA KESLER FINE ART
Paintings
Pages 245, 392

My works on paper and canvas integrate printmaking, collage and painting. I find inspiration by experimenting with materials and techniques and am intrigued by the repetition of pattern. In my artwork, I stylize forms into simpler geometric shapes and juxtaposes bold colors into fanciful compositions. Contrasts between light and dark remain central to my art. My work can be found in private and corporate collections throughout the United States and abroad. Commissions welcome. Slides and catalog available upon request. Commissions include: Zax Restaurant at the Golden Nugget, 2002, Las Vegas, NV; Best Western, San Francisco, CA and Alexis Hotel, Seattle, WA. Collections include: Evergreen Medical Center, Kirkland, WA; Riversoft Corporation, San Francisco, CA; Microcrafts, Redmond, WA and Eli Lilly, Indianapolis, IN. Publications include: *Florida Design* magazine and *Art World News.*

MARK LEVIN
Furniture
Page 57

I use solid wood in my work for its sculptural malleability and creative viability. The aesthetic linchpins that drive my creations are sensuality and delicacy. My work has a mellifluous dynamic similar to that of a Beethoven passage, weaving melodic filigree out of molten steel. Work is executed on a commission basis for both residential and commercial clients. Exhibitions and awards: First Place Niche Award, 2003 and 2002; First Place, National Custom Woodworking Business Design Portfolio; First Place, Artisans of the New Forest National Exhibition. Recent publications: *Wood Art Today, The Custom Furniture Source Book, Furniture Studio: The Heart of the Functional Arts, Fine Woodworking, Woodwork, Woodworker West, Woodshop News, New Mexico* magazine. Commissions: Bank of Hong Kong; Occidental Petroleum; Baird & Warner Real Estate; Temple Solel and Congregation Israel.

LIGHTSPANN ILLUMINATION DESIGN
Lighting
Page 105

In 1989 I crossed the fence from fine art painting to the world of hot glass. The fluid movement of blown, fused and slumped glass ignited my passion for creating glass art. Since my painting background had instilled the significance of light in my work, I soon started using electric light to accentuate the fragility of glass and the rigidity of metal. I started bringing together a community of glass and metal artisans to complement my skills and founded Lightspann Illumination Design. In the last decade, we've emulated the artisan's guild approach, bringing together top craftspeople from various disciplines to create illuminated sculptures from high-quality art materials. Today, Lightspann has ten employees and over 50 fixtures in its product line, which is distributed throughout the United States and Canada.

STEVE LOPES
Windows, Doors & Railings
Pages 5, 159–160

For over two decades, the focus of my work has been the design and execution of unique, top-quality, hand-forged architectural metalwork. I encourage a collaborative design process with clients so that they may understand the possibilities of metal, and thus commission a body of work that meets their specific aesthetic ideals. As such, I am not trying to sell any individual pieces in my portfolio, but rather to show how certain design challenges were met. I am comfortable working with architects, designers and clients who have time, design and budget constraints and welcome the challenge that each project brings.

ARTIST STATEMENTS

LOTTON ART GLASS
Lighting
Page 108

It is my pleasure to create beautiful and exotic artwork that graces many homes across America.

LISA AND LORI LUBBESMEYER
Tapestry, Fiber & Paper
Page 350

As twin sisters who studied printmaking and oil painting respectively, we symbiotically influence each other through our collaborative work in fiber appliquéd wall hangings. While we were attempting to combine the conventional elements of our individual disciplines, it was actually our interest in working together that brought us to the unique, painterly qualities of fiber. Because our interpretation of architecture and nature reflect the interaction of light, color and dimension, our compositions have a textural quality that we achieve through the process of layering and overstitching pieced fabrics. Our award-winning representations of domestic, urban and natural environments can be found in corporate and private collections nationally.

DEAN LUDWIG
Furniture
Page 93

When I turned 40, I decided to follow my heart. I gave up secure business and faculty positions (I hold an M.B.A. and Ph.D. from Wharton) to pursue furniture making full time. Today, the bulk of my work involves the creation of key furnishings such as altars and pulpits for churches across North America. Still, my favorite piece to build is the rocking chair. There is no piece of furniture as technically challenging in form and function as the rocker, and I am honored that people consider mine among the most beautiful and comfortable in the world. More importantly, rocking chairs call us to pause and reflect amidst our hurried culture. I hope the works of my heart will give comfort, refreshment and inspiration for generations to come.

ELIZABETH MacDONALD
Doors, Windows & Screens
Page 102

I produce tile paintings that suggest the patinas of age. These compositions are suitable for indoors or outdoors and take the form of freestanding columns, wall panels or architectural installations. Commissions: Conrad International Hotel, Hong Kong; St. Luke's Hospital, Denver, CO; and the chapel at Mayo Clinic, Scottsdale, AZ. Public Art: Wilbur Cross High School, New Haven, CT; and Department of Environmental Protection, Hartford, CT. Awards: State of Connecticut Governor's Arts Award. My work has been featured in previous GUILD sourcebooks.

CATHERINE A. MAHONEY
Paintings
Page 262

I invite the viewer to dance in my paintings, partnering with the excitement that moves my soul. As a multimedia artist, I express light as it impacts color, pattern and texture: dramatic skies and dynamic landscapes through windows and doors, or around the sensitive human form. Over the past 35 years, national and international collectors have included the Ella Carothers Dunnegan Gallery of Art, Missouri Public Service, Ballas-Clayton Standard, Inc. and First Bank. I've won numerous awards and have appeared in many juried exhibitions. Recently, the Missouri Arts Council awarded me a grant to complete an 20' Gasconade County historical mural. Publications include: *Best of Watercolor: Painting Texture, Our Missouri Heritage,* the *Missouri Symphony Society* cover and *Waldechesche Landeazeitung.*

KELLY BURKE MAKUCH
Sculpture
Page 199

Through varied media, my art has always been influenced by a fascination with my own link to all living things, thus irretrievably connecting me to the larger world. A constant seeker of new materials and methods of expression, I discovered kiln-formed glass, a medium I find exhilarating! Glass has enabled me to comfortably express subliminal powers of abstract description, as well as realistic representation. It is therefore a wonderful medium for various residential and commercial applications, from tabletops and tiles to bowls and sculpture. My work has been shown at Scenario Gallery, Westhampton Beach, NY; Washington Art Association, Washington Depot, CT; and Garrison Art Center, Garrison Landing, NY. It is also found in private collections.

BRENT J. MARSHALL
Doors, Windows & Screens
Page 98, 101

Having returned to the United States after an inspiring three-year stay in England, I am currently developing architecturally based glass panels and windows. These timeless pieces are individually designed, catering to each client and the space he or she wishes to enhance. The tiles are carefully crafted using several distinct methods of casting, giving each element a unique surface. Customizing my sculptures to each environment frees me to create unique pieces for public, corporate and residential spaces. Acknowledgment of my artwork has come both locally and internationally in the way of inclusion in corporate collections, the Lilly Endowment Grant and a recent fellowship at the Creative Glass Center of America, among others. The two screens featured in this book are approximately $10,000 each.

THERESE MAY
Art Quilts
Page 338

My "puzzle interchange" technique starts with one small drawing, which I repeat throughout the quilt. Using this pattern, each piece is cut and rearranged so that each block is a combination of all of the selected fabrics. This idea began with the *Therese* quilt in 1969. I am now working on a series of quilts that uses the technique in a new, updated way. The *Therese* quilt was chosen in the year 2000 as one of the 100 Best American Quilts of the 20th century. My work has been exhibited, published and collected extensively. Prices range from $1,000 to $12,000.

PAVLOS MAYAKIS
Tapestry, Fiber & Paper
Page 349

I hand-weave and surface design unframed 28" x 60" ARTpieces as wall art. Producing rich colors and striking that important balance between the elements in a controlled, yet somewhat spontaneous manner, comes naturally to me. Working with multiple dye classifications, I especially enjoy working with fiber-reactive dyes in tandem with vat dyes. My work appears throughout the United States and Europe, and has been featured in the 2002–2003 *New Art International* and *The Artful Home I: Art for the Wall.* Awards include a Mendocino College full-time faculty scholarship and the Mendocino College Foundation Scholarship of Promise. I welcome collaborations with architects, designers and individuals.

ARTIST STATEMENTS

TERESA McCUE
Paintings
Page 258

My work really has two components. The first involves my spiritual connection with the outdoors. I am enamored of the sights and sounds of nature—the patterns, rhythms, textures and the almost tangible quality of light. The second component to my work is an enchantment with color. Using pastel I am able to fully explore an infinite variety of the hundreds of hues and values that are at my fingertips. It fascinates me that a color will appear altered depending upon the other colors that surround it. I am also intrigued by the ability of color to evoke emotion—be it passion, exhilaration or serenity. My pastel paintings, both intimate and large in scale, can be found in private and corporate collections nationwide. Commissions are welcome.

CLAUDIA McKINSTRY
Paintings
Pages 220–221

My paintings begin and end with a passion and sensitivity to light and how it affects a variety of subjects. My works are stories, statements, reflections and studies. I fully explore my themes, even to the point of observing the growth of the plants that I will paint or watching the movement of light through days and seasons. My process involves innumerable layers of transparent color (whether in watercolor or oil), which results in luminous, rich values. Many of my paintings are available as high-quality archival giclé prints, which may be viewed on my website, www.claudiamckinstry.com. My work lives in many private and public collections around the world, including the Narita Airport in Tokyo and the San Francisco International Airport.

BRENDA McMAHON
Objects
Page 131

By merging primitive pit firing with a technique from 17th-century Germany, my saggar-fired porcelain is born. Surrounding my porcelain vessels with a variety of organic materials in the firing chamber yields a splendid combination of smoky blacks and grays, with a fumed palette of orange, salmon, pink and burgundy. The alchemy between potter and fire always yields surprise. These thrown and burnished vessels have a quiet elegance that is complimented by the dynamic, smoky surface. My tile work is the canvas for fire paintings, perfectly capturing the mystical depth of this alchemy. Abstract landscapes and cosmic stellar explosions are revealed, and it gives me great joy to see nature's patterns repeated on my porcelain vessels and tiles. My work is a drop in the ocean of humanity's creativity, one that continually compels me forward.

MEG BLACK
HANDMADE PAPER PAINTINGS
Tapestry, Fiber & Paper
Paper 355

My landscape, seascape and garden paintings are created exclusively from fibrous paper pulp: there is no "paint" of any kind on the surface. Each pulp painting is pigmented with 100% pure, non-fading, acid-free pigments and is carefully treated so that it can be hung with or without glass. This unique process, combined with masterful craftsmanship, provides a seductive, textured surface that lends itself to the natural subject matter of my paintings. I work on a commission basis of $425 per square foot. A portfolio of available works can be viewed through my website. My collections include: Fidelity Investments, Solomon Smith-Barney and Harvard University.

MEKO DESIGNS
Mixed Media
Page 325

We have been refining our unique style of fused glass artistry since 1995. Designing vibrant, lively masks that convey emotion, personality and human experience has provided a solid foundation for our current artistic focus. Presently we are exploring the fragmented nature of the human psyche using the fused glass medium. Our process involves kiln-firing very large face masks made from carefully cut geometric and irregular shapes of opaque glass. The components of the human face are dissected and rearranged, and the elaborate metalwork that surrounds the glasswork serves as both a frame and as an extension of the emotional mood of each piece. Our prices range from $135 to $3,500.

MERRYWOMAN STUDIOS
Murals, Tiles & Wall Reliefs
Page 313

I incise clay with my hands, my being. The raku process so honors me in the same way. Each piece is illustrated by drawing directly into the clay's surface. Then it's raku fired, bringing the clay to life with beautiful textures, crackling and, of course, the gorgeous metallic luster created during the process. The fire and I must respect (not control) each other; we become Zen partners in the creation of something that is beyond what either of us could create alone. From simple textured wall tiles to beautiful landscapes to detailed Japanese figures, from your kitchen to your foyer, these pieces will sing out with the fire's energy and beauty. The wonderment never ends.

GINA MICHAELS
Garden Sculpture
Page 207

I create my bronze "Hand Plants" by pressing my hands, arms, legs and feet into casting sand. The expressive energy of the body is thus directly imprinted in the mold. I then ladle or pour molten bronze into the hollows of sand created by the body. The immediacy of the flowing metal—and the happy accidents that occur—are an integral part of the work and help to make each piece unique. The process starts in a sandbox, in a spirit of meditation and play. The work has a sense of lightness, pushing up and reaching out into space. "Hand Plants" are hybrid forms incorporating animal (body), vegetable (plant) and mineral (bronze). My work has been featured in numerous solo and group exhibitions in museums, galleries and cultural centers.

DUANE MICKELSON
Sculpture
Page 184

My sculptures have been described as "exploring the boundaries between human imagination, invented culture and natural form, with many of the sculptures depicting fantastically hybrid figures that witness . . . the human capacity to create and destroy." I work in bronze, welded steel, found wood and mixed media in sizes ranging from small tabletop pieces to those that are monumental. Work is priced between $500 and $10,000, with all works being one of a kind. My sculptures have received numerous regional and national awards and are in the collections of colleges, universities and regional museums in the Midwest, with private collectors from the East to West coasts. A portfolio of images is available upon request.

MILLEA FURNISHINGS
Furniture
Page 73

Millea Furnishings represents a sophisticated approach to art. We combine art and furniture into the same thought process, offering a daring line of home furnishings that are three-dimensional, functional art pieces. Intrigued by the concept that art is an interactive process, our furnishings provide energy and movement to an environment. We create furniture that makes a statement. Each piece is its own canvas of bold, abstract design. The structures are sleek and unencumbered since it is the marriage of form to surface design that is the focus of our artwork. Colors can be customized, and commissions are always welcomed.

ARTIST STATEMENTS

AMOS MILLER
Paintings
Page 225

I paint in oil and acrylic on canvas. My primary focus is to record and convey images of our time or current events. I follow the news from around the world through various mass media, often using newspaper photos and stories as starting points for my pictures. My work has appeared in numerous exhibitions and is collected throughout the United States, France, Jamaica and South Africa.

APRYL MILLER
Furniture
Page 78

A love of color and movement are brought to my work through the use of collage. Altering forms of recycled furniture, the conventional becomes unexpected, exuberant and whimsical. The boundaries are crossed between unbridled expression and functionality. Texture, shape, color and pattern are juxtaposed to free the inanimate. Dissonance creates its own harmony. My furniture art is created on a commission basis for collectors and members of the trade. Please visit www.aprylmillerstudios.com for more information.

MORGAN MILLER
Photographs
Page 299

My photographs are starkly simple and are most often described as "painterly." I come in close with my camera to isolate light, shadow and form in order to evoke the sense of quiet, strength and peace I see in my subjects. I show that this beauty exists in even the most humble of objects, be they man-made or from nature. I use a Nikon D1X and print large, limited-edition giclée prints up to 26" × 42" on a very heavy archival watercolor paper. My work is found in private collections across the United States and Canada.

CLAUDIA MILLS
Floor Coverings
Page 122

In my 1880s carriage house studio in Massachusetts, I work on five-foot looms to create rugs showcasing beauty and durability. Updating an age-old craft using new fabrics, I weave contemporary rag rugs for today's homes. I work with two styles: log cabin rugs highlight the fabric interplay, while double block rugs emphasize geometry. My leather rugs, which provide an unusual twist on tradition, offer a modern floor covering option. My custom lines provide trade and private clients with simple, exciting ways to design unique rugs. Claudia Mills Custom Rugs offers one-of-a-kind rugs to accommodate all sizes and colors. My *Runner Project* custom rugs offer custom-sizing based on two-foot widths of 100% cotton or leather, are well priced, easy to care for and have short turnaround times. My rugs are well received at prestigious craft shows and are sold in stores as well as through my studio.

LEN MORRIS
Photographs
Page 296

As an artist, part of my job is to create opportunities for people to see and think differently. I create and photograph assemblages of objects that are often viewed as disposable or ordinary, like scraps of newspaper, dried leaves, flowers or, as featured in this book, a dried Casablanca lily. My art reveals an extraordinary beauty in what may have been otherwise overlooked. My photographs are generic in subject, but specific in concept: ordinary objects viewed with consideration and passion. Corporate and private collectors around the world, including the Boca Raton Museum; the Miyako Osaka Hotel, Japan; and WNYC Radio, New York, have enthusiastically embraced and acquired my work.

MIRANDA MOSS
Paintings
Page 235

In life, many things go on under the surface, worlds of things are hidden … until you have the insight to see them. These hidden dimensions fascinate me, and I like to paint around this theme. Large, bold and expressionistic, my canvases are richly layered with suggestions of animals, personal and cultural icons, landscapes and figures. Some images are overt and some are hidden through positive-negative juxtapositions. The longer you look, the more you see. I received a B.F.A. from the Maryland Institute of Art and have taught at the Minneapolis College of Art and Design. My work can be seen in my studio/gallery; prices range from $600 for prints to $7,500 for original paintings. I also accept commissioned work.

LORETTA MOSSMAN
Paintings
Page 230

I have expanded my artistic vocabulary by exploring new materials and processes, to which I bring my own personal content. Inherent elements in the media allow a range of expression. Subtleties and ambiguities within my images become apparent and articulate my reality. I use symbols to access what lies within me. I express my views through metaphor, visual suggestions, textures and tonal sensuality. Recent work includes lithographs, etchings, woodcuts, multimedia paintings and drawings. I continue to design and produce unique wool rugs and tapestries with the weavers of Teotitlan del Valle, Mexico. These works vary in pricing according to complexity and color. My work is displayed in public, corporate and private collections.

ALAN MOWREY
Paintings
Page 280

My work comprises landscapes, portraits and abstract works. Regardless of the genre, I incorporate devices such as layering, light effects and color harmonies to convey impressions of distance, depth and a flow of natural forces to evoke an emotional response from the viewer. Commissions accepted for portraits, public spaces and private collections. I have a wide selection of works available for immediate purchase. Prices start at $500.

ANDREW MUGGLETON
Furniture
Pages 11, 55

I combine extraordinary woods with metal and glass to create furnishings with spare, elegant lines. Dining room tables and chairs, console tables, beds, entertainment units and sets of drawers have been crafted with a nod to comfort and an eye towards beauty. Simplicity is a hallmark of my design. Keeping design simple—and avoiding the trap of filling empty space with unnecessary clutter—is my hardest and most rewarding challenge. Exhibitions include: *Living with Art*, Sedona, AZ; American Craft Council Show, Baltimore, MD; The Philadelphia Furniture and Furnishings Show, Philadelphia, PA; Best of Show at the Boulder Arts Festival, CO; Sculpture, Objects and Functional Art (SOFA), Chicago, IL; and *Furniture on the Park*, Denver, CO. Publications include: *Architecture & Design of the West*, *Fine Woodworking* magazine and *Northern Home* magazine.

ARTIST STATEMENTS

STEVEN J. MURPHY
Objects
Page 133

I have been in Boston for over a decade, creating high-fired stoneware and porcelain pottery for the home. My work is highly influenced by my experience as a potter's apprentice in Japan, and continues to be founded upon the traditions of tea ceremony and the artistry of Japanese cuisine. The colors and textures come from a variety of natural sources, including ashes from leaves, wood, rice straw and volcanoes. These materials, along with a special firing process, combine to produce what I consider "gifts from the fire." My work can be found in galleries in New York, Boston and the Jersey Shore. I have been published in *The Art of Contemporary Pottery* by Kevin A. Hluch; *Chanoyu: Landscapes in a Tea Bowl* by Kathleen Fink; and *Asian Wraps* by Nina Simonds.

NANCY NICHOLSON
Objects
Pages 18, 145

I love the visual and tactile qualities of glass and lead—the illusive and the solid, respectively. Using traditional techniques, I design and fabricate traditional and contemporary stained glass pieces for both residential and corporate interiors. I am particularly attracted to the interplay of pattern, shape and color in the urban landscape, and create vignettes (as one would create a painting) that are designed to be viewed in a window setting. Prices range from $500 to $10,000.

NOMA
Paintings
Page 236

The ability to make known who we are exists in all of us. Seldom does one have the strength to disentangle the puzzle of his or her identity. Through art I explore not only my silent thoughts but the concealed perception of others, which ignites my capacity to execute prolific works of art. Art exposes honesty and truth. My art is expressionistic, executed primarily in oil, or sometimes acrylic. Sizes vary from small (5" x 7") to large (144" x 72") or larger by request. My paintings are simplistic in design but generate a powerful message of dignity, integrity and dedication to the spirit of creation. My art has been published in books, magazines and advertising all over the world, and purchased by private collectors and businesses.

MARLIES MERK NAJAKA
Prints & Drawings
Page 288

I am an award-winning watercolorist and signature member of AWS and NWS, known for my dramatic use of light and shadow. My work has appeared in numerous publications and is included in private and corporate collections. My work can also be seen in previous GUILD source-books. My luminous watercolors, with their multiple glazes, are reproduced as limited-edition giclée prints and can be viewed on my website: www.watercolorart.com. Slides, catalog and resume are available upon request.

NANCY EGOL NIKKAL
Tapestry, Fiber & Paper
Page 351

My collage paintings are inspired by my love of paper. I work with handmade imported papers as well as appropriated papers. My works are abstract, yet inspired by my love of birds, animals and the environment. I start each collage by painting a palette of collage papers. Sizes range from 7" x 7" to 80" x 56"; prices range from $300 to $3,000. My works have been commissioned for clients throughout the United States and Japan. Selected public collections include Hewlett-Packard, Pfizer Inc., Sun Chemical and Cablevision. My dominant medium is collage on paper. Additional media include monotype and giclée prints, and oil paintings on canvas. A color catalog and a CD of recent works titled *The Cactus* are available upon request. My work has appeared in previous GUILD sourcebooks.

ROBERT ODDY
Windows, Doors & Railings
Page 167

In 1983 I began working in stained glass part-time while working as a professor of information sciences at Syracuse University. I resigned from my professorship in 1997 to concentrate on my art. A distinctive quality of my work is a feeling of depth and subtlety in the representation of natural subjects, though I retain recognizable traits of traditional stained glass art. In some work I combine glass with other materials, such as carved wood and cast bronze, thereby extending my stained glass art in three dimensions. Most of my work is found in private dwellings. Each commission is an original design that takes into account the wishes and ideas of the individual client and the nature of the site.

KATHLEEN NEWMAN
Paintings
Pages 7, 232

Whether painting landscapes, cityscapes or water scenes, I am intrigued by the quality of light and inspired to express its effect on color and atmosphere. Using oil or pastel, I often paint on location and complete larger pieces in the studio. I studied at Chicago's American Academy of Art, The School of the Art Institute and worked as a designer/illustrator before making a recent transition to fine art. Signature memberships: Pastel Society of America, American Society of Marine Artists and American Transparent Watercolor Society. Awards: *International Artist,* 2003; *Pastel Artist International,* 2002; *Pastel Journal,* 2002 and 2001; *Artists Magazine,* 2003 and 2000. Publications: *Best of Portraits, Northlight Books* and *The Chicago Art Scene,* CrowWoods Publishing. Corporate collections: Ritz Carlton Orlando, Ameritech, IBM, MCI and Disney.

JAMES NOCITO
Paintings
Page 231

I received my B.A. in art from Carnegie-Mellon University and did graduate work at Columbia University. Since then I've seen two themes consistently recur in my work: our relationship to nature and the nature of memory. Using primarily tempera paint, I've created a vast, ever-growing supply of small paintings that I combine into larger pieces. I like the idea of ordering the chaos of experience into some kind of visual narrative. My paintings are published by The Winn Devon Art Group and have been exhibited at the California Museum of Art, the Palm Springs Desert Museum, the Riverside Museum of Art, Littlejohn-Smith Gallery, New York, and 80 Washington Square East Galleries, New York. Commissions are welcome. Painting, mural and fabric design images are available upon request.

ORKA ARCHITECTURAL ART GLASS
Mixed Media
Pages 322–323

My ability to interpret the true human form in sand-carved glass not only stems from my 22 years of experience in the medium, but also from my painting, sculpting, airbrushing and graphic design career. My approach to portrait work not only reflects the true likeness of the subject but the layout and embellishments allude to the subject's personality. My style extends beyond portrait work to encompass a vast array of subjects. My company's commissions of interest include: World Map, a 25,000-lb glass sculpture, Enron Headquarters, Houston, TX; Contemporary Interpretation of Today's Athletes, sixteen 8' x 12' panels, University of Iowa, Iowa City, IA; and Tapestry of Life, five full-size portrait panels exhibiting ethic diversity, WellStar Kennestone Hospital, Marietta, GA.

ARTIST STATEMENTS

OUT OF THE MAINSTREAM DESIGNS, INC.
Tapestry, Fiber & Paper
Page 348

I have been designing and weaving for 25 years and have worked with many traditional and nontraditional techniques. My focus for most of the last 15 years has been commissioned tapestries and rugs. I enjoy research in historic textiles and graphic designs of the past century. Each of my pieces is created with the client's needs, location and architectural space in mind. My framed wall pieces usually include layered fabric (which is hand-dyed or felted), as well as handwoven bands of silk and antique buttons and beads. Please contact my studio for slides, pricing and additional information. I am currently designing a series of oriental garments for Delnor-Community Hospital, Geneva, IL. These garments will be auctioned at its annual fundraising gala.

BINH PHO
Objects
Page 157

My work primarily reflects the Far East culture and my journey to the West. I love to bring the beauty of nature and hand-creation techniques together to create character and soul in a piece. I accept limited commissions due to nature of the wood; please inquire about this type of work. My works have been included in major exhibitions, such as SOFA (Sculpture Objects Functional Art) New York, NY, and Chicago, IL, and are also in the collections of the White House, the University of Michigan Fine Art Museum, the New York Museum of Contemporary Art and Design and the Long Beach Fine Art Museum, as well as in corporate and private collections throughout the United States, Europe and Japan.

RICHARD M. PARRISH
Doors, Windows & Screens
Page 163

Much of my fused glass work draws directly on my architectural education and practice, both formally and conceptually. As an architect and glass artist, I am inspired by the long tradition of architectural glass. My fused glass installations include custom panels, tiles, windows and wall panels. Commissions allow me to collaborate with homeowners to make a work of art that speaks to their vision. I have completed several large commissions in private residences and public places that are integral to the spaces for which they were designed. Some of my works investigate ideas about site, map or place in imagery and the projection of that imagery to another space. Others explore notions of insight and reflection. Fused glass is a medium that allows wonderful explorations in transparency, lightness, texture and color.

KURT PIPER
Furniture
Pages 1, 96

Mankind has always, for celebration or function, blended styles and materials to create objects of beauty and utility intimate to daily life. I attempt to continue this convergence in my work, paying tribute to influences both historical and cultural. It is my goal to create contemporary design details that will be experienced in a meaningful way. The integration of extraordinary woods with timeless materials such as petrified wood, steel, stone and bone (elements common to our visual world, but uncommon to our everyday experience) reinforces an inner sense of balance. Opportunities to collaborate with designers and clients allow the development of projects that leave an enduring impression on our lives.

LEO PECK
Furniture
Page 74

Over 15 years ago, after working for several years as a functional potter, I ventured into custom tile design. More recently, I have merged my ceramics expertise, welding skills and passion for furniture design to create artistic, highly functional tables and light fixtures. I enjoy the challenge of turning an artistic design into a well-made furnishing that can last for generations. Years of fine-tuning have accomplished this, and I am proud of the craftsmanship that goes into my work. Using my custom clay to make the individual ceramic pieces and building a sturdy table substructure suitable for the outdoors are examples of this craftsmanship. My custom tile and sculpture have also been incorporated into pools, fireplaces, kitchens, bathrooms, waterfalls and restaurants. To explore this work, visit www.pecktile.com.

BOB POOL
Objects
Page 130

I was merrily pursuing a career in biological research when, in 1979, I took a casual course in pottery. I immediately fell in love with clay and the transformation of amorphous blobs of mud into beautiful forms. In 1982 I gave up my life in science for that of a studio potter. I am inspired by natural forms, as well as Asian and African motifs, particularly as expressed in fabrics. I like to emphasize the surface of the pot, as if it's a piece of fabric suspended in space. I throw a light, well-balanced pot and decorate with layers of glaze in geometric, organic patterns. Fired in a reducing atmosphere to stoneware temperatures, the pot has a surface of great depth and intense color.

WILLIAM POULSON
Doors, Windows & Screens
Page 100

My unique folding screens and lamps are inspired by the Asian masters of *ukiyo-e* and *sumi* brush painting. As a third-generation woodworker, I pay very close attention to detail and fine craftsmanship. More than 25 years ago, I joined my skills in cabinetry and furniture making with my love for art glass to create functional art that combines the beauty and softness of wood with the brilliance of glass. My public and private art glass commissions incorporate my original designs which are based on natural themes. Lamp prices range from $2,500 to $3,500. Screen prices range from $5,000 to $12,000. Private collections include: William Randolph Hearst II, Christopher Titus and Byerly Aviation.

CAROLINE RACKLEY
Windows, Doors & Railings
Page 173

I am marketing a line of tapestry doors, an idea built on 35 years of professional textile design. Tapestry doors contribute rich, textured ambiance to rooms, hallways, small spaces and cabinetry. Every door has symbolic meaning, however subtle. With unlimited design potential, these tapestry doors offer an imaginative adventure. My woven image is permanently mounted on the door; it is stabilized and glazed with a clear acrylic medium for safe handling and cleaning, hence a highly durable textile. Featuring a collaboration of many mediums, this line involves the IMAGENM.COM design team: fine woodwork by Bob Hernandez, carvings by Linda Kaysing, and tin and embroidery embellishment by Beatrice Maestas-Sandoval.

JOHN RAIS
Furniture
Page 81

I create contemporary forged metalwork that combines centuries-old techniques with a progressive design sensibility. The process of forging (heating and hammering) enables me to dance with the metal, squeezing, pushing and pulling it into forms like taffy. After the forging I begin a long series of finishing techniques that gives the work a distinguished level of refinement. I earned a bachelor's degree in sculpture, then a master's degree in metalsmithing from the Cranbrook Academy of Art in Bloomfield Hills, MI. The furniture and fireplace elements are evidence of a marriage between sculpture and craftsmanship, for which I have been commissioned internationally. I also create sculpture and vessels for galleries and private clients. I often teach and lecture on my art throughout the United States.

ARTIST STATEMENTS

HOLLIE HELLER RAMSAY
Tapestry, Fiber & Paper
Pages 339, 341

My wall pieces are a result of my fascination with manipulating materials and exploring the contrasts that I find so exciting, such as matte versus shiny, intuitive versus labor intensive, kitschy versus elegant, historical versus contemporary, and colorful versus neutral. I am interested in the production of constructed and layered surfaces and use a variety of materials to give the viewer segments of information using color, texture, photography and pieced imagery. My work is included in the following collections: Hyatt Hotel, Philadelphia, PA, and Sedona, AZ; HBO World Headquarters, New York, NY; Mohegan Resorts, Rutgers University, NJ; Ortho Biotech of Johnson & Johnson, NJ; as well as many private collections. Pieces are priced between $300 and $4,000. Commissions are accepted.

KEVIN B. ROBB
Sculpture
Pages 175, 195

I create individual contemporary sculptures in stainless steel or bronze, as well as limited-edition cast bronze for intimate environments or large-scale public arenas. I bring a natural curiosity to my work, combined with the understanding of how positive and negative spaces, shadow and light work together. Recent projects include: Borgata Resort Casino Spa, Atlantic City, NJ; Harrison Point Shopping Center, Cary, NC; Franke Consumer Products, Hatfield, PA; Rocky Mountain College of the Arts, Lakewood, CO; and Westbank Community Library, Austin, TX.

GRETCHEN ROMEY-TANZER
Tapestry, Fiber & Paper
Page 347

I am a textile artist of wall pieces. My weaving has been streamlined to the point where image and material harmoniously join in abstract clarity. Dynamic, contrasting colors help create depth and evoke emotion. I weave together fine cotton or linen threads in a dense and flat-textured, multi-block double-weave structure. With the use of analogous and complementary colors, I am able to create the illusion of movement and volume. The woven fabric is of sound structure and is decorative in nature. Smaller pieces are stitched to a stretched canvas frame for a formal presentation. My weavings are included in the collections of Jack Lenor Larsen and the Boston Museum of Fine Arts, among others.

KIM RITTER
Art Quilts
Pages 333, 390

My newest body of work features wild horses and wild women. *Spirit Horses*, a series of silk-screened quilts, explores my lifelong love of horses. My interest in the horse is influenced by my childhood in Oklahoma and an inspiring trip to the Uffington White Horse, a 1,000-year-old abstract chalk carving of a horse in rural England. My horses are imaginary spirits of strength and freedom. The women in my quilt series, *Attitudes*, share these same spirited qualities.

WILLIAM ROBBINS
Furniture
Page 61

Fine art can be sat upon, spilled on or closed with a satisfying click. At William Robbins we call that furniture. Built to use easily and designed to be contemplated, our furniture stands in homes and offices throughout the United States. Production is limited to commissions, which are tailored to the individual needs of our customers. Prices range from $2,000 for a coffee table to $12,000 for a freestanding liquor cabinet. We work with expertly selected solid woods and use fine wood veneers where it makes sense. We expect our furniture to last 200 years. You may request additional information by contacting the workshop directly.

CYNTHIA ROOT
Paintings
Page 274

My inspiration comes from the spiritual connection I feel to the beauty and power of nature. Sunlight on trees and the fragmented patterns of light in the forest are the dominant subjects of my paintings. International and national exhibitions include the San Diego Watercolor Society International, the National Society of Painters in Casein and Acrylic, the Salmagundi Club and the Hyde Collection. My most recent award was from the Adirondack National Exhibition of American Watercolors. I work primarily in aqua media and have had ten solo shows since 1976. My paintings have been represented by galleries in Germany, the United States and Canada and are in many private collections. Prices range from $600 to $2,000. Brochure, resumé and slides are available upon request from my studio in the Adirondacks.

RIVERSIDE ARTISANS
Furniture
Page 60

Our studio is built on the principle of "following your bliss." A move brought Riverside Artisans to a historic building in downtown Paterson, New Jersey, in 2002. Defining a style that embraces curves and flowing shapes while maintaining balance and weight has helped keep our studio satisfying for high-end residential customers. Kerry Pierce chose our studio for inclusion in his acclaimed book, *The Custom Furniture Sourcebook*, published by Taunton Press in 2000. Close, personal attention is a hallmark of our design philosophy. Design is always viewed as the coming together of beauty, function and the personality of the client. I, along with my son, Aaron, infuse my business with a respect and love for our work, our clients and each other.

ROBERT PULLEY SCULPTURE
Garden Sculpture
Page 210

My handbuilt stoneware sculptures have evolved during a 30-year journey with clay. The forms reflect forces and structures of nature, organic growth and geologic age, as well as human gesture, through sculptures that exude strength and powerful presence. I like to see the sculptures in the garden, where they resonate with the changing colors and textures of nature. They look great indoors too. Outdoors the work is unaffected by weather. I can answer questions about siting and installation. My work is found in private and public collections around the world, including the Canton Art Institute, the Wright State University Art Museum and McDonald's Corporation, and has been featured in publications such as *Sculpting Clay* and *Smashing Glazes*. Prices range from $500 to $2,500.

ALAN ROSEN
Furniture
Page 64

Since 1974 I have been creating distinctive original and custom furniture known for its simple elegance, uncompromising craftsmanship and attention to detail. The careful selection of woods, traditional joinery and signature hand-rubbed finish ensure enjoyment by future generations. I consider myself fortunate to have found work I truly enjoy. I am excited by the challenge of designing and building furniture. While building my own designs is rewarding, I also find great satisfaction in creating personalized custom furniture for my clients. Commissions: William Gates III, 1999, Medina, WA; Paul Allen, 1999, Mercer Island, WA; David Usher, 1995, Carmel, CA; Sacred Heart Church, 1993, Bellevue, WA. Collections: Grizzly Industrial Inc., Bellingham, WA, Columbus, MD, and Williamsport, PA.

ARTIST STATEMENTS

MARK ROSENBAUM
Lighting
Page 106

Since 1979 I have been intrigued by the physical and creative properties of blown glass. I try to capture the uniqueness of the material by applying up to 16 layers of colored and clear glass to convey a sense of depth within each piece. My lighting further incorporates these qualities by introducing transmitted light and its reflective properties. My work is shown nationwide, and I have been profiled on HGTV's "Modern Masters" series. I received a grant from the Louisiana Division of the Arts to establish the first privately owned glassblowing studio in the state. I have since moved to an award-winning vintage art deco movie theater, which I've converted into my studio and gallery/showroom. Prices range from $185–$575.

MELANIE ROTHSCHILD
Furniture
Page 77

I thrive on color and believe that fashion is too often the enemy of art. I feel like my work is at its best when I am feeling irreverent or reckless. I am inspired by a huge spectrum, ranging from natural to urban forms—a dozen eggs lined up in their carton or the configuration of cars in traffic, for example. I admire the legacy of outsider artists, whose work always inspires me because it's free of the rigors of style and trend, and exudes a genuine artistic exuberance. That is what I strive for. Since 1990 my work has been sold throughout the United States, in stores, galleries and museum shops.

LINDA GAIL RUDELL
Home Accessories
Pages 115, 120

The color, shape and texture of the ribbons and fabrics I use create a rhythm that is my artistic language. I am Linda Rudell, president, artist and well-known designer. I have exhibited at many one-of-a-kind art and craft shows in the United States and, as a result, have received numerous commissions for my pillows and accessories for the home. My work is in private collections from New York to California. The silk or velvet pillows are made by weaving or knitting silk ribbons, creative beading and antique lace. The luxurious feel of the fabrics I use for scarves, throws, pillows and the new *For Socks Only™* footstools and ottomans adds a sensuous feeling to my art. Art is a large component of life; incorporating it into our everyday living enhances our lives exponentially.

ANDY SÁNCHEZ
Furniture
Page 97

Our unique juniper designs begin in the forests of New Mexico, where we find ancient juniper trees (sometimes over 1,000 years old) that have died from old age. I first determine how best to use the wood, employing its natural features as much as possible. If there is a natural hole in the wood, we often fill it with polished marble, turquoise or other semiprecious stones. After hours of sanding and polishing, we finally apply several coats of oil and wax to build an inviting finish. Rough edges create a rustic illusion, contrasting with the smooth finish and quality craftsmanship. My sons and I work together, and we have shown our work in art shows all over the United States, including the Philadelphia Furniture and Furnishings Show, PA; the Western Design Conference, Cody, WY; and the Beaver Creek Art Festival. Recently, I was featured on the Home & Garden Television network.

JOAN SKOGSBERG SANDERS
Paintings
Page 254

Fresh Paint is my new series of paintings. I have temporarily put aside my fascination with Morocco, which was the subject of a recent, large series. This new series is a natural segue from the muted earth colors that I concentrated on for so long. Another side of my persona is evident in two of these new pieces, *Long Beach* and *Emmental*, which are responses to California and Switzerland, respectively. I wanted to capture the warm feelings I have about both places and transfer that feeling to the viewer. Before I begin painting with my vibrant acrylics, my wood panel "canvases" are heavily processed, texturized and glazed. My award-winning artwork has been exhibited widely, both in the United States and in Europe. Many pieces are available as giclée prints.

JOY SAVILLE
Art Quilts
Page 336

Have you ever had your breath taken away by the color of dogwood trees, autumn leaves, a sunset or a view of the landscape as you drive over a hill? These are the frozen moments I strive to express in my work. Piecing cotton, linen and silk in an impressionistic, painterly manner, I use the inherent quality of natural fabrics to absorb or reflect light, producing a constant interplay of light, texture and color. Commissions include: Johnson & Johnson; Ortho Pharmaceutical and The Jewish Center, Princeton, NJ. Collections include: American Craft Museum; the Newark Museum; Bristol-Myers Squibb; Time-Warner Inc.; H. J. Heinz; PepsiCo and Art in Embassies, 2000, Brunei. My work has been featured in GUILD sourcebooks as well as solo and group exhibitions throughout North America and internationally since 1976.

KAREN SCHARER
Paintings
Page 253

My expressive contemporary paintings combine bold color with strong design to convey moods from dramatic to contemplative. Working primarily in acrylic, I use multiple layers of color to produce pieces that radiate light and often create the impression of stained glass. Whether examined closely or enjoyed from across the room, my work draws the viewer in with rich textures, line and movement, enlivening the imagination and inviting the viewer to become part of the creative process. Since 1987 I have produced paintings on paper, board and canvas ranging in size from miniature to 3' × 7'. Selected images are available as limited-edition giclée reproductions. My work has earned numerous awards in juried festivals and exhibitions and is currently held in hundreds of private and corporate collections. Commissions are welcome.

SCHULTE STUDIOS
Garden Sculpture
Page 217

I forge dramatic art and unique metalwork from my studio in Sugar Grove, Illinois. My passion for metalwork developed as an artsmith apprentice in Germany under the guidance of K.T. Neumann. When Neumann retired five years ago, I brought his handmade tools to America. Specializing in diverse metals and subject matter, I use my unique vision to create powerful images designed to move the soul. I also choose materials to match my subject. By blending the traditional techniques of the artsmith with modern tools and materials, I use my work in stainless steel, carbon steel, brass, copper and bronze to create a distinctive aesthetic.

MICHAEL J. SCHUNKE
Sculpture
Page 201

My creative process always begins on paper as a drawing or watercolor painting. I use the time during drawing to refine shape, proportion and color. When the actual glassblowing begins, however, I leave myself open to whatever change may take place in attempting a particular form. Sometimes a piece comes out almost exactly as I had drawn it, sometimes completely different. My series *Weight, Float and Hope* has been ongoing. These are pieces inspired by my time near the water when I was a child. The simple yet complex shapes of buoys, fishing net markers and anchors always seem to come back to my imagination as inspiration for new pieces. Making my work is both cathartic and frustrating. I'm never completely satisfied with anything I create, and that's what keeps me going.

ARTIST STATEMENTS

JOHN SEARLES
Mixed Media
Page 318

My wall sculptures reflect my enduring interests in mathematics, visual pleasure, energy and freedom. Working with copper, brass, stainless steel or aluminum (sometimes melting one on the other), these wall sculptures are puzzle pieces. I cut up one piece of patinated metal into many, then reassemble them into a more visually stimulating, higher level of order, often as large-scale work. Some of my sculptures are weavings, but all have some component of under/over dimensionality. My purpose is to delight the brain and visual centers in a noncerebral manner as "music for the eyes."

PETER SECREST
Objects
Page 146

My murrini vases resonate with techniques that span the entire history of glass. The use of murrini (short cross sections of decorative rods of glass) predates the invention of glassblowing by several thousand years. I begin a piece by first making the murrini canes, chopping pieces of this cane and then laying up a pattern with the murrini. These murrini are heated, fused, attached to a blowpipe and formed into a cylinder. The cylinder then has a blown bubble attached to it, which becomes the lower part of the vessel. This process is called incalmo. Ever since I pulled my first murrini cane almost 25 years ago, the process has spoken to me with a special voice. This fascination with murrini has led me to explore its use in many forms throughout my years of glassblowing. Price range: $950–$1,500.

KAREN ELISE SEPANSKI
Windows, Doors & Railings
Page 162

I have been exploring the realm of kiln-formed glass since art school in the late 1970s. My glass panels and forms are often combinations of geometric and organic bas-relief sculptural elements over textured background surfaces, which resemble stone or rippling water. I combine a variety of processes and materials, often metal and stone, to reflect the abstract imagery. I have created a signature style for numerous clients and locations, covering everything from tabletop pieces, murals and lighting to architectural features such as windows and doors. In designing site-specific work, every attempt is made to complement the existing space or location. Recent projects include the altar, pulpit and baptismal font for a new church, and the complete redesign of a residential entrance. Other work can be found in previous GUILD sourcebooks.

MK SHANNON
Sculpture
Page 191

We are all interconnected; our lives are interrelated and intertwined in ways we cannot even begin to imagine. I strongly believe wherever we are and whomever we are, we share the same basic feelings and hopes. My sculpture honors the human spirit and our extraordinary capacity to reach beyond ourselves. I attempt to capture these emotions in bronze. Collectors and corporations all over the world have embraced this vision. Commissions are my passion, and I have created over 60 different pieces in the last 20 years. My sculptures can be displayed indoors or outdoors. I am self-taught by an intense desire to capture feelings in metal. My work is a celebration of life, conveyed through the medium of clay by my hands, then captured in metal. Finally, the pieces are ready to be realized by anyone open to experience another's vision.

JUDITH SHAPIRO
Objects
Page 140

Exceptional quality, vivid colors and a sensuous matte finish characterize my art glass vessels, many of which have seasonal or nature-inspired themes reflecting my childhood on an East Coast barrier island. I have studied glass at Pilchuck Glass School, the Studio at Corning and in workshops nationally. I teach kiln-formed glass at the Torpedo Factory in Alexandria, VA, and work full-time in my studio, which is nestled in a picturesque industrial park just 10 miles from the White House. My work is exhibited nationally and held in private collections, including the Lincoln Center in New York.

RICK SHERBERT
Lighting
Pages 103, 107

I have always wanted to capture the brilliant colors of a sunset in glass. I knew it would have to have luminescence from within to achieve this goal. My line of blown glass lighting is a beautiful combination of brilliant colors, classic shapes and unique designs that one client described as "better than looking through the Hubbell telescope." Pendant and wall sconce designs, both custom and stock, are available to fit your dcor. These functional art pieces come complete and ready to install with UL approved hardware. My studio and home are located in suburban Washington, DC, where I create my work and teach the art and craft of glassblowing.

GERALD SICILIANO
Sculpture
Page 178

Gerald Siciliano has created a full range of unique and limited-edition sculptures for the discriminating collector. Attractively priced, these elegant and enduring works are offered in bronze, marble, granite and stainless steel. Available in sizes ranging from the intimate to the monumental, they will enhance any collection or setting. His classically inspired figurative and nonrepresentational sculptures are meticulously crafted to the highest standards for discerning collectors worldwide. We invite your inquiries, via telephone, e-mail or the Internet, for our featured sculpture or for your personalized commission. Collections: American Airlines; American Axle & Manufacturing de Mexico; Bristol-Myers Squibb; the Brooklyn Museum; Canon Corporation; Chang-Won Provincial Government, Korea; Dong Baek Art Center, Korea; John Templeton Foundation; Mozart Companies; Pusan Olympic Park, Korea; and Sparks Exhibits & Environments.

STEVE SINNER
Objects
Page 154

When I was a preteen, my father gave me a used wood lathe, which kindled my love of working with wood. After many years of avocational furniture making and turning, I read Dale Nish's *Creative Woodturning*. His book shaped my passion for the fascinating and absorbing pursuit of creating art with fine woods. In 1998 I realized my dream and became a full-time artist, establishing a studio in Bettendorf, Iowa. Today my works are in private and corporate collections from coast to coast. I specialize in hollow vessels, often embellished with silver and gold leaf, and accompanied by chemical patina, acrylics, dyes and pen and ink. Sizes range from a few inches to nearly three feet in height. Prices range from $300 to $10,000.

BJORN SJOGREN
Prints & Drawings
Pages 20, 284

"The power of simplicity." This comment—made by a viewer of my art at an exhibition in New York—is perhaps the best way to describe the way I work. I use color, rhythm and form to express the essence of a subject and awaken the senses, allowing the viewer to feel the emotion of my work. Many times my art is the spontaneous response to a subject or an event; the title is the unity between subject and emotion. I work in gouache, acrylic and mixed media. My work can be found in Scandinavia, Germany, Russia and the United States. I used the pseudonym B Padrick early in my career, from 1987 to 1990. In the fall of 2001, I moved from Sweden to Wisconsin.

ARTIST STATEMENTS

SLAMMING SCREEN DOOR FUNCTIONAL ART CO.
Home Accessories
Page 117

My hand-painted shower curtains came about from a desire to paint bigger pieces. I discovered that the shower curtain is a perfect location for art and makes a terrific canvas. They're shower curtains, but more importantly, they're works of art, with no two exactly alike. Some of the curtains have objects incorporated in the design, such as an actual picture frame, twigs wrapped with colored thread or taillight reflectors. All are painted with acrylic paint on heavy vinyl and then sealed for protection. Prices range from $385 to $450. My shower curtain paintings have been well received at every exhibit and have been featured on HGTV's program "Your New Home." The curtains are made to order, so please allow several weeks for completion.

COLETTE ODYA SMITH
Paintings
Page 271

My paintings spring from what excites and intrigues me. Approaching nature with humble attentiveness, I find complexity and subtlety in intimate scenes and push my compositions to reveal this. I am particularly fond of painting rocks and water. They speak to me of mysteries that are both personal and universal, while visually providing an endless source of aesthetic delights. I work in soft pastels, which are thickly layered over watercolor, to achieve a lush, inviting surface. Exhibitions and awards include: Pastel Society of America, signature member and purchase award, 2002 and 2000, NY; Wichita Center for the Arts, purchase award, 2002; Pastel Society of New Mexico, award, 2002 and the Northwest Pastel Society, award, 2002. Publications include: *Pastel Artist International*, grand prize cover, 2002 and *The Pastel Journal*, awards, 1999–2001.

SPHERICAL MAGIC REVERSE GLASS
Windows, Doors & Railings
Page 170

BJ and I have fused our artistic abilities to forge Spherical Magic and have had the opportunity to create some truly unique, stunning and inspirational works of art. Our main focus is creating architectural, artistic accents or showcase pieces, which are installed in corporate, public and private spaces all over the world. Our works are created from blown, molded, carved, etched and painted glass, and can contain a lighting system. Each installation is created specifically for the site and client, giving each piece a beautiful individuality. These works range from two-dimensional paintings to three-dimensional sculptures—and everything in between, in any size required by the client. We gladly accept commissions and enjoy working with our clients to create their visions in glass.

SLICES OF LIFE BY G. BUTEYN
Prints & Drawings
Page 290

My *Slices of Life* series began during my early years on a Wisconsin farm and continued to develop during my teaching years as I observed and captured on camera "slices of life" around Wisconsin. After completing a wide range of commissioned work and teaching art for 18 years at a private school, I retired in the fall of 2002 to concentrate on this series and to coordinate Vintage Works, a family framing business. My original oils and prints with custom framing are displayed in several galleries across Wisconsin. Original oils average 16" x 50" in size and $2,000 in price. My canvas giclée prints range from $160 to $750 and offered in various sizes, with or without custom framing.

STEVE SMULKA
Prints & Drawings
Page 292

My subject matter is light. I have always been fascinated by the elusive and ephemeral quality of natural light. Following in the genre of painting everyday objects, I give my paintings a contemporary edge by painting the objects larger than life size. Beginning with a detailed drawing before painting with oils on linen, I allow my hyper-realistic vision of glass to tell its own story: the time of day, atmospheric conditions, etc. I studied under renowned photo-realist Chuck Close, who inspired me to begin painting in the photo-realist manner. My paintings and prints are in numerous corporate and private collections all over the world. Limited-edition archival giclée prints are available from $300 to $2,000. I also accept commissions for originals.

STEPHANIE ANN STANLEY
Paintings
Page 249

I seek to represent a spiritual experience, so I invoke the power of color and texture in all my work. A true "color field" painter (like Rothko and Noland), I am concerned with exploring the effect of pure color on canvas. Being the daughter of artists, I was compelled to express myself at an early age. Inspired by my dreams, meditations and experiences, my collection is filled with variant textures and vibrant colors. I think that while abstract impressionism is nonrepresentational with regard to form, my work nevertheless represents very real and specific ideas. My work is created with oil or acrylic on canvas, in varying dimensions, and all edges of the canvas are painted. A sample of my work can be viewed at www.sangitaart.com.

BRAD SMITH
Furniture
Page 67

My furniture incorporates the old and the new. I was born in 1954 and raised on a farm in Pennsylvania, where I learned that nothing should be wasted. While studying at the Rochester Institute of Technology, I developed this idea into my design aesthetic. Since 1980 I've given old lumber new life in a chest of drawers or an armoire. Pitchforks become the backs of benches and chairs, and ax handles are made into the legs of stools. The reworking of these unusual parts creates my distinctive "Bradford look." I produce a small line of furniture, which may be seen in many galleries throughout the country. Prices range from $200 to $3,000. Each year I also produce a number of one-of-a-kind pieces on speculation and commission.

MICHAEL GRANT SOLOMON
Home Accessories
Page 118

I am most fortunate that I can make my living doing something I love. I create colorful, functional mosaics with lots of movement. The unique sliver shapes that I hand cut from sheets of hand-made American art glass are assembled into a distinctive mosaic with an emphasis on veining (the grout line). The outer borders are decoratively soldered with textures, dots or plain antique finishes and are available in copper, pewter and silver. If you send me a swatch of fabric, wallpaper, tile or paint, I'll send you a mosaic color sample that best fits your decor. For additional examples, visit my website: www.reflectiveart.com.

TODD STARKS
Paintings
Page 237

Beginning with sketches of landscape or still life, I paint with a palette knife to build up impasto layers of subtly altered realities, revealing my deep spiritual, emotional and sensory connection to my surroundings and a dynamic interplay between conscious and subconscious thought. Formally, the works are about shape, color and process. I allow shards of underpainting to show through, revealing both a recorded path to the finished piece and a permanent blueprint of the painting structure. My work has been included in national and international juried exhibitions and has received merit awards. Artworks are part of private collections nationwide. Sizes range from 12" x 12" to 40" x 55". Prices range from $750 to $1,800. For a complete catalog of available work, go to www.ToddStarks.net.

ARTIST STATEMENTS

ELINOR STEELE
Tapestry, Fiber & Paper
Page 342

My design process is an adventure of observation and discovery, with an eye toward images that translate naturally and gracefully into the woven form. Subjects include abstract and impressionistic images, landscapes, cityscapes and geometric compositions. I weave by hand on a high-warp loom, combining several strands from my large palette of wool yarns to achieve the desired colors and gradients. I like to take advantage of the richness of tone and texture that is inherent in the medium of woven tapestry. I have exhibited work nationally for over 25 years and have been commissioned to create numerous tapestries for residential and corporate settings. I often incorporate colors and design elements from the surrounding architecture, as well as images that are relevant to the personal experience of the customer.

ARTHUR STERN
Prints & Drawings/Windows, Doors & Railings
Pages 165, 281–283

I am an internationally known, award-winning glass artist. I also create one-of-a-kind oil pastels on Arches paper, on which I build up layers of oil pastel, then carve down to layers below, revealing complex graphic patterns and textures. For the past several years, I have also been working on two distinct series of prints. Collaborating with master printmaker Rob Reiter, very small editions (based on the oil pastels) have been created. These are offered as numbered and signed giclée prints, or as "enhanced prints," which are hand-embellished versions on which I draw improvisational additions in oil pastel and colored pencil, then collage handmade paper (and sometimes glass details) onto the print. The end result is a one-of-a-kind piece: mixed media on Arches paper.

MARTIN STURMAN
Furniture
Page 84

I create original contemporary sculptures and furniture in carbon steel or stainless steel, suitable for indoor or outdoor placement. Stainless steel surfaces are burnished to achieve a beautiful, shimmering effect. Carbon steel sculptures are painted with acrylic and coated with polyurethane to preserve color vitality. I encourage site-specific and collaborative efforts. Corporate commissions include: Tesoro Galleries, Beverly Hills, CA; Hyatt Westlake Plaza Hotel, Westlake Village, CA; Manhattan Beach Car Wash, Manhattan Beach, CA. Collections include: McGraw-Hill Publishing Company, Columbus, OH; McDonald's Corporate Art Collection, Oakbrook, IL. Please review previous GUILD sourcebooks and my website for additional work.

STEL OBJEKT STUDIO
Furniture
Page 87

Sensual, captivating, functional. Our studio creates works of art that transcend the ordinary. Engulfed in flame and forged in the mind, we create modern works, shaped by hand, that will become heirlooms for the future. From our Chicago studio, we design and handcraft pieces that will help you satisfy your design challenges. We are committed to culminating artistic expression, with a focus on the client's individual needs. Commissions include: Indianapolis Colts, The Red Room, Talbott Street, Crystal DeHann Family Foundation, and the City of Highland, IN.

STEVEN BOONE STUDIO
Paintings
Pages 276–277

I have a firm foundation in the basics of art, which I gained through years of study and culminating in a degree in painting from The Maryland Institute, College of Art, class of 1976. Being unconstrained in expression and continuing to experiment keeps me fresh, and my paintings benefit. The main thing is that each of my works has vigor, and that my knowledge is expressed— knowledge I have gained from years trying many approaches and techniques. My work is featured at Adieb Khadoure Fine Art, Santa Fe, NM; Rice Gallery, Denver, CO; Gallery 7000, Tucson, AZ; in private collections throughout the United States and Europe and in the permanent collection of the U.S. Department of Interior.

MARK J. SUDDUTH
Objects
Page 142

I have operated a private glass studio for 20 years. I blow and hot form all of my work. The work represented in this book plays largely on the glass itself, making use of depth, transparency, reflection and refraction. I am also very interested in form. A clean or flowing line that defines the shape from top to bottom allows the piece to sit prominently, then ends the work in a manner that does not appear cut off or incomplete. I believe these concepts enable the work to compliment the environment in which it resides.

LARRY STEPHENSON
Paintings
Pages 10, 239

My most recent body of work combines nostalgic imagery with a flair for contemporary pop culture. These are fun subjects executed in vivid primary colors. My paintings are created on paper using a blend of watercolor, gouache and egg tempera. Over the years I have worked professionally as a studio painter, a college professor at Northern Oklahoma College, a freelance illustrator and a fine art publisher (Third Street Art Publishing). My art has allowed me to work inside my chosen field while making a living doing what I most love to do. I was elected into signature membership of the American Watercolor Society, New York, NY, in 1990. I am an art graduate of the University of Central Oklahoma, 1972. Visit my website: www.lstephenson.com.

LANSE STOVER
Lighting
Page 111

I want my lighting to breathe life into a room. At rest on the wall, a sconce is a spark of color that can harmonize and animate space. When in use, light spills from inside, lending volume and depth to the surrounding wall. I have been working in clay for over 30 years and began making sconces five years ago. I delight in exploring the interaction between light and color, form and shadow, and the way a simple source of light can become the focal point of a room or an active partner of a harmonious decor. My work is exhibited in galleries across the United States. Design challenges and unique settings inspire me, and I welcome custom work.

SUN & EARTH POTTERY STUDIO
Objects
Page 132

For the past 15 years, I have been creating both functional and decorative pieces at the wheel. My line of stoneware combines the simplicity of Asian design with warm earth tones. Although my work has been shown in galleries throughout the United States, I still believe in using functional art in the home. The experience of eating from handmade dinnerware is unique and pleasing to the senses. Working with clay, for me, is about more than making cups and plates; there is an inner journey that takes place. I am reminded of this as I drink tea each morning from one of my cups. Set of four dinner plates $120; set of four tea bowls $72. Additional pieces for the table are available at www.sunandearthpottery.com.

ARTIST STATEMENTS

SUTTMAN STUDIO
Furniture
Page 59

I love art and art history. I love industrial design. The design process for me is about reconsidering and playing with classical and contemporary design motifs. I do enjoy designing some pieces that present engineering challenges. My primary medium is metal. Fabrication involves saw cutting, plasma cutting, cold forming, welding and some machining. Many of the details I create in the forge. I use wood, glass and other media as necessary to make a piece work. The finishing process takes at least two weeks for each piece of furniture. I use age-old patina techniques with a variety of chemicals to color my pieces. I follow this with many layers of pigments and urethane to get a number of rich finishes, one of which is difficult to distinguish from wood. Prices for my sculptures start at $800. Furniture pieces begin at $5,500.

WIKTOR SZOSTALO
Sculpture
Page 200

With an M.F.A. from the Academy in Fine Arts, Krakow, Poland, I came to the U.S. as a political refugee in 1983. I started out as a painter because of my love for color, but I always wanted to be a sculptor. You can find my welded stainless steel and wood sculptures throughout the United States. Steel and wood did not hold enough color for me, however, so the magic of light directed me to glass sculpture. This new medium crowns my 30-year journey as an artist. It is the hardest, most sweat-inducing and back-breaking physical labor there is, but when you take the glass out of the kiln, touch it up, put it in the stand, light it and then sit down to look at it, all of a sudden your own work gives you goose bumps. At such moments you know that you must be on the right track.

STEVE TEETERS
Windows, Doors & Railings
Page 172

From architectural details to large-scale public artworks, I am known for artwork that is site specific. From "This Old House" to New York to Seattle, I have the unique ability to make the artwork match the site and the client. My studio is located on a historic street in the hometown of legendary rocker Buddy Holly. Expect only the very finest in artwork and architectural details.

THOMAS THROOP
Furniture
Page 58

I want my furniture to be simple and direct, with line, surface, mass and proportion performing together, always working toward harmony. The forms that interest me are visually powerful, yet delicate, airy and open. They unify elements that sometimes seem incongruous, but ultimately merge and enhance one another. The character I look to foster within a piece dictates my visual and manual approach. Wood, a material of transcendent character, guides my designs, while the species I choose for a piece dictates its shape. My designs instill the theme of simple elegance, but each work has an individual subtlety that continues to reveal itself over time. Art is as much the nature of the process and the materials chosen as it is the outcome.

TIMOTHY HAGLUND STUDIO
Murals, Tiles & Wall Reliefs
Page 316

Sister Wendy said: "To look—as opposed to merely seeing—takes time and concentration. It is most richly rewarded." For me, being an artist is an ongoing process of study, work, concentration and reflection. It is a way of being in the world that allows me to look at and be inspired by art, the natural world and day-to-day interpersonal existence. My studio, open since 1990, is a fine art studio specializing in interior design consultation, decorative painting, trompe l'oeil murals, custom paintings and unique hand-dyed canvas wall coverings. Our work is innovative yet classic, artistic, beautiful and transformative. We have experience in a wide variety of residential and corporate settings, and we work well with interior designers, architects and homeowners. Our portfolio is available on request.

INGE PAPE TRAMPLER
Doors, Windows & Screens
Page 171

My experience and love for working with glass began over 30 years ago while I was employed at Rohlf's Studio in New York, where I designed and restored windows. I create skylights, dividers and windows for private homes, public buildings, churches and synagogues using both stained glass and dalle de verre. For the past 15 years, I have enjoyed working with glass—in both abstract and realistic styles—from my own home studio. My work includes three-dimensional sculpture, which incorporates various techniques such as combining bronze with blown, slumped, fused, laminated and cast glass. Displaying God's beautiful creations through light and color in autonomous panels and windows is another passion of mine. My work can be viewed in previous Guild sourcebooks.

JEFF TRITEL
Sculpture
Page 183

A bronze sculptor for over 30 years, I have artwork in over 800 private and corporate collections. My work is appreciated for its formal sensibilities, its sense of whimsy and its keen psychological insight. Sculptures range in size from 3" to 100'. Recent projects include: Tritel Sculpture Park, CA. Commissions include: lobby, Wells Fargo Bank, Salt Lake City, UT; 22' sculpture, San Jose, CA. Collections include: City of Anaheim, CA. Exhibitions include: Rosicrucian Museum, San Jose, CA. Awards include: Best of Show, 2000, 1999, 1987, Art on the Main, Walnut Creek, CA; first place, 2000, 1991, Art Festival, Hermosa Beach, CA. Publications include: Millionaire magazine, July 2000; "Arts Alive," PBS TV, 1988-1990; and Easyriders magazine, May 1995.

TURNER SCULPTURE
Sculpture
Page 193

Since 1983 our father-and-son team has been designing and casting wildlife sculptures in bronze. We both grew up and currently reside on the shore of Virginia. Our studios, gallery and foundry are located on Route 13 near Onley, Virginia. To date we have created more than 500 different limited-edition bronzes and more than 50 large public commissions. Ranging in size from life-size mice to full-size bears and dolphins, our sculptures can be made to fit the smallest niche in a home or to enhance the entrance of a zoo or museum. Whatever the case, our work is a reflection of our deep appreciation and understanding of nature.

TUSKA INC.
Garden Sculpture
Page 215

Our studio represents the work of artist John R. Tuska (1931–1998). We offer Illuminates, two-dimensional cutworks of the human form engaged in the motion of dance and suspended on open screens. Each screen is assembled by hand in custom dimensions and materials ranging from woods, steel, aluminum or bronze to contemporary polymers. Each screen is meticulously executed and rendered in exceeding detail. True craftsman quality makes them ideal for use as window or wall hangings, room dividers, gates, shutters, landscape decorations or other custom applications. We also offer reproductions of the artist's most engaging work: Illumine, a series of 11 distinct figures. Each figure is cast in bronze with a patina finish and is 36" tall.

ARTIST STATEMENTS

JOHN T. UNGER
Furniture
Page 86

My furniture, sculpture and ironwork portray simple yet highly expressive figures engaged in joyous dance. Joining steel, copper and glass mosaic, these graceful figures suggest both the motion of their dance and the music that moves them. The visual rhythm of this series draws from the staggered accents and off-beat phrasing of jazz. My work has shown in numerous national and international exhibitions and is included in many private and public collections including Northeastern University, Boston, MA, and Manley Career Academy High School, Chicago. Recent commissions include *City Gates*, two pairs of 8' x 8' gates patterned on street maps for the Lakeview Baseball Club and *The Story of Howie and JoAnn*, a garden fence that tells the story of the clients' relationship in four sections.

HELEN VAUGHN
Paintings
Pages 12, 223, 358–359

I specialize in pastel and oil paintings of landscapes, figures and still lifes. The works feature rich, velvety textures and vivid colors wrapped in carefully arranged compositions. As a painter I am continually fascinated by the properties of color, light and shadow as they affect both the image and my own sense of time, place and inner harmony. While this fascination influences both the visual elements of the work and my needs as an artist, the paintings stand or fall on their own. My work is included in museum, corporate and private collections and has been widely exhibited. Many of the paintings are also available as limited-edition giclées. My work has been featured in the following publications: *Pastel Artist International*, 2002, and *American Artist*, November 1998.

RICHARD WARRINGTON
Sculpture
Page 190

As an impressionistic sculptor, I design two- and three-dimensional original and limited-edition hollow form and silhouette sculpture. My designs emulate an outpouring of my emotional and spiritual response to my daily environment and relationships. My simple, human-like forms work as a unit, entwined and playing off each other, sometimes whimsically, other times dramatically. Line, balance and strong composition are the hallmarks of my work, as are color, buffed finishes and extreme attention to detail. Powder-coated aluminum is my preferred medium, but I also work in stainless steel, Cor-Ten steel, bronze and cast acrylics. Sizes range from tabletop to monumental and are suitable for corporate settings, residences, gardens and public sites. I specialize in site-specific commission work. My work has appeared in previous GUILD sourcebooks.

VAJRA GLASSWORKS
Objects
Page 135

My name is William L. Henry. I've been lampworking glass for over six years. My first hands-on experience with glass was an introductory stained glass course. Through this class I started to see the possibilities of glass. After a short time, I discovered Corning, New York, the home of Steuben crystal and the Corning Museum of Glass. Without hesitation I packed up and moved there. Within a year and a half, I had completed intense coursework from such talents as Robert Mickelsen, Emilio Santini, Roger Parrimorer, George Kennard and many other modern masters of glass. Over the past two years, I've been applying to as many art shows as I can find, so as to familiarize others around the world with my work.

KERRY VESPER
Furniture
Page 62

Every piece I make in wood is, to me, a sculpture. I strive to capture the flow and movement of nature that I find in flowing water, desert canyons and mountains. I equate my method of layering and shaping wood to the way nature builds up layers of earth, and then shapes it with wind and water. Using imported plywood and exotic hardwoods, I stack and glue layers together to approximate the form I intend to create. I shape each piece by hand with carving, grinding and sanding tools, then apply a clear oil/urethane finish. I exhibit and sell my work in galleries and at fine craft shows. I especially enjoy creating commission pieces.

JASON WATTS
Paintings
Pages 19, 244

My personal belief is that painting should be like good music. A great song has a catchy melody and a solid musical structure. But without meaning and substance to the lyrics, the song will fail to inspire any further thought. I hope my paintings are not only visually dynamic, but also bring an inspiring message and concept to the viewer. My goal is to capture the American experience of my generation. I find much of this in the sprawling suburbs, the vast stretches of highways and in the revitalization that is occurring in our cities. Cars figure into my work very prominently because they have become the vantage point for most of today's daily routines and experiences. Although I am a Midwesterner, I have been showing my work primarily through galleries on the East Coast, with solo and group shows in New York, Washington, DC, and Maryland.

ALICE VAN LEUNEN
Tapestry, Fiber & Paper
Page 356

My artworks explore pattern, texture and reflection. My approach is light-hearted. Many of the artworks make musical or literary allusions and feature calligraphic marks and symbols. Works range in size from small, intimate pieces to major architectural installations. Commissions are welcome. Commissions: Mulia Bank Complex, Djakarta, Indonesia; National High Magnetic Field Laboratory, Tallahassee, FL (with Walter Gordinier); Fairview Auditorium, Fairview, OK; Kaiser Medical Services, San Diego, CA; Kodiak Auditorium, Kodiak, AK; Playboy Towers, Chicago, IL. Collections: Atlantic County Office Building, Atlantic City, NJ; General Motors, New York, NY; City Light Collection, Seattle, WA; Calvin Klein Cosmetics, Wayne, NJ. Awards: Oregon Individual Artist Fellowship, 1993. My work is featured in previous GUILD sourcebooks.

GLEN WANS
Photographs
Page 294

I try to create images that have a sense of peace and order about them. Something that lets one stop for a moment and enjoy the textures and beauty of nature, or the interesting characteristics of a found object or everyday item, but on a higher level. The ability to create and control the look and feel of an image through the use of, and sensitivity to, studio light has always been very important to me. From idea to composition to lighting, the process is similar to starting with a blank canvas. In my case, however, the canvas is an empty studio floor upon which something is created from nothing.

JOAN WEISSMAN
Floor Coverings
Pages 2, 52–53, 121, 125

My rugs and tapestries continue my long-standing commitment to functional art. After many years as a porcelain sculptor, I turned first to tile murals, and then to painting. The paintings evolved into floor cloths, and then into hand-woven rugs. I now consider myself a textile designer. I specialize in hand-tufted and hand-knotted rugs, but I also design fabrics and embroidered tapestries. All my rugs are made to order. I work closely with my weavers in Nepal, the United States and Pakistan to create unique pieces in wool and silk that are customized for each client. Asian art has always been my biggest influence, althoughI absorb ideas from daily life and frequent wide travels. I like to combine balance and harmony with a fresh, bold treatment of design and color. I have been commissioned to make rugs throughout the United States for residential and commercial settings.

ARTIST STATEMENTS

KIRK L. WELLER
Photographs
Pages 293, 306

My photography unveils vistas far off the beaten path. I often visit a location repeatedly until I capture a sublime moment of light and shadow. Panoramas are one of my specialties. My large panoramic prints are vivid portrayals of our gorgeous planet. I produce fine art giclée prints, ranging in size from 10" x 13" to 40" x 60", with prices ranging from $200 to $1,200. My prints are matted superbly with archival integrity in mind. For more information about me and to see more of my work, visit www.gorgeousplanet.com.

STEWART WHITE
Paintings
Page 261

I am drawn to the idea that all of nature can be translated with a repertoire of brush marks, as in the Chinese tradition of painting. By focusing on the simple aspects, I can bring out the more spiritual aspects of an image. In addition to landscapes, I have created many murals for private residences and institutions throughout the United States and the Caribbean. Collections include: 70 murals for the Texas Rangers baseball club; eight murals for the Baltimore City Life Museum, MD; and background murals for the Smithsonian's Museum of Natural History and National Museum of American History. Prices for paintings range from $800–$8,000.

JOE STEELY WHITE, JR.
Furniture
Page 91

I am a craftsman who designs and builds furniture that is easy to live with and exemplifies timeless beauty. Communication and creativity are my strong points. With your input, I will create furniture that fulfills your expectations.

DONNA JILL WITTY
Paintings
Page 222

"Strong images filled with light and color." This statement is only a surface description of my work. By making passion what it is all about, I attempt to paint the extraordinary within the ordinary that is around us all. With many awards to their credit, my watercolor paintings have been featured in numerous publications and included in national and international exhibitions, including the American Watercolor Society, the National Watercolor Society, the Transparent Watercolor Society of America, Watercolor USA and many others. Prices for original paintings range from $400 to $5,000. My open-edition giclée prints are produced on acid-free watercolor paper with archival pigment inks, and are available for $65 or $130. Visit www.donnajillwitty.com to view a current selection of available paintings and prints.

BEATRICE WOOD
Objects
Page 129

At the time of her death in 1998, age 105, Beatrice Wood was a legend in the art world. The Beatrice Wood Studio in Ojai, CA, presents a permanent exhibition of the artist's work in addition to a sales gallery of fine pottery (including vessels, ceramic tiles and figurative works) and original drawings. Wood, also known as the "Mama of Dada," first took pottery classes in 1933 at the Hollywood High School in Los Angeles, and subsequently studied with Glen Lukens, and Gertrud and Otto Natzler, before developing her own personal and uniquely expressive art form. She is represented in numerous museum collections around the world. Prices for her fine pottery range from $1,200 to $35,000, and $1,000 to $3,500 for works on paper.

TERRY WOODALL
Sculpture
Page 192

Interpreting the natural flow and beauty of wood and transforming it into wildlife sculpture is my lifelong artistic endeavor. From my studio/woodshop on the Pacific coast of Oregon, I enjoy observing migrating whales, seals, sea lions, spawning salmon and the neighborhood elk herd. This visual inspiration results in lifelike renditions carved from rare woods recovered from local forests and waterways. Carved portions show a beautifully polished grain with lacquer finish, while a black or weathered gray stain highlights the rustic forms. Since establishing Pacific Carvings in 1981, I have exhibited my work in Mexico, Japan and the United States. Wildlife Art Magazine and a prominent woodworking magazine in Japan have featured my work, which has also been exhibited in the Oregon state capitol. My wide spectrum of carving ranges in price from $300–$3,000.

WOODLAND STUDIOS
Photography
Page 305

Our studio creates custom original artwork to fit the architectural design of any property. We mix art and photography with digital and natural mediums. Tools include cameras, computers, watercolors, pastels, colored pencils and acrylics. Applying graphic skills, we abstract the photographic images and over-paint each one until the brush strokes take over and the photo "melts" into the background. Even with a magnifying glass, it is difficult to see where the photo ends and the graphic image begins. Call to request an image catalog of our complete portfolio.

DAVID WOODRUFF
Objects
Page 155

I create one-of-a-kind hollow-formed vessels and other art objects from woods that possess great character as a result of trauma in the growing environment. This combination of genetic and environmental forces provides the raw material for the multidimensional beauty found in my art objects. Using a wood lathe and museum-quality lacquer, I create art pieces that reveal the beauty of nature's variety. Commissions: Weaver-Cooke Construction, Greensboro, NC; Novant Healthcare, Winston-Salem, NC. Exhibitions and awards: Top score, Krasl Art Fair, St. Joseph, MI; Top score, Tennessee Association of Craft Artists Crafts Fair, Chattanooga, TN; Piedmont Craftsman Guild, NC; Ann Arbor Street Fair, MI. My work has been featured in previous GUILD sourcebooks.

WOODSILKS STUDIO
Lighting
Page 114

I am Barbara Woods. My husband, Tom Thomas, and I create lighted sculptures and lamps. By combining color, texture and light on a canvas of silk, I create images of beautiful winged creatures, landscapes and seascapes that mimic a playful vision of the world. Each clay-bodied sculpture is unique, a combination of hand-formed and painted ceramics and hand-painted silk. The lighted sculptures make exceptional conversation pieces and provide ambient lighting for entryways, entertainment rooms, galleries and other living areas. Tom's wood lamps are made by combining native and exotic hardwood segments in ways that capture the inner structure and beauty of each wood. We complete every lamp with a handmade shade, which I design to complement each base. The result: a classic work of art that can be enjoyed in the home or on an executive's desktop.

ARTIST STATEMENTS

STEPHEN YATES
Paintings
Page 273

My paintings are nature-based abstractions that suggest water, plants and landscapes. They range in size from 12" x 18" to 5' x10' and are part of private and public collections including: The University of Washington and Cascadia Community College, Bothell, WA; The City of Seattle, WA; The City of Portland, OR; Evergreen State College, Olympia, WA, Microsoft Corporation, Redmond, WA. Awards include fellowships from Artist Trust, Seattle, WA; Art Matters, New York City; and Corporate Collectors Project, WESTAF, Santa Fe, NM, as well as a number of juror's awards in competitive exhibitions. I accept commissions for a broad range of sizes and imagery. A portfolio of past and recent work is available on my website or can be sent as a CD upon request.

YVETTE SIKORSKY STUDIO
Paintings
Page 272

After years of experimentation, I came upon a technique of sensuous abstraction that explores color and form. The images strike the viewer visually to reveal a true sense of design. The use of luminous color plays across the spectrum while balancing a complex tension in design. I received an Honorable Mention and a bronze medal from the City of Paris, France, my native country, and an Award of Excellence from Manhattan Art International. From 1985 to 2002, I showed my work at the Paris International Exhibition, and in New York, Colorado and California. My work may currently be viewed in the World Fine Art Gallery, New York, NY, and the Schacknow Museum of Fine Arts, FL. Paintings range from 18" x 24" to 36" x 48" and are acrylic. Prices ranges from $800 to $10,000. In addition to being an artist, I have also been a textile designer for upholstery fabrics.

LAURA ZINDEL
Objects
Page 134

I believe that some objects can carry a personal history through a family from year to year. I hope that I can make art that a family member can buy to be handed down the line. Something bought on a whim that becomes the platter for the family turkey or that sits on the mantel. I can hear it now: "Crazy old Uncle Larry bought that peculiar spider platter, and we just can't throw it out for some reason." I would like to be part of that. All work is handbuilt with earthenware and fired with nontoxic glazes.

KEVIN ALBERT YEE
Murals, Tiles & Wall Reliefs
Page 309

You are invited to explore the fascinating sculptural art of my studio, Terrathena. Set in beautiful Three Rivers, California, at the entrance of the majestic Sequoia National Park, I and my equipe d'artistes design and build award-winning neoclassical and transitional pieces in ceramic tile, stone and copper. These intricately sculptured bas reliefs, set in functional designs and finished with masterful antiquing, create a focal point for any setting. Every tile is uniquely handcrafted and finished in such a way that the entire piece, whether a fireplace, mural, mirror or table, creates an ambiance of intriguing beauty and classical harmony that arises from the thoughtful integration of all design elements. Over 20 years of studying and creating art and architectural works in Europe, India and the United States have provided me with an encyclopedic background to design these works of fine art.

STEPHEN ZEH
Objects
Page 158

I hand craft baskets from brown ash, which I find in the forests of northern Maine. The brown ash's beautiful and subtle tones are enhanced by hand scraping, which brings out the highlights and natural sheen. I learned the art of basket making from Eddie Newell, a Penobscot Indian basket maker. In my work I use the tools and methods of the Maine woodsmen, Shakers and Native American basket makers. Only one in 100 brown ash trees will meet my standards for quality. Through hand selection of the tree and careful craftsmanship, the baskets I make are designed to last for generations and will become even more beautiful through the years.

ZINGARA YULI GLASS STUDIO
Furniture/Mixed Media
Pages 76, 324

My goal as an artist is to meld traditional glassmaking with unique visions for utility and art. Through fusing, etching, carving, casting, sandblasting and laminated sculpting, I create hanging art for private residences and businesses. I love to incorporate illuminating, clear and colored glass with textures, drawings and various materials (including metal, plastic, paints and enamel), to push the conventional boundaries of glasswork. I appreciate form and expression and am influenced by the art of Calder and Picasso. My most unique work is found in my geometric panels, creative configurations of both balanced and random texture. My installations are found in Brazil, Germany and the U.S., and recent exhibits include ArtExpo International, 2003 and 2002, New York; Agora Gallery, NY; Kips Bay, NY; Martha Hewett Gallery, KY and Mod Décor Gallery, MD.

DARCY YOUNG
Art Quilts
Page 334

My first love is the dyeing, painting, quilting and embellishment of fiber (primarily silks). My work is always evolving and now includes airbrush and screen printing techniques. Dramatic in color, my pieces are heavily embellished with free-motion thread painting, beading and intricate quilting designs. Selected images are available as limited-edition giclée reproductions. Several of my pieces are in private collections around the country. One of my works was selected for the Art in Embassies program and is currently showing in the American embassy in Islamabad, Pakistan. My work was commissioned for the permanent exhibit for children in the Little Rock Territorial Restoration Museum, AR. Prices begin at $150 per square foot. Commissions and exhibition opportunities are welcome. Completed works are available for purchase.

LARRY ZGODA
Windows, Doors & Railings
Page 161

From my earliest years of interest in stained glass, I had regular inspiration from the stained, beveled and jeweled windows of the Victorian era. There are many kinds of stained glass jewels readily available. Most jewels are made in a mold and simply polished on the flat side. I go to great lengths to obtain full-cut jewels in which the flat side is cut, and each of the facets is cut and polished, as if it were a precious stone. The facets cast a strong spectral smear and imbue the work with vivid kinetics. I use Swarovski machine-cut crystal jewels or hand-cut jewels of comparable quality. If our intention is to assemble beautiful environments in sympathy with elemental forces and materials of nature and human imagination, cut jewels impose a radiance not found anywhere else.

BARBARA ZINKEL
Prints & Drawings
Page 287

Barbara Zinkel is known for her dramatic use of color in her limited-edition silkscreen prints, and in her professionally hand-tufted and hand-carved custom wool rugs for residential and corporate interiors. Zinkel's work has been featured in decorators' show houses in Detroit and Columbus, on several television programs, and in the Detroit News (1994), Hour Detroit magazine (1999), and Better Homes and Gardens Decorating magazine (1987). While featured in various collections in the Netherlands, Hong Kong, Venezuela and Spain, Zinkel's domestic collection placements include General Motors, Daimler Chrysler Corporation Headquarters, Ford, Dupont, Steelcase, CBS, Chase Manhattan Bank, Texas Instruments, Honeywell, Ericcson and Verisign.

GLOSSARY OF ART TERMS

Alabaster
George Westbrook, *Stone Vessel.*

Appliqué
Kim Ritter, *Spirit Horse #2.*

Burl
Christian Burchard, *Black Baskets, Three Parts.*

Celadon
Amber Archer, *Celadon & White Fruit Bowl.*

ACRYLIC	A water-soluble paint made with pigments and synthetic resin; used as a fast-drying alternative to oil paint.
ALABASTER	A fine-textured, usually white, gypsum that is easily carved and translucent when thin.
ALUMINUM	A lightweight, silver-colored metal used extensively in commercial applications, and occasionally by metal artists. In a process called anodizing, aluminum is given a tough porous coating that can be colored with dyes.
APPLIQUÉ	A technique whereby pieces of fabric are layered on top of one another and joined with decorative stitches.
AQUATINT	Printmaking process used to create areas of solid color, as well as gradations of white through black tones. Usually has the appearance of transparent watercolor.
BAS-RELIEF	Literally, "low-relief." Raised or indented sculptural patterns that remain close to the surface plane.
BATIK	A method of applying dye to cloth that is covered, in part, with a dye-resistant, removable substance such as wax. After dyeing, the resist is removed, and the design appears in the original color against the newly colored background.
BEADING	The process whereby decorative beads are sewn, glued or otherwise attached to a surface.
BEVELED GLASS	Plate glass that has its perimeter ground and polished at an angle.
BONDED GLASS	Glass pieces that have been adhered together by glue, resin or cement.
BRASS	An alloy of copper and zinc. Brass is yellow in color, and though harder than either of its constituents, it is appropriately malleable for jewelry making.
BRONZE	Traditionally, an alloy of copper and tin widely used in casting. The term is often applied to brown-colored brasses.
BURL	A dome-shaped growth on the trunk of a tree. Intricately patterned burl wool is often used by wood turners and furniture makers.
CASTING	The process of pouring molten metal or glass, clay slip, etc. into a hollow mold to harden. Some casting processes permit more than one reproduction.
CELADON	French name for a green, gray-green, blue-green or gray glaze produced with a small percentage of iron as the colorant.
CERAMICS	The art and science of forming objects from earth materials containing or combined with silica; the objects are then heated to at least 1300°F to harden.
CHASING	A technique in which steel punches are used to decorate and/or texture a metal surface.
CHINA PAINT	A low-temperature overglaze fired onto previously glazed and fired ceramic.
DICHROIC GLASS	A thin metallic coating on any type of glass. The coating is applied at a high temperature in a vacuum chamber.
DIE FORMING	The process of placing metal between two steel dies or stamps and squeezing them together under high pressure. This process shapes and strengthens the metal.
DIGITAL IMAGING	Refers to the creation, manipulation and production of images by use of computer technology, including software and printers.

390

GLOSSARY OF ART TERMS

DIPTYCH — Artwork on two panels that are hung together. Historically, a hinged, two-paneled painting or bas-relief.

EARTHENWARE — Ceramic ware with a permeable or porous body after firing (usually to a temperature of 1600°F to 1900°F).

EMBOSSING — A decorative technique in which a design is raised in relief.

ENAMELED GLASS — Glass decorated with particles of translucent glass or glass-like material, usually of a contrasting color, which fuses to the surface under heat. Multicolored designs can be created, as well as monochrome coatings.

ENGRAVING — An intaglio printing process in which a design is incised into a metal plate. Characterized by sharp, clean lines and high definition. Also called line engraving.

ETCHED GLASS — Glass decorated, carved or otherwise marked by sandblasting or the use of hydrofluoric acid. The glass is partially covered with an acid-resistant wax or gum and the exposed area is etched.

ETCHING — A printing process in which chemical agents are used to deepen lines drawn onto a printing plate.

FIRING — Heating clay, glaze, enamel or other material to the temperature necessary to achieve a desired structural change. Most ceramics are fired in a kiln to temperatures ranging from 1600°F to 2300°F.

FORGED — A blacksmithing technique in which metal is shaped by hammering, usually while at red or white heat.

FUMING — A vapor deposition process in which a thin film of metal (usually silver, platinum or gold) condenses on the surface of a hot piece of glass or clay, resulting in an iridescent surface.

FUSED GLASS — Glass that has been heated in a kiln to the point where two separate pieces are permanently joined as one without losing their individual color.

GICLÉE — French term meaning "sprayed." A process by which an image is rendered digitally by spraying a fine stream of ink onto archival art paper or canvas. Similar to an airbrush technique.

GLASSBLOWING — The process of gathering molten glass onto the end of a blowpipe and forming it into a variety of shapes by blowing and manipulating it as the glass is rotated.

GLAZE — Glassy melted coating on a clay surface. Glaze has a similar oxide composition to glass, but includes a binder.

GOUACHE — An opaque watercolor paint, or work so produced. Gouache is applied like watercolor, but reflects light due to its chalky finish.

HUE — The pure state of any color.

ILFOCHROME — A trademarked photographic paper and the process of making prints with such paper. Ilfochrome prints are produced from slides or transparencies, not color negatives.

IMPASTO — A thick, uneven surface texture achieved by applying paint with a brush or palette knife.

INCALMO — The glassblowing technique used to create horizontal or vertical bands of color by forming and connecting cylinders of colored glass.

Earthenware
David Heaps, *Pouring Vessels*.

Etched Glass
David Van Noppen,
Leaf Vase with Etched Bouquet.

Giclée
Jane Sterrett, *Three Apples Pink*.

Incalmo
Dari Gordon and Bruce Pizzzichillo,
Bubble Incalmo Cylinders.

All glossary illustrations are from the GUILD.com website. Visit www.guild.com.

GLOSSARY OF TERMS

Intaglio
Nicolette Jelen, *Golden Afternoon V.*

Lampwork
Ellie Burke, *Pig With Wings.*

Linocut
Lisa Kesler, *Vessels–2.*

Luster
Gail McCarthy, *Lustered Vessel #121*

INCLUSIONS	Particles of metal, bubbles, etc., that occur naturally within glass or are added for decorative effect.
INLAY	A decorating technique in which an object is incised with a design, a colorant is pressed into the incisions, and the surface is then scraped to confine the colored inlay to the incisions.
INTAGLIO	A printmaking process in which an image is created from ink held in the incised or bitten areas of a metal plate, below the surface plane. Engraving, etching, mezzotint and aquatint are examples of the intaglio process.
IRIDIZED GLASS	Flat or blown glass sprayed with a vapor deposit of metal oxides for an iridescent finish. The iridized layer, which resembles an oil slick, can be selectively removed for a two-tone effect.
IRIS PRINT	The trademarked name for a digital print produced by an Iris Graphics inkjet printer. (See "Giclée.")
KILN	A furnace for firing clay, forming glass or melting enamels; studio kilns can achieve temperatures up to 2500°F and can be fueled with gas, wood or electricity.
KILN-FORMING	A glass-forming process that utilizes a kiln to heat glass in a refractory or heat-resistant mold, slump glass over a form, or fuse two or more pieces of glass together.
KINETIC	Active. Kinetic sculpture has parts that move, whether by air currents (as with a mobile) or by motors and gears.
LAMINATED	Composed of layers bonded together for strength, thickness or decorative effect.
LAMPWORK	The technique of manipulating glass by heating it with a small flame. An open flame is advantageous in very detailed work.
LEADED GLASS	Glass containing a percentage of lead oxide, which increases its density and improves its ability to refract and disperse light. Leaded glass is used for ornaments and for decorative and luxury tableware.
LIMITED EDITION	Artworks produced in a deliberately limited quantity. All items in the edition are identical and each one is an original work of art. The limited size of the edition enhances the value of each piece.
LINOCUT	A relief print process similar to woodcut. Wood blocks covered with a layer of linoleum are carved with woodcut tools, coated with ink and printed by hand or in a press.
LITHOGRAPHY	A planographic printmaking process based on the repellence of oil and water and characterized by soft lines and blurry shapes.
LOW-FIRE GLAZES	Low-temperature ceramic glazes, usually associated with bright, shiny colors.
LUSTER	A brilliant iridescent film used on ceramic glazes; formed from metallic salts.
MAJOLICA	An opaque glaze, usually white, with a glossy surface. Typically decorated with bright overglaze stains.
MARQUETRY	Decorative patterns formed when thin layers of wood (and sometimes other materials, such as ivory) are inlaid into the surface of furniture or other wood products.
MEZZOTINT	An intaglio printing process that produces areas of tone rather than clean lines.

GLOSSARY OF TERMS

MONOPRINT A print produced by painting directly onto an already-etched surface and printing the image by hand onto paper.

MONOTYPE A print made when an artist draws or paints on a glass or metal plate and then prints the image onto paper.

MOSAIC The process of creating a design or picture with small pieces of glass, stone, terra cotta, etc.

MURRINI A small wafer of glass bearing a colored pattern. Formed by bundling and fusing colored glass rods together and then heating and pulling the resulting cylinder to a very small diameter. When cut into cross-sectioned wafers, each piece bears the original pattern in miniature.

OIL PAINT A paint in which natural oil—usually linseed—is the medium that binds the pigments.

PALLADIUM A photographic process in which the image is produced by palladium crystals deposited on the paper.

PASTEL A crayon of ground pigment bound with gum or oil. Pastel crayons have varying ratios of pigment to chalk and gum; the more pigment, the more intense the color.

PATE DE VERRE A "paste" of finely crushed glass that is mixed, heated and poured into a mold.

PATINA A surface coloring, usually brown or green, produced by the oxidation of bronze, copper or other metal. Patinas occur naturally and are also produced artificially for decorative effect.

PHOTOETCHING A printmaking technique in which a light-sensitive metal plate is exposed to photographic film under ultraviolet light.

PHOTOGRAVURE A printing process based on the production, by photographic methods, of a plate containing small ink-receptive pits.

POLAROID TRANSFER A trademarked name for the process by which an image recorded by the camera's lens is reproduced directly onto a photosensitive surface, which functions as both film and photograph.

PORCELAIN A clay body that is white, strong and hard when fired. When sufficiently thin, it is also translucent.

PRINT An image made from an inked surface. Prints are usually, but not always, produced in multiples.

RAKU The technique of rapidly firing low-temperature ceramic ware. Raku firings were used traditionally in Japan to make bowls for tea ceremonies.

RELIEF PRINT A process in which a print is produced from the relief carving on a metal plate or a wood or linoleum block.

REPOUSSÉ An ancient process in which sheet metal is hammered into contours from both the front and the back.

REVERSE PAINTING A technique where paint is applied to the back side of a surface (typically glass) and viewed through the front. This process requires the painting to be done in reverse order; what appears closest to the viewer as a detail or highlight must be painted first rather than last. Any lettering must likewise be painted in the mirror image so it will appear right facing when viewed from the front.

Monotype
Susan Lawson-Bell, *Sunset*.

Oil Paint
Daniel Lang, *Sunset Valley*.

Porcelain
Peter Saenger, *Tea for Two*.

Woodcut
Barbara Leventhal-Stern, *Games We Play*.

GLOSSARY OF TERMS

Sepia
Allan Baillie, *Calla #3.*

Stoneware
Tom & Sara Post, *Patchfish Platter.*

Turned
Jack T. Fifield, *Elevated Bowl.*

Watercolor
Helen Klebesadel, *Quilter's Hex.*

SALT GLAZE	A glaze created during high-temperature firings. Sodium, usually in the form of rock salt, is introduced into the fully heated kiln and forms a clear coating on the clay, often with an orange-peel texture.
SAND CASTING	An ancient and still widely used casting method in which moistened sand is packed against a model to make a mold—usually for metal.
SANDBLASTING	A method of etching the surface of a material by spraying it with compressed air and sand.
SEPIA	Warm, reddish-brown pigment produced from octopus or cuttlefish ink, used in watercolor and drawing ink. In photography, some toning processes produce a similar color in the print.
SILKSCREEN PRINTING	A printing process in which paint, ink or dye is forced through a fine screen onto the surface beneath. Different areas of the screen are blocked off with each layer of color. Also known as "serigraph."
SILVER GELATIN	A photographic process that uses silver halide crystals suspended within the photographic emulsion to produce the image. The most popular type of black-and-white photograph produced today.
SLUMPED GLASS	Preformed flat or three-dimensional glass that is reheated and shaped in a mold.
SPALTED	Wood that contains areas of natural decay, giving it distinctive markings. Spalted wood is used for its decorative effect.
STILL LIFE	A depiction of a group of inanimate objects arranged for symbolic or aesthetic effect.
STONEWARE	A gray, red or buff clay body that matures (becomes nonporous) between 1900°F and 2300°F.
TERRA COTTA	Low-fired ceramic ware that is often reddish and unglazed.
TERRA SIGILLATA	A thin coating of colored clay or clays applied like a glaze. A terra sigillata solution is composed of fine particles of decanted clay and water.
TRIPTYCH	A three-paneled artwork. Historically, triptychs were hinged together so that the two side wings closed over the central panel.
TURNED	Wood or other materials shaped by tools while revolving around a fixed axis, usually a lathe. Cylindrical forms (dowels, rungs) and circular designs (bowls) are made in this way.
TROMPE L'OEIL	Literally, "fool the eye" (French). An object or scene rendered so realistically that the viewer believes he or she is seeing the real thing.
VITREOGRAPH	A print made from a glass plate that has been prepared by sandblasting or etching.
VITREOUS	Clay fired to maturity, so that it is hard, dense and nonabsorbent.
WATERCOLOR	Watercolor paints are made with pigments dispersed in gum arabic and are characterized by luminous transparency.
WHITEWARE	A generic term for white clay bodies.
WOODCUT	A relief printing process in which a picture or design is cut in relief along the grain of a wood block.

Boris Bally, home setting, recycled traffic signs. Photograph: Jeff Johnson. Find Bally's work at GUILD.com.

A commissioned work of art is a uniquely individual way to celebrate a family milestone, fill an unusual space or make everyday objects artful. This book gives you the essential tools to make that happen: photographs showing a range of products, media and art forms, and contact information so that you can connect directly with the artists whose work you want to own. For many Artful Home users, the path to custom-designed artworks is just this simple.

However, you may want to make use of another service available through the GUILD.com website. The GUILD Custom Design Center enables you to broadcast a description of your dream project to suitable artists via the Internet. Interested artists submit proposals free of charge, and you are under no financial obligation until you decide to proceed with a project.

What kinds of projects pass through the Custom Design Center?

SAMPLE COMMISSIONS

- Lamps for a California bedroom
- Bar stools for a New York apartment
- Ceramic tiles for an Oklahoma kitchen
- Wall sconces for a California walkway and garden
- Indoor fountain for a Canadian home

Visit the GUILD Custom Design Center at www.guild.com/cdc, or call 877-344-8453 to discuss your idea with one of GUILD's Design Consultants. They can recommend candidates for a specific job, assess the qualifications of individual artists or help draft a letter of agreement.

INDEX OF ARTISTS & COMPANIES

INDEX OF ARTISTS & COMPANIES

INDEX OF ARTISTS & COMPANIES

LOCATION INDEX

LOCATION INDEX

LOCATION INDEX

LOCATION INDEX

Vermont

Virginia

Washington

Wisconsin

Wyoming

Canada